THE POLITICS OF PLACE IN POST-WAR GERMANY

Essays in Literary Criticism

'Faust and Mephistopheles ascending to the Brocken on Walpurgnis Night' by Moritz Retzsch (1812). Courtesy of www.goethezeitportal.de

THE POLITICS OF PLACE IN POST-WAR GERMANY

Essays in Literary Criticism

Edited by

David Clarke

and

Renate Rechtien

With a Foreword by
Karen Seago

The Edwin Mellen Press
Lewiston•Queenston•Lampeter

Library of Congress Cataloging-in-Publication Data

The politics of place in post-war Germany : essays in literary criticism / edited by David Clarke and Renate Rechtien ; with a foreword by Karen Seago.
    p. cm.
  Includes bibliographical references and index.
  ISBN-13: 978-0-7734-4736-3
  ISBN-10: 0-7734-4736-9
  1. German literature--20th century--History and criticism. 2. Politics and literature--Germany--History--20th century. 3. Place (Philosophy) in literature. 4. Germany--Intellectual life--20th century. 5. Germany--In literature. I. Clarke, David (David John), 1972- II. Rechtien, Renate.
  PT405.P5785 2009
  830.9'35843--dc22

                                          2009016735

hors série.

A CIP catalog record for this book is available from the British Library.

Front cover photo: 'Leipzig, November 2007' © David Clarke, 2007

The Edwin Mellen Press   The Edwin Mellen Press
Box 450   Box 67
Lewiston, New York   Queenston, Ontario
USA 14092-0450   CANADA L0S 1L0

The Edwin Mellen Press, Ltd.
Lampeter, Ceredigion, Wales
UNITED KINGDOM SA48 8LT

Printed in the United States of America

For our grandparents and their places

Für unsere Großeltern und ihre Orte

CONTENTS

LIST OF ILLUSTRATIONS

FOREWORD

In 2003, the German historian Karl Schlögel asserted in his book *We Read Time in Space* (*Im Raume lesen wir die Zeit*) that history does not only happen in time but also in space. Local and global developments, the dissolution of borders and creation of new boundaries, the re-orientation of social, cultural and political landscapes have provided a context for critical and literary focus on the topographical. The wide-ranging contributions in the present volume offer eloquent evidence of the way literature engages with space and its (historical) meanings, how individuals interact with their environment and attempt to make sense of it and the self.

As David Clarke outlines in his brilliant introduction, space and place are constructed in subjective experience – they are a process rather than familiar, static and contained indicators of identity. German history, German territory and conceptions of German-ness in the 20th century and beyond are complex and fraught – how do Germans make sense of who they are: whether they are coming to terms with the National Socialist past, the SED past or the post-unification present? And how does this past, or present, sediment itself in place, visibly or 'below the ground', bearing evidence to history? Juliane Parthier peels apart the layers of invisible spaces which are repressed in public memory but which contain material reminders of uncomfortable pre- and post 1989 history in the shadow of the wall. Andrew Webber reads Berlin as a case history through its psycho-topographical symptoms where place becomes a carrier of clues for memory, triggered by catastrophe. Similarly, Simon Ward examines the function of Berlin as an imaginary place in the work of novelist Wolfgang Koeppen.

Trauma, memory, imposed forgetting, repression and appropriation are central issues from the perspectives of both West-, East- and post-unification German writers. Helmut Schmitz shows how landscape functions as an iconography of historical trauma, closely linked to family history and an overcoming of the past through an imaginary restitution of the destroyed *Heimat*.

Dora Osborne discusses how Sebald uses the archive as access to the traumatic past of the Holocaust through fragmentary and almost immaterial evidence, which threatens to dissolve on contact. The ghetto Theresienstadt is constructed as a heterotopic space of confinement and marginalisation outside the normal social order and linked to London as Austerlitz traverses the city in his attempts at recovering his childhood.

Foucault's concept of heterotopia as an 'other space', a utopian countersite which links to and contests other cultural sites, is a tool used by a number of contributors to engage with places outside reality. Ute Wölfel reads Angela Krauß's 'sceneries of fulfilment' as a reaction to the post-1989 loss of the industrial milieu with its daily routine, where the protagonist produces a 'bio-map' of heterotopias through a remembered childhood, linked to concrete places but overlaid by an internal vision of paradise: a big white ship which is also a representation of the narrator as ice skater. In Stephan Krause's chapter, Budapest is presented as a heterotopic space across time and through the underground labyrinth of the city's steam bath. Intertextual webs establish Budapest as an eloquently literary place in which the interpretation and writing of texts occurs and where Fühmann's mythopoetics give access to another space away from the world of the real, constructing experience.

Literature and the act of writing are also central in Thomas Möbius's and David Clarke's chapters. Möbius shows how we perceive landscape through the literature about it, and discusses how authors appropriate places and their history in the representation of the Harz mountains as ritual and cultural site (Goethe's Walpurgisnacht), as a symbolic model of national unity and German division (Rosenlöcher's wanderer) or as a model for the deconstruction of power and history in Heine and Irmtraud Morgner. Clarke explores Gert Neumann's political poetics of resistance to the discursive imposition of reality in a close analysis of how the disjointed and fragmentary experience of working and writing in Leipzig iconically represents the open-ended process of encountering reality as every-day lived experience rather than ideological rhetoric. Strategies of engagement/evasion and attempts to find spaces for living a life, constructing an identity (as writer) off the beaten path of SED ideology inform Dennis Tate's and Renate Rechtien's chapters on Günter de Bruyn's and Christa Wolf's dis/identifications and shifts of allegiance articulated through a tension between the country and the city, or the idyllic chronotope of the garden and the no-place of Berlin in 1989.

Emily Jeremiah's contribution engages with the question of gendered space and a perception and representation of German-ness through emigration. She shows how Vanderbeke articulates a critical refusal through the creation of a women's space and female relationality which challenges traditional perceptions of femininity through an assertion of mobility, crossing borders and challenging boundaries.

This is a wide-ranging collection, giving us fascinating access to how well-known and less well-known writers engage with conceptions of place, identity and cultural memory. It offers a coherent account of the complex interactions between the private and the public, engaging the reader in a stimulating interdisciplinary dialogue with the theoretical frameworks underpinning the case studies, with the texts and their authors, and – in the case of this reader – my own dis/locations and dis/engagements with place and identity.

Dr Karen Seago
Centre for Language Studies
City University London, England

ACKNOWLEDGEMENTS

The editors would like to thank the authors for their hard work and patience; the German Academic Exchange Service (DAAD) and the Department of German of the University of Cambridge for financially supporting the symposium which was the starting point for this volume; Ute Wölfel (Reading) for organizing the symposium; Dr Karen Seago for providing the foreword; Professor Jan Berendse (Cardiff) and Dr Jon Hughes (Royal Holloway) for kindly agreeing to read and recommend this book before publication; Professor Dennis Tate (Bath) for assistance and advice during the production of the book; Dr Nina Parish (Bath) for her helpful comments; Alex for the author photographs; Malcolm and Rick for their encouragement and support.

INTRODUCTION

Place in Literature

David Clarke

This collection of essays on post-war German-language literature brings together contributions from a symposium held at the University of Cambridge in 2005, along with a number of commissioned pieces, all of which reflect on the function of place in the work of a range of authors from the Federal Republic, from the German Democratic Republic and Austria after 1945. The point of departure for the original symposium was a visit to the UK by the author Angela Krauß and the impetus to interrogate the notion of place as it expresses itself in literature was, to begin with, very much a response to this individual author's work, which offers a striking example of an artistic engagement with the relationship between place and identity, between geographical situatedness and self. From Krauß's earliest autobiographically inflected texts such as *The Service* (*Der Dienst*, 1989/1990), which is based upon the author's own childhood in the *Erzgebirge* mountains, to more recent reflections on place and self in times of rapid social transformation and increased global mobility, such as *Flying over Countries* (*Die Überfliegerin*, 1995), *Summer on Ice* (*Sommer auf Eis*, 1998), *A Billion New Stars* (*Milliarden neue Sterne,* 1999) and *Kissed Away* (*Weggeküsst*, 2002), Krauß's entire *oeuvre* offers itself as a meditation on Gaston Bachelard's adage that 'we do not change place, we change our nature'.[1] Krauß's work is explored in depth in Ute Wölfel's chapter in this volume, but her explorations of the situatedness of personal identity have in many cases also provided a point of departure, even if not explicitly acknowledged, for the wider debate about the function and meaning of place in post-war German writing that occupies this collection of essays.

---

[1] Gaston Bachelard, *The Poetics of Space*, trans. Maria Jolas (Boston: Beacon, 1994), 206. For an account of Krauß's autobiographical project, see Dennis Tate, *Shifting Perspectives: East German Autobiographical Narratives Before and After the End of the GDR* (Rochester: Camden House, 2007), 58-60.

Nevertheless, and compelling though the example of Krauß's work is, there are a number of other good reasons for exploring the experience of place in literature at this particular point in time. As Philip E. Wegner points out in an introductory essay on 'spatial criticism', the last three decades have seen the publication of an ever increasing range of often interdisciplinary projects by geographers, cultural theorists, sociologists, philosophers and others that amount to a 'spatial turn' in the humanities and social sciences.[2] Taken together, such work seeks to move away from a conception of space as an empty stage on which the events of history can (literally) take place, unconditioned by and unconditioning of their location. This inattention to the role of space is not only the result of a privileging of an engagement with time and history in the Western philosophy of the nineteenth and twentieth centuries, from Hegel and Marx to Bergson and Heidegger, but also the result of that tradition's tendency to regard space as an infinitely extended, passive and homogenous container, which Edward Casey, in his philosophical defence of the notion of place, traces back to origins of modern thought.[3] Broadly speaking, the thrust of the 'spatial turn', or the 'topographical turn' as Sigrid Weigel has called it,[4] has been to see space as simultaneously socially produced and productive. That is to say that the organization of space in a particular social order is regarded as the product of that society in terms of its economics and its ideology, but that this relationship is seen as a dialectical one: space does not passively bear the marks of its construction by society (and especially by economic and political power), but simultaneously helps to shape the social order as it is expressed in space. The chief source of this notion is undoubtedly Henri Lefebvre in his seminal *The Production of Space* (1974). In what is on the whole an optimistic work, Lefebvre points to capitalism's increasing tendency to treat space in much the same way that Casey's

---

[2] Phillip E. Wegner, 'Spatial Criticism: Critical Geography, Space, Place and Textuality', in Julian Wolfreys (ed.), *Introducing Criticism in the 21ˢᵗ Century* (Edinburgh: Edinburgh UP, 2002), 179-203.
[3] Edward W. Casey, *The Fate of Place: A Philosophical History* (Berkeley: U of California P, 1997), 131 and 141.
[4] Sigrid Weigel, 'Zum "Topographical Turn"', *Kulturpoetik*, 2.2 (2002), 151-65.

modern philosophers do, in other words as a neutral background to its activities. Anticipating contemporary discourses on the phenomenon of globalization, Lefebvre points to this 'abstraction' of space, in which the world becomes a network of characterless sites at the disposal of a world economy, as potentially destructive of individual identity, community and the local.[5] Yet, he also seeks to demonstrate that capitalism will not get everything its own way. The spaces it produces are also lived in by subjects who are by no means condemned to be subordinated to the functions assigned to those spaces by economic and political power; rather, spaces are always also 'lived' and therefore contain 'potentialities'.[6] Lefebvre's study takes as its primary focus the elaboration of such resistant 'potentialities', amongst which, as we will see later, art has a particularly privileged position.

Another reason for looking at place is that the 'spatial turn' described above has been closely allied to theorizations of the 'post-modern' condition of Western societies in this same period, which have sought to interpret the alleged distinctness of the epoch in terms of the way it organizes space and the way in which space is experienced in it.[7] As Doreen Massey observes, this can almost create the impression that issues around space and place have only become important with the dawn of the 'post-modern' age:

> the debate about the postmodern has brought with it a sudden recognition of, indeed a revelling in, the importance of space and place. It is a realization, a sudden discovery, which seems to have dawned on intellectuals across much of the social sciences.[8]

Whilst we can share Massey's scepticism at this 'discovery' of space and place amongst analysts of the 'post-modern' and recognize instead, along with

---

[5] Henri Lefebvre, *The Production of Space*, trans. Donald Nicholson Smith (Oxford: Blackwell, 1991), pp. 52-53.

[6] Lefebvre, *Production of Space*, 349.

[7] Three key figures here are Fredric Jameson, David Harvey and Edward W. Soja. Jameson, *The Postmodern Condition or The Cultural Logic of Late Capitalism* (London: Verso, 1991) Harvey, *The Condition of Postmodernity: An Enquiry into the Origins of Cultural Change* (Oxford: Blackwell, 1989). Soja, *Postmodern Geographies: The Reassertion of Space in Critical Social Theory* (London: Verso, 1989).

[8] Doreen Massey, *Space, Place and Gender* (Cambridge: Polity, 1994), 135.

Lefebvre, that the production of space is a feature of every human society, the renewed emphasis on the spatial in critiques of contemporary society provides a further impetus to investigate the function of place in our chosen period of German literature.

Alongside both the 'spatial' and the 'post-modern' turns, it is furthermore possible to identify an intensified engagement with cultural production in the work of both the analysts of the 'production of space' and theorists of the 'post-modern'. Whilst on the one hand the ramifications of the 'post-modern' condition are often demonstrated using artefacts from the cultural sphere, such as films, novels and architecture, on the other geographers and cultural historians now seek to explore the ways in which human societies think about topography in and through cultural products such as landscape painting or photography.[9] Furthermore, geographers in particular have increasingly become conscious of the fact that the physical world is also a text transversed by competing signifying discourses, rather than merely an objectively measurable phenomenon, and have turned to the insights of cultural studies in order to come to meet the challenge of engaging with the world in these terms.[10] At the same time, the relationship between culture and the 'imaginative geographies' of the Western world has also been central to analyses of its colonial practices, most famously in Edward Said's *Orientalism* (1978), which demonstrates how writing about 'the Orient', not only by historians and administrators, but also by novelists and poets, helps to create 'the very reality they appear to describe' and thereby participates in the subordination of the colonized.[11] The continued currency of these debates about the relationship between culture, ideology and geography provides yet another

---

[9] See, for example, the following two collections of essays: W. J. T. Mitchell (ed.), *Landscapes and Power* (Chicago: U of Chicago P, 1994) and Joan Schwartz and James Ryan (eds.), *Picturing Place: Photography and the Geographical Imagination* (London: I.B. Tauris, 2003).

[10] For an outline of this position from the perspective of geographers, see Trevor Barnes and James S. Duncan, 'Introduction: Writing Worlds', in Barnes and Duncan (eds.), *Writing Worlds: Discourse, Text and Metaphor in the Representation of Landscape* (London and New York: Routledge, 1992), 1-17.

[11] Edward W. Said, *Orientalism: Western Conceptions of the Orient* (Harmondsworth: Penguin, 1995), p. 94. See Larry Wolff, *Inventing Eastern Europe: The Map of Civilization on the Mind of the Enlightenment* (Stanford: Stanford UP, 1994).

motivation for engaging with the experience of place in the literature that our contributors have made their area of specialism, in the expectation that post-war German fiction can be connected to some of these wider discussions.

However, whilst the interdisciplinary work mentioned above is clearly extremely valuable, the decision to focus our discussion on literary texts in itself throws up an important question. All of the contributors to this volume are at home in literary studies and the focus of their work implies that there is something specific to be gained by examining the function of place in literature. In other words, though there are certainly points of contact with other disciplines, the scope of this volume implicitly makes a claim to some particular contribution of literature to our understanding of place and its possibilities. In the context of German literary studies, this is a question that Hermann Meyer was to some extent already posing in the early 1950s, when he asked whether it was possible to speak of a specifically literary 'organization of space' ('Raumgestaltung').[12] I will attempt to address this question in more detail below, although my answer is not necessarily programmatic for every contribution in this volume, all of which engage in different ways with the theory of space and place.

The critical reader will already be uneasy with my apparently indiscriminate and interchangeable use of the terms 'space' and 'place' in the above. This is a problem of much writing about the topographical, not least because there is no real consensus about what might distinguish these two neatly rhyming opposed terms. The attraction of this juxtaposition is apparently largely confined to Anglo-Saxon academia. In a German context, the corresponding contrast between *Raum* and *Ort* is not so readily made. Whilst the term *Raum* is common in German literary criticism, it is in itself a problematic term, given that it can mean 'space', 'region' and 'room', the latter in the double sense of a room in a building as in 'room to manoeuvre'. Even in the English-speaking world, as the editors of the volume *Key Thinkers on Space and Place* explain, '[space and

---

[12] Hermann Meyer, 'Raumgestaltung und Raumsymbolik in der Erzählkunst', in Meyer, *Zarte Empirie: Studien zur Literaturgeschichte* (Stuttgart: Metzler, 1963), 33-56 (here 35).

place] remain relatively diffuse, ill-defined and incohate concepts'.[13] In this section of this introductory chapter I will nevertheless propose a working definition of place that will hopefully be of particular use for a discussion of place in literature.

Some of the confusion over the definition of place in literary studies can be seen in other volumes that seek to engage with this theme. For example, in *The Literature of Place*, edited by Norman Page and Peter Preston in 1993, and *Literature and Place 1800-2000*, edited by Peter Brown and Michael Unwin in 2006, the definition of place is left either inclusively open or vague, depending on your point of view.[14] Taken together, these volumes contain contributions on literary *topoi* (e.g. particular kinds of dwelling as a motif in literature), the writing produced by an individual author in and about a particular region or country, the personal attachment of an individual author to an area or region, regional identity as expressed in the work of a number of authors, and constructions of national identity in literature. The problem is clearly that place has a common-sense meaning that can be applied to a whole range of geographical units, from the nation state to the hearth and every point in between, whilst the commonality of the 'places' in terms of the human experience of them and the particular function of that experience in literature remains untheorized. It appears, then, that the same kind of confusion reigns in terms of the use of 'place' terminology as Armin von Ungern-Sternberg observes in relation to terms like 'space' and 'region':

> There is a lot of talk at the moment about 'spaces' and 'regions',
> including in literary studies. It is unclear, however, what is really
> being talked about. The discussion often suffers from the terms

---

[13] Phil Hubbard, Rob Kitchin and Gill Valentine (eds.), *Key Thinkers on Space and Place* (London: Sage, 2004), 6.

[14] Brown and Irwin acknowledge and justify this openness as an indication 'that it [literature and place, DC] is a field of study, as yet in its early stages'. Peter Brown and Michael Irwin, 'Introduction', in Brown and Irwin (eds.), *Literature and Place 1800-2000* (Bern: Lang, 2006), 13-23 (here 15). Page and Preston do not specifically address the question of defining place in their brief introduction. Norman Page and Peter Preston (eds.), *The Literature of Place* (Houndmills: MacMillan, 1993).

being used in a number of different ways and consequently from a chaotic growth of arguments.[15]

One explanation for this confusion, of course, is that a general term from everyday speech is being imported into an academic discourse for which it lacks the necessary precision. Nevertheless, the common experience reflected in our everyday understanding of place should not be dismissed: human beings do have a complex sense of place that applies not just to their own particular location at a given point in time, but that also understands that location in relation to other locations, which they do not necessarily have direct personal experience of, and within larger geographical units such as neighbourhood, city, region, nation or some supranational entity such as 'Europe'.

This complexity is missing from definitions of the relationship between place and space that present place as the contained and the familiar and space as the inhospitable expanse of the unknown. For instance, anthropologist Yi-Fu Tuan argues for this distinction as follows:

> To be open and free is to be exposed and vulnerable. Open space has no trodden paths. It has no fixed pattern of established human meaning; it is like a blank sheet on which meaning may be imposed. Enclosed and humanised space is place. Human beings require both space and place. Human lives are a dialectical movement between shelter and venture, attachment and freedom.[16]

Such definitions idealize on three fronts. Firstly, the notion of the 'enclosed' and therefore 'humanized' place suggests that we all have a single demarcated (and implicitly private) place in which we feel at home, rather than living lives that traverse a number of distinct but often relatively discreet locations, in which we perform different functions and adopt different identities.

Secondly, the notion of the outside space as entirely blank fails to take into account the extent to which even moving through unfamiliar locations is

---

[15] Armin von Ungern-Sternberg, *"Erzählregionen": Überlegungen zu literarischen Räumen mit Blick auf die deutsche Literatur des Baltikums, das Baltikum und die deutsche Literatur* (Bielefeld: Aisthesis, 2003), 17.
[16] Yi-Fun Tuan, *Space and Place: The Perspective of Experience* (London: Arnold, 1977), 54.

conditioned by our own cultural background and experiences: it is actually quite difficult to experience any place as entirely without meaning for us or to be entirely disorientated. Leisure travellers adopt a number of strategies when in other countries, for example, from the most extreme forms of 'holidaymaking', to use Julian Baggini's term, in which the traveller demands a more or less exact reproduction of already familiar leisure activities and home comforts with the bonus of better weather, to the more 'touristic' experience of sampling aspects of local colour as recommended by the guidebook bought back home.[17] Even the exile, it can be argued, is not confronted with an entirely meaningless environment, even if that environment is difficult to master and alienating: finding oneself in entirely unfamiliar territory is in fact a process of negotiation between one's cultural origins and expectations and an unfamiliar culture, although, as Hamid Naficy points out, such a negotiation can undermine any sense of the naturalness of one's own cultural identity and that of one's hosts.[18]

Thirdly, as Doreen Massey has argued, the binary opposition between closed, familiar and, by implication, unchanging place and open, unknown and, again by implication, fluid space ignores both, on the one hand, the fact that place itself is always in a process of change (social, political, economic and even geological) and, on the other, that the open space perceived from one point of view is in fact made up of places experienced in terms of local specificity by others. As Massey demonstrates, this kind of opposition between space and place encourages a view of the world which tries to impose an unproductive stasis on the place of origin whilst at the same time taking an essentially colonizing view of the world beyond.[19]

The idealization of place as enclosed, known and sheltering is not infrequently allied with assumptions about the relationship between place and community, which are the starting point for a critique of modernity's tendency to

---

[17] Julian Baggini, *Welcome to Everytown: A Journey into the English Mind* (London: Granta, 2007). Chapter 6 deals with the distinction between 'holidaymaking' and 'tourism'.
[18] Hamid Naficy, *An Accented Cinema: Exilic and Diasporic Filmmaking* (Princeton: Princeton UP, 2001).
[19] Doreen Massey, *for space* (London: Sage, 2005).

create 'placelessness'. French anthropologist Marc Augé, to take a recent example, defines place in terms of relationships, shared identities and common histories bound to the location of the group, and compares such places with the spaces or 'non-places' of 'supermodernity', in which the relationship of human beings to locations is increasingly (if not exclusively) mediatized and devoid of real human interaction.[20] Whilst Augé recognizes that the experience of place is not entirely erased by 'non-place',[21] the general rhetorical thrust of his argument is that human beings in Western societies are moving ever closer to a point where they will only experience the outside world as motorway drivers and media consumers, whose identities are no longer formed through integration into a community of others in a particular location. As such, his position chimes in with that tradition in sociology and cultural anthropology that regards place, as Mike Featherstone puts it, as the locus of 'a stable homogenous and integrated cultural identity' based on 'day-to-day interactions',[22] and that interprets the process of modernization as a gradual decaying of such a sense of place and belonging, and thus of identity.

This notion is central, for example, to Otto F. Bollnow's conceptualization of space in his *The Human Being and Space* (*Mensch und Raum*). Although Bollnow consistently uses the German term *Raum* rather than *Ort*, his frame of reference is clearly translatable into that set up by writers like Augé who valorize place over space. Bollnow emphasizes, after Heidegger, the necessity of 'inhabiting' ('Wohnen') in a healthy human relationship to space: human beings, he states, need to establish a place of habitation that is part of a 'larger whole'.[23] For pre-modern societies, Bollnow claims, the sense of a geographical and cultural 'centre' was given and unquestioned. However, the process of

---

[20] Marc Augé, *Non-Places: Introduction to an Anthropology of Supermodernity*, trans. John Howe (London: Verso, 1995), 101.
[21] Augé, *Non-Places*, 79.
[22] Mike Featherstone, 'Localism, Globalism and Cultural Identity', in Rob Wilson and Wimal Dissanayake (eds.), *Global/Local: Cultural Production and the Transnational Imaginary* (Durham, NC: Duke UP), 46-77 (here 47).
[23] Otto Friedrich Bollnow, *Mensch und Raum*, 2nd edn (Stuttgart: Kohlhammer, 1971), 310.

modernization brings with it the loss of such a centre and therefore the danger of 'deracination' ('Entwurzelung'), which must be compensated by the embedding of the home in a series of 'zones of familiarity' emanating outwards through the neighbourhood, and the region to the nation.[24] Like Augé, Bollnow sees processes of modernization, such as increased mobility and communication, as the enemy of such familiarity and a sense of being at home in the world.[25] This emphasis on the sense of place as the source of rootedness and connection to human community is generally a feature of conservative discourses on modernization, which equate the sense of place with integration into a local and or national community that is also the embodiment of shared values.

There are a number of objections that can be raised to such a definition of place. The first, as Massey observes, is that '"place" and "community" have rarely been coterminous'.[26] To assume that all subjects inhabiting a particular bounded locale, even the most traditional of villages, universally share a sense of common identity or values is an idealization that ignores a number of factors, not least divisions of class, religion, ethnicity, gender or the exclusion of sexual difference.

Secondly, a location may appear to be a piece of fragmented, emptied out, alienating and meaningless space (a 'non-place') only from a particular point of view. Augé, for example, cites the supermarket car park as one such space, but this can only be as it is experienced by the transient consumer. For those people who collect the trolleys in the supermarket car park and who are part of a larger workforce, which is itself probably drawn from the surrounding area, this space can be the site of interactions with a particular group of people over a period of time, where friendships and a sense of familiarity and belonging, if not automatically a sense of shared values, might develop. Although this may appear to be a banal example, such ordinary experiences are a counterweight to high theory that assumes that the meaning of places is univocal, and that a locality is

---

[24] Bollnow, *Mensch und Raum*, 124 and 131.
[25] See, for example, Bollnow's comments on the development of motorways. Bollnow, *Mensch und Raum*, 101-7.
[26] Massey, *Space, Place and Gender*, p. 147.

resistant to identification and the development of a specific character because the theorist has no access to these.

Thirdly, the pessimistic narrative of the erosion of place by space underestimates the presence of both the familiar and the anonymous in everyday lives: a lifestyle that includes package holidays, media consumption, high-speed travel and visits to out-of-town shopping malls can also include visits to local events, participation in local clubs and societies, journeys on foot, visits to the local shop (where one is recognized) and conversations over the garden fence.

The problematic nature of the discourse of modern 'placelessness' has been further demonstrated in recent years in the context of discussions of the phenomena of 'globalization'. Following on from the pessimistic narrative of modernization in relation to place, the negative image of globalization is that of homogenization, a 'McWorld', in which local cultural specificities are erased by the development of a uniform world-wide consumer market. This 'mythology' about globalization,[27] has been challenged in a number of ways, not least by theorists who seek to understand the process of 'glocalization': that is to say the process by which increased global cultural and economic interchange acts upon the local, which nevertheless retains its specific character as a hybridization of the global and the local.[28]

If the equation of place with the familiar, the home-like and the collective proves to be something of a dead end, if not also implicitly conservative and restricting, what model for a notion of place can be identified in its stead, particularly bearing in mind the focus of this volume on literary studies? It seems essential to take into account two key factors: firstly, and as the phenomenologists remind us, we are all always somewhere, that is to say that our bodies and thus

---

[27] Marjorie Ferguson, 'The Mythology about Globalization', *European Journal of Communication*, 7 (1992), 69-93.

[28] Robert Robertson, 'Glokalisierung: Homogenität und Heterogenität in Raum und Zeit', in Ulrich Beck (ed.), *Perspektiven der Weltgesellschaft* (Frankfurt a.M.: Suhrkamp, 1988), 192-220. For a useful overview of the debates around the relationship between the global and the local with particular reference to the German context see Karoline von Oppen, 'Introduction', in Von Oppen and Renate Rechtien (eds.), *Local/Global Narratives* (Amsterdam: Rodopi, 2007), 1-17.

our selves are situated in a particular place that is always relative to the rest of the world;[29] secondly, that the world that we all exist in relation to is not only a physical world, but also simultaneously a symbolic world which 'gives particular places and regions as well as their interrelationship symbolic functions' and covers 'the totality of space with a semiotic net'.[30] In other words, each place has a specific meaning for us as individuals because we are in it and uniquely so, but that it is only because particular places have a culturally determined meaning that we can experience them as places at all. Places are culturally produced geographical entities, which are always also experienced subjectively. Part of the cultural 'imagining' of such entities is that the difference of subjective experience and individual identity is often erased by the fantasy of a collective experience and identity. The prime example of such 'imagining' is, of course, the nation, as Benedict Anderson's famous study demonstrates.[31]

The example of the nation highlights a further important factor in the cultural construction of place: namely, the extent to which such constructions cannot be value-free. Subjects have an unequal relationship to 'imagined' places, in that they are more or less able to influence the symbolic meanings attached to particular places. We should also not forget that the interests of power are not only expressed symbolically in place, but that power has the actual means to change the physical make-up of particular places for its own purposes and control their use by the population: urban planning, surveillance and attempts to impose 'public order' are the contemporary expressions of this unequal distribution of power.

---

[29] See Jean-Paul Sartre, *Being and Nothingness: An Essay in Phenomenological Ontology*, trans. Hazel E. Barnes (London: Methuen, 1969), 308: 'Man and the world are relative beings, and the principle of their being is in relation. [...] [K]nowledge can only be an engaged upsurge in a determined point of view which one *is*. For human reality, to be is to-be-there; that is "there in that chair," "there at that table," "there at the top of that mountain, with these dimensions, this orientation, *etc.*" It is an ontological necessity'.
[30] Norbert Mecklenburg, *Erzählte Provinz: Regionalismus und Moderne im Roman* (Königstein: Athenäum, 1982), 34.
[31] Benedict Anderson, *Imagined Communities Reflections on the Origin and Spread of Nationalism*, revised edn (London: Verso, 1991).

Nevertheless, despite the many apparent barriers to an individual experience of space, this is precisely what that experience remains: individual. To return to Lefebvre's notion of space as something both produced and productive, much the same could be said of our definition of place. Subjects do not individually make place – even Robinson Crusoe's transformation of the wilderness of his island into a 'civilized' habitation was conditioned by his own cultural assumptions – but they do live it, as Lefebvre says of space more generally, and therefore potentially have it in their power to 'appropriate it' either in a concrete or a symbolic way to their own needs, whether individually or collectively.[32] In a similar, if more qualified fashion, Michel de Certeau has described this process of appropriation in terms of 'tactics', which he opposes to the 'strategies' of power. Although individuals and groups do not necessarily have the resources to challenge the spatial strategies of power, he argues, they can, through their everyday, lived used place, divert it to their own ends.[33] One might add that this living and appropriation of place is necessarily a 'process', as Massey puts it, that is to say not directed towards something static and stable, but, like the cultural identity of which it may be a component, open and always being produced.[34] As I will argue below, it is precisely this notion of place as process that speaks to the possibilities of literature.

Before attempting to apply this definition of place to literature, however, it will be useful to briefly summarize the varied approaches that both German and non-German critics have made to the role of the topographical or the spatial as a feature of literary texts.

To begin with, it is clear that literary texts themselves have certain spatial qualities. In as far as they are written down, all texts constitute a physical space: the reader's eye moves along the lines of the page, from the top to the bottom, and from page to page through the book, although some readers move through this

---

[32] Lefebvre, *Production of Space*, p. 39.
[33] See Michel de Certeau's, *The Practice of Everyday Life*, trans. Steven F. Rendall (Berkeley, California and London: U of California P, 1984).
[34] Massey, *Space, Place and Gender*, 171.

textual space in unconventional ways, jumping back and forth and skipping from place to place. In his attempt to outline a general theory of 'spatial form' in literature, W. J. T. Mitchell has gone as far as to argue for an approach to literary texts that sees this movement through the work, following the 'track' of the narrative, as producing a meaning-generating 'spatial pattern', which is not necessarily linear.[35] Variations of this tendency to define the qualities of a literary space that belongs only to the text can be found in Maurice Blanchot's attempt to define a specific literary space that exists outside and beyond the constraints of the physical space of everyday experience,[36] Ernst Cassirer's definition of 'aesthetic space',[37] or Cary Nelson's contention that literature aspires to a 'pure spatiality' or 'visionary space', that is to say that it creates a space that the reader enters into in a comparable fashion to the way she enters bodily into a physical space, but which is separate from the spatial experience of the world.[38] Whilst these approaches have the virtue of focusing our attention on a form of spatiality specific to literary form, they are not immediately useful for my purpose, in that they do not explicitly consider the construction and function of geographical place in literature.

If a narrowing of focus onto the spatial properties of the text itself or a spatiality specific to the experience of reading leads us away from our real object of interest in one direction, we also need to avoid the reduction of literature to a straightforward reflection of certain places, regions or landscapes, or indeed the reduction of certain places, regions or landscapes to direct reflections of the content of literary texts. This is the approach of numerous literary guidebooks,

---

[35] W. J. T. Mitchell, 'Spatial Form: Toward a General Theory', *Critical Enquiry*, 6.3 (1980), 539-67 (551-53).

[36] Maurice Blanchot, *The Space of Literature*, trans. Ann Smock (Lincoln: U of Nebraska P, 1990). For an overview of Blanchot's thinking, see Peter Boxall, 'Beckett, Blanchot and the black hole', in Glenda Norquay and Gerry Smyth (eds.), *Space and Place: The Geographies of Literature* (Liverpool: Liverpool John Moores UP, 1999), 45-54.

[37] Ernst Cassirer, 'Mythischer, ästhetischer und theoretischer Raum', in Alexander Ritter (ed.), *Landschaft und Raum in der Literatur* (Darmstadt: Wissenschaftliche Buchgesellschaft, 1975), 17-35 (here 29-30).

[38] Cary Nelson, *The Incarnate Word: Literature as Verbal Space* (Urbana: U of Illinois P, 1973), 3 and 6: 'Visionary space is the child born of our cohabitation with the language on the page. We shape our bodies to the rhythms of literature'.

which, whilst entertaining, operate on the principle that reading a novel tells us as much about a place as visiting a place will help us to understand a novel (and to understand its author even better), on the assumption that the work of literature will allow us access to 'the reality it subsumed [aufgehoben]'.[39] This approach is more properly seen as an aspect of the 'heritage industry', an off-shoot of tourism that sells destinations according to their literary and historical associations, although there is of course no requirement that visitors must have read Jane Austen to experience 'Jane Austen's Bath' or that they must have read Goethe to enjoy a visit to the *Goethehaus* in Weimar.

Having said this, Franco Moretti has presented a much more subtle and intriguing approach to the relationship between geography and the narrative structure of literary texts in his *Atlas of the European Novel 1800-1900* (1997). Here Moretti proposes a 'geography of literature' that will demonstrate the ways in which narratives are shaped by the production of space in their epoch, working from the thesis 'that *each space determines, or at least encourages, its own kind of story*'.[40] This approach would certainly provide a productive avenue for literary studies, although it is not one actively pursued in this volume.

A further approach that can be identified in writing on literature and place is to investigate historically the greater or lesser extent to which different literary periods tend to foreground the geographical specificities of the settings of their narratives, and to make causal links between the characteristics of the places in which those narratives are played out, the shape of the narrative itself and the development of the characters: in other words, the purpose of such analyses is to decide whether setting determines character and plot at a certain point in literary history or whether it merely functions as a neutral backdrop. As examples of this approach, Leonard Lutwack's study of the English and American novel and Bruno Hillebrand's spatially-oriented account of the history of the German novel reach strikingly similar conclusions, but also share, despite their claims to merely

---

[39] Albert von Schirnding, *Literarische Landschaften* (Frankfurt a.M.: Insel, 1998), 39.
[40] Franco Moretti, *Atlas of the European Novel 1800-1900* (London: Verso, 1999), 70. Emphasis in original.

describe and classify, a strong sense of what they see as the proper relationship between place and literature, which in both cases can be broadly defined as 'realism'. To summarize the developments they describe, both Lutwack and Hillebrand subscribe to a three-step model, whereby an initial disregard for place in literature, with geographical setting as a merely sketched-in backdrop to action centred on the self of the protagonist (for Lutwack in the eighteenth century English novel and English Romanticism and for Hillebrand in German Classicism and Romanticism), gives way to nineteenth century realism, wherein the place of the action gains a relative autonomy and becomes essential to the development of the narrative and its protagonist, only to be dissolved again into the 'placelessness' of modernism.[41]

Lutwack and Hillebrand differ in their notion of what the ideal of the interrelationship between literature and place in the context of realism should be. Lutwack, taking Henry James as his model, describes this ideal as follows:

> Here, finally, we have woven together place in its literalness, a character's response to this place in both its concreteness and its symbolic relation to his life, and an important action transpiring in this place. This is a proper use of place in a measure not too meagre to do justice to the importance of place in narrative nor so concrete as to overwhelm the imaginative power in the art of fiction.[42]

Although Lutwack's approach is prescriptive in its restriction of these qualities to a particular style of nineteenth century realism, we can perhaps already see some points of contact between the model of place I outlined above and a potential function of place in literature. The elements I identified in the experience of place find an equivalent expression in literature according to Lutwack: place is concretely and symbolically given, that is to say that characters are situated in a specific place that has a localized reality, physically and symbolically constructed by forces beyond their control; at the same time, literature is concerned with the

---

[41] Leonard Lutwack, *The Role of Place in Literature* (Syracuse: Syracuse UP, 1984). Bruno Hillebrand, *Mensch und Raum im Roman: Studien zu Keller, Stifter, Fontane mit einem einführenden Essay zur europäischen Literatur* (Munich: Winkler, 1971).
[42] Lutwack, *The Role of Place*, 26.

response of characters, who are neither passive products of physical and symbolic place nor masters of it.

It is worth noting that Hillebrand's ideal of the relationship between literature and place, although in many respects working from a similar model to Lutwack's, points to an engagement with place in German culture that can be read in terms of a problematic national tradition. Whilst also locating the ideal of literary representations of place in the era of realism, Hillebrand defines this ideal in quite different terms to Lutwack, namely as

> a naming of spatial relationships and things from a unified perspective, which is not only an optical one, but which is also rooted in the incommensurable centre of the personal.[43]

This centering is not merely a matter of perspective, however. It is also a centredness of an existential quality, in that certain realist authors are credited with creating a relationship between protagonist and place in which their environment serves as a 'compensation and opposite pole to latent doubts' and a 'basis for harmony'.[44] Such realism, Hillebrand goes on to argue, affirms a positive relationship to place, in which, although the environment is portrayed as a reality independent of the consciousness of the protagonist, that environment is fortuitously revealed to be in tune with and accommodating of that consciousness.[45] This notion of centredness and harmony immediately recalls Bollnow's conception of the ideal relationship between human beings and place, which Norbert Reichel has interpreted, alongside the work of thinkers such as Bachelard, as an attempt to compensate an existential 'loss of centre' in modernity by retreating to a bounded space of supposed harmony and order.[46]

---

[43] Hillebrand, *Mensch und Raum*, 86.
[44] Hillebrand, *Mensch und Raum*, 95.
[45] Hillebrand, *Mensch und Raum*, 98.
[46] Norbert Reichel, *Der erzählte Raum: Zur Verflechtung von sozialem und und poetischem Raum in erzählender Literatur* (Darmstadt: Wissenschaftliche Buchgesellschaft, 1987), 16-17.

This attempt to make good the supposed 'spiritual homelessness'[47] of the modern individual by seeking to centre oneself in a place, which is idealized as holding no potential for conflict with the subject, is not just a feature of conservative thought in general, as already observed, but has a specific German history in relation to the notion of *Heimat*. This link is evident in Hillebrand's key example, the first part of Gottfried Keller's novel *Green Henry* (*Der grüne Heinrich*, 1855), which is centred on the protagonist's childhood experiences in his Swiss provincial home town, and which represents, as Hillebrand puts it, a 'unity of man and place'.[48] *Heimat* is a complex notion that implies simultaneously the regional, the provincial (in the sense of the non-urban), a resistance to the rationalized and instrumental human relationships of modernity through recourse to a rooted, stable and homogenous community, and a nostalgia for the secure world of childhood and home.[49] All of these elements are present in Hillebrand's valorization of a carefully selected section of Keller's text (he is more critical of the second part, in which Heinrich leaves the ideal place of childhood).

Returning to Lutwack's definition of the function of place in literature, however, and informed by my earlier definition of place itself as an open-ended process, it is clearly possible to be concerned with place without falling back into such essentialism or simply into a nostalgia for the supposedly 'intact world' ('heile Welt') of the provinces, which, as Stuart Taberner observes, still resonates today as one possible conservative response to the threatening 'placelessness' of

---

[47] For an influential discussion of this notion in the context of German literature, see Hans Egon Holthusen, *Der unbehauste Mensch. Motive und Probleme der modernen Literatur* (Munich: Piper, 1951).
[48] Hillebrand, *Mensch und Raum*, 121. The original German reads 'Einheit von Mensch und Raum', which means literally 'unity of human being and space'. In this context, however, given that Hillebrand is talking about a male character, and that the problem of alienation from place is exclusively (if not consciously) portrayed as a masculine one, I have opted for the more outmoded translation of 'Mensch' as 'man'. Equally, since Hillebrand is talking about a bounded space with specific qualities, it seems reasonable to translate 'Raum' as 'place' in this instance.
[49] For an enlightening discussion of *Heimat* in German culture, see Elizabeth Boa and Rachel Palfreyman, *Heimat: A German dream: Regional Loyalties and National Identity in German Culture, 1890-1990* (Oxford: OUP, 2000).

globalization.[50] Key to Lutwack's approach, and to my own view of place, is that of 'response', in other words the individual engagement with place in its concrete and symbolic specificity. Because that specificity is also experienced by a potentially large number of other subjects, this is not merely a solipsistic enterprise. Rather, those multiple and sometimes incompatible experiences are what contribute to the ever developing identity of a place, which may not be, as Massey notes, 'a seamless and coherent identity, a single sense of place which everyone shares', but can nevertheless be recognized as something specific by all those who participate in and contribute to it.[51]

Literary works can show us the engagement of individuals with place as a contribution to that ongoing process of place and, as such, represent a particular kind of contribution in themselves. They too are ways of 'imagining' place, which is equally an element of that 'imaginative power of fiction' that Lutwack emphasizes, and can offer models of appropriation or, as Hartmut Böhme puts it, orientation.[52] What characterizes the most interesting writing about place, as the contributions to this volume demonstrate, is not the portrayal of place as a stable given, but as something to enter into a dialogue with, to produce one's own version of, often in opposition to the colonization of place by power and its ideologies. In this respect, literature can take on the special function, which Lefebvre assigns to all art, of working on space, appropriating it and creating 'potentialities',[53] possible other ways of seeing, understanding and living space, or, in the context of this volume, a particular place.

As contributions to this volume demonstrate, literature engages with place as process in a number of specific ways. If we regard place as a cultural construct traversed by competing signifying discourses, then literature can engage with

---

[50] Stuart Taberner, 'The German Province in the Age of Globalisation: Botho Strauß, Arnold Stadler and Hans-Ulrich Treichel', in Taberner (ed.), *German Literature in the Age of Globalisation* (Edgbaston: Birmingham UP, 2004), 89-109.

[51] Massey, *Space, Place and Gender*, 153.

[52] Hartmut Böhme, 'Einleitung', in Böhme (ed.), *Topographien der Literatur: deutsche Literatur im transnationalen Kontext* (Stuttgart and Weimar: Metzler, 2005), ix-xiii (here xxii).

[53] Lefebvre, *Production of Space*, 349.

these discourses, bring them into dialogue and in so doing relativize their claims to hegemony. This is particularly the case where these discourses are historical in nature, an issue of central concern to a number of the contributions contained in this volume. If, as theorists of 'cultural memory' and 'collective memory' like Pierre Nora and Jan Assmann have argued, such memory is often inscribed into concrete sites, landscapes and monuments in order to buttress a group identity,[54] then literature can help to uncover multiple and possibly resistant memories through an engagement with place that seeks not to reinforce, but rather to problematize and challenge the collective. As an extension of this, literature can also approach place not just as the location of collective history, but equally in terms of a literary history, seeing place as a palimpsest of texts which participate in its own cultural construction. Indeed, by writing authors modify and contribute to that construction. Finally, although this is by no means an exhaustive list, literature can show how everyday interactions with place, and with our co-inhabitants of place, help to refashion our understanding of it, and how these interactions, informed as they are by questions of gender, nationality, ethnicity, class, generation and so on, might produce 'tactics', in De Certeau's sense, for turning place to our own ends.

Clearly, all of these potential contributions of literature to an understanding and negotiation of place are played out in specific socio-historical contexts, and this is very much reflected in the analyses collected here. The discussion of place, particularly as a constituent of belonging and identity, is especially complex in the context of German culture following the National Socialist period, when place, in the guise of *Heimat*, became implicated in the National Socialist vision of a racial community (*Volksgemeinschaft*) that sought its identity in its rootedness in a particular soil, and in which the specificity of place and the specificity of race were seen as interdependent. One of the intellectual products of this equation of place and identity was the planned

---

[54] Pierre Nora, 'Between Memory and History: *Les Lieux de Mémoire*', *Representations*, 26 (1989), 7-24. Jan Assmann, 'Collective Memory and Cultural Identity', *New German Critique*, 65 (1995), 125-33.

reshaping by German geographers of occupied areas of Poland into an ideally 'German' landscape, in order to provide a suitable home for resettled Rhineland farmers; this programme also necessitated the 'cleansing' of such regions of their native populations.[55]

Yet the legacy of National Socialist ideology is not the only specifically German issue which approaches to place in German culture have to contend with. The end of the Second World War brought with it a number of political developments that had consequences for the experience of place in Germany. Firstly, around 12 million ethnic Germans fled or were forced to flee territories in central and eastern Europe for what were to become the Federal Republic or the German Democratic Republic in the months following the end of the war. Thus both fledgling German states had to socially and economically integrate substantial immigrant populations, many of whom maintained a connection with and a nostalgia for the places they had left and who were not always readily accepted in their new homes. In the Federal Republic, these immigrants were joined throughout the 1950s by those who chose to leave their homes in the GDR. From the years of the German Economic Miracle in the 1950s and 1960s, Germany also had to come to terms with, and is indeed still coming to terms with, its status as a multicultural society, with a significant number of German citizens now negotiating hybrid, transnational identities, that often express themselves in terms of complex relationships to multiple sites of belonging.[56] This development is mirrored to an extent, although under very different circumstances, by the increased mobility of Germans themselves, now inhabitants of a wealthy and increasingly cosmopolitan society. Emily Jeremiah's chapter in this volume addresses the experience of migration from Germany in the work of Birgit

---

[55] Dennis Cosgrove, 'Landscape and Landschaft', in *GHI Bulletin*, 35 (2004), 57-71 (here 66).

[56] The films of German-Turkish director Fatih Akin, including *Head On* (*Gegen die Wand*, 2004) and *The Edge of Heaven* (*Auf der anderen Seite*, 2007), are a particularly striking example of such negotiations. A number of recent publications address Turkish-German writing in particular, including Leslie A. Adelson, *The Turkish Turn in Contemporary German Literature: Toward a New Critical Grammar of Migration* (Houndsmills: Palgrave Macmillan, 2005) and Tom Cheesman, *Novels of Turkish German Settlement: Cosmopolite Fictions* (Rochester, NY: Camden House, 2007).

Vanderbeke in order to investigate the complex construction and meaning of place for the German migrant, an undertaking made still more complex by the feminist elements of Vanderbeke's work.

Another historical factor has been the division of Germany, particularly after the closure of the GDR border in August of 1961, which had significant consequences for the experience not just of nation but also of place, with towns, villages and landscapes finding themselves politically resituated on a heavily fortified border, with communication between neighbouring localities severed: what had previously been close and familiar, as the case of divided Berlin in particular demonstrates,[57] seemed suddenly to be on the other side of the world. Within the GDR itself, spatial issues took on a particular political dimension in the quest of citizens to carve out for themselves a place where they could experience a respite from the demands of the state. In this context, Juliane Parthier's analysis of the work of Helga Schütz is particularly intriguing, in that it shows how the border area itself, despite its tight control by the GDR security forces, could be reimagined as a site of resistance to their claims to spatial and ideological control. In Dennis Tate's chapter on Günter de Bruyn and in Renate Rechtien's discussion of Christa Wolf, the importance of finding a place 'off the beaten track', whether physically or in the imagination, becomes an essential (if not unproblematic) precondition of the maintenance of a sense of creative freedom for some writers under state socialism.

Thirdly, the experience of place was and still is implicated in a coming to terms with the National Socialist past and the Second World War, which were the ultimate causes of German division. Not only did devastated cityscapes have to be rebuilt, but the entire landscape bore traces of the horrors of National Socialism, and of the war itself. Both Helmut Schmitz's chapter on the fiction of Hanns-Joseph Ortheil and Dora Osborne's chapter on W.G. Sebald's novel *Austerlitz* (2001) focus on the legacy of the National Socialist past in the lives of the

---

[57] A number of German works of fiction about Berlin have addressed this situation, such as Peter Schneider's *The Wall Jumper* (*Der Mauerspringer*, 1983) or, more recently, Sven Regener's *Herr Lehmann* (2001).

children of its victims through an exploration of topographies of memory. Place figures here as the locus of forgetting but also of the attempt to recover memory against the imposition of such forgetting, whether that imposition has its source, as in the former case, in the repressive silence of the family, or, as in the latter, in the institutionalized forgetting that saw the agencies of the Third Reich seek to destroy any physical traces of their crimes. Questions of history and memory are equally central to the contributions by Andrew Webber and Simon Ward, who both take the city of Berlin as their particular focus and demonstrate how the engagement of post-war German-language authors such as Wolfgang Koeppen and Ingeborg Bachmann with this cityscape becomes a meditation on the relationship between place and history that seeks to explore alternative conceptions of national and personal identity.

Three of the contributions to this volume show a particular interest in the formal strategies developed by authors addressing the experience of place and in the politics of those literary strategies. Thomas Moebius analyses texts by GDR authors to show how their literary description of particular landscapes, and in particular the Harz mountains, mounts challenges to the political status quo, both pre- and post-unification, through the use of intertextual practices that recall earlier canonical representations and appropriate them to their own political ends. Stephan Krause's discussion of GDR author Franz Fühmann's *Twenty-two Days or Half a Life* (*Zweiundzwanzig Tage oder die Hälfte des Lebens*, 1973) similarly shows how Fühmann's description of his stay in Budapest is less an account of the place itself than an exploration of the modernist literature still regarded with suspicion by the authorities through the medium of the city. David Clarke's essay on Gert Neumann's engagement with the city of Leipzig in the 1970s and 1980s, on the other hand, shows how Neumann uses his daily experience of working, living and writing in the city as a starting point for a poetics of resistance to the hegemonic claims of the ruling socialist ideology.

A Note on Translations

The present volume is designed to be equally as accessible to scholars and students working in German language culture as it is to literature specialists who do not read German. With this in mind, quotations from all of the literary texts discussed are given first in English and then in German, using an extant translation where one was accessible. All other quotations from secondary literature in languages other than English are given in English only.

The chapters by Möbius and Krause were translated from the German for the purposes of this volume and contain explanatory notes from the translator in square brackets where necessary.

CHAPTER 1

'Walking and Gazing':
Autobiography, Spatiality and Heimat in Hanns-Josef Ortheil's 'Post-War' Cycle

Helmut Schmitz

Hanns-Josef Ortheil was born in 1951 as the fifth and only surviving child of a family from the *Siegerland* in West Germany. Both parents were deeply traumatized by the war, the father due to his experiences as a soldier at the Eastern front and the mother as a result of the bombing raids on Berlin, during which she experienced her first miscarriage. Her second child was killed by a grenade splinter at the age of three in the last days of the war; two more died at birth or shortly afterwards as a result of the mother's traumatization. Ortheil's mother lost the ability to speak for several years and enveloped her surviving son in a symbiotic relationship; he grew up in the shadow of the dead brothers, unwittingly inheriting his parents' wartime trauma. Ortheil has explored this family constellation in his autobiographical novels *Hedge* (*Hecke*, 1983) and *Farewell to the Combatants* (*Abschied von den Kriegsteilnehmern*, 1992), pre-empting the contemporary academic discussion of transgenerational family trauma by a good two decades.[1] I have written on the issue of transgenerational traumatization and coming to terms with the past in Ortheil's work elsewhere;[2] here I want to pursue the question of how the issues of family history, writing, subjectivity and trauma manifest themselves in the concept of landscape and the perception of environment in Ortheil's novels. I will first focus on Ortheil's autobiographical

---

[1] On the issue of transgenerational trauma see, for example, the essays by Brigitte Rauschenbach, Werner Bohleber und Michel B. Buchholz in Jörn Rüsen and Jürgen Straub (eds.), *Die dunkle Spur der Vergangenheit: Psychoanalytische Zugänge zum Geschichtsbewusstsein* (Frankfurt a.M.: Suhrkamp, 1998), 242-55, 256-74 and 330-53.

[2] See the chapter on Ortheil in my *On Their Own Terms: The Legacy of National Socialism in Post-1990 German Fiction* (Birmingham: U of Birmingham P, 2004), 27-54.

essay *The Element of the Elephant* (*Das Element des Elephanten*, 1994), before I pursue the development of a number of motifs in the narrative works.

For Ortheil's writing, the idea of self-location, both in three-dimensional space and in writing is central. Ortheil's metaphor for his existence as writer, for writing and the relation of writing to the self is emphatically spatial. It invokes less the idea of the public space in which the writer situates himself than that of the infinite space of literature, an experience that oscillates between self-creation and extinction of the self, attainment of contours and loss:

> To publish means to reproduce oneself in these artificial, refracted and fleeting images. [...] [F]inally, everything that is private and intimate is extinguished, it has dissolved into the dominance of Writing, [...] into the space of mirrors and labyrinths, into the space of infinite dialogues.

> Veröffentlichen heißt, sich in solche künstlichen, gebrochenen und flüchtigen Bilder zu vervielfachen. [...] [S]chließlich ist alles Private und Intime ausgelöscht, es hat sich aufgelöst in die Herrschaft der Schrift, [...] in den Raum der Spiegel und Labyrinthe, in den Raum der unendlichen Dialoge.[3]

The Element of the Elephant describes the experience of language and Writing[4] as both disorderly chaos and ordered (as well as ordering) system. Ortheil's concept of spoken language and Writing opens up a spatial system of coordinates in which each concept is doubly encoded and symbolically located in relation to mother and father. The mother represents the symbiotic 'sound-proof room' ('schalldichten Raum', EE 27) of a silent, pre-symbolic understanding. Ortheil, who grows up in this silence without language experiences the voices of others as 'disordered, ephemeral, importunate, [...] a kind of rough chaos' ('ungeordnet, ephemer, zudringlich [...] eine Art grobes Chaos', EE 45). On the other hand, these voices represent the first experience of the 'infinite murmuring' that, according to Michel Foucault, makes up the space of literature, into which the

---

[3] Hanns-Josef Ortheil, *Das Element des Elephanten* (Munich: Piper, 1994), 126-7. Referred to in the following as EE.
[4] I have capitalized Writing here to distinguish it from the mere act of writing (*schreiben*).

writer enters and 'in which the writing subject disappears again and again' ('in dem das schreibende Subjekt immer wieder verschwindet').[5] Ortheil connects the mother-pole of writing explicitly with the restitution of the symbiotic state in the mother's womb, in an image that recalls Oskar Matzerath's desire in Günter Grass's *The Tin Drum* (*Die Blechtrommel*, 1959) to disappear under his grandmother's skirts: 'where language grows from its chaotic underground [...] there the *fissure* opens, into which I want to slip, singing and writing' ('wo die Sprache aus ihrem chaotischen Untergrund wächst [...] dort öffnet sich der *Spalt*, in den ich, schreibend und singend, hineinschlüpfen möchte', EE 40, emphasis in original).

Writing is similarly experienced as chaotic; as long as the letters do not fall into line with the 'art of naming' ('Kunst der Benennung', EE 58) they appear as 'fiends, little lively spirits' ('Unholde, kleine springlebendige Geister', EE 37). Ortheil describes the relationship with his mother as an enclosed space, a 'manageable terrain with borders and fences' ('gut überschaubares Terrain mit Grenzen und Zäunen', EE 43). The mother, who has to laboriously learn to speak anew encloses the child in a silent world of letters that she cuts from coloured paper. In their three-dimensional material form the letters threaten to invade the symbiotic space between child and mother; but as Writing (*Schrift*) they disappear into the 'white pages of my exercise book. Outside of the exercise book, the paper scraps were destroyed' ('in die weißen Seiten meines Heftes. Außerhalb des Heftes aber wurden die Papierschnipsel vernichtet', E 38).

For the young Ortheil, this silent separation results in the dissociation of spoken language and sign system, sign and referent and he subsequently refuses to speak. In analogy to the chaotic and disordered experience of language, he experiences open spaces as terrifying and unstructured, due to growing up in the protective environment of his parents' house enclosed by a garden surrounded by dark hedges. As a remedy, the father, a land surveyor by trade, undertakes long

---

[5] See Michel Foucault, *Das unendliche Sprechen*, in *Schriften zur Literatur* (Frankfurt a.M.: Fischer, 1988), 90-103 (here 96).

walks with the child during which he names all the visible signs of the landscape, effectively a programme of re-connection of sound and referent. In paradigmatic Lacanian manner, Ortheil connects language and Writing explicitly to the subordination under the Law of the Father, the entrance into the symbolic order. On the walks with the father Ortheil experiences language as an Adamic system of domination, a system that regulates domination via the name: 'The art of naming was the art of ordering and the subordination of things' ('Die Kunst der Benennung war die Kunst des Befehls und der Unterordnung der Dinge', E 59). Words are as material as the things they denote, they are 'hard living things that were under *supervision*' ('feste Lebewesen, die unter *Aufsicht* standen'' (E 64, emphasis in original).

While the mother thus embodies the experience of writing as never fully attained restitution of the original symbiosis, the father represents '*realism*, the art of exact naming, the words under supervision of the gaze' ('*Realismus*, die Kunst der genauen Benennung, die Worte unter der Aufsicht des Blicks', E 65, emphasis in original). The figure of the land-surveyor becomes the central symbol for Ortheil's cycle of novels that explore the psychological and spiritual foundations of the post-war generations; the project of writing the traumatized history of his family as the 'inner history of the post-war generations who grew up in the West' ('innere Geschichte der im Westen aufgewachsenen Nachkriegsgenerationen') is articulated in the topographical metaphor of mapping:[6] 'I will be an excellent land-surveyor, I will perfect the instinct inherited from my father and use it within my limits', the first person narrator in *Farewell to the Combatants* says of himself ('ich werde ein ausgezeichneter Vermesser werden, ich werde den von meinem Vater erworbenen Instinkt ausbilden und in meinen Grenzen zur Anwendung bringen').[7] The genre of the novel is itself described in spatio-temporal and topographical terms: the novel is 'a path through a landscape [...]. The novel is

---

[6] Hanns-Josef Ortheil, 'Werkstatt-Poetik', in *Schauprozesse. Beiträge zur Kultur der 80er Jahre* (Munich: Piper, 1990), 21. Referred to in the following as S.
[7] Hanns-Josef Ortheil, *Abschied von den Kriegsteilnehmern* (Munich: Piper, 1992), 48. Referred to in the following as AK.

the landscape set in motion and action' ('ein Weg durch eine Landschaft [...] Der Roman war die in Bewegung und Aktion versetzte Landschaft', EE 66-7)

Ortheil's writing oscillates between two poles that can be denoted as a post-structuralist experience of disappearance into the text and a modern position of the *Zeitroman*, which attempts to offer a representative picture of a particular era.[8] Both poles are described in *The Element of the Elephant* in the biographical experience of writing as 'crossroads of all the voices' ('Wegkreuzung der Stimmen', E 102): it is a space of disappearance and infinite murmur on the one hand, and of writing as naming, ordering, and self-location on the other.

This double binary encoding of Writing, speaking and writing corresponds to a double binary encoding of space as both protective space/confinement and openness/threat, originating in the ambiguous symbiotic parental relationship. Constitutive for the self-location of the subject in space in Ortheil's narratives is the possibility of a distance-creating gaze that keeps the phenomena at bay and allows the subject to visually structure the space, both actually and symbolically. The experience of the 'art of naming', looking and collecting are constitutive for the concept of world-appropriation and experience in Ortheil's first novel *Fermer* (1979) and reappear in variation in the subsequent novels *Hedge, Lady-Killer* (*Schwerenöter*, 1987), *Agents* (*Agenten*, 1989) and *Farewell to the Combatants*. In *Fermer* there are three characters who embody Ortheil's 'aesthetics of memory relating to landscape'.[9] Lotta, who grows up in the countryside appropriates the landscape through drawing, thereby establishing a sense of order and control. While she is within the apparently unstructured landscape, the environment 'remained undisclosed for a long time; it was an indecipherable secret of

---

[8] With respect to *Hedge*, Elmar Locher has exemplified how much Ortheil's experience of writing and learning to write coincides with the theoretical positions of French post-structuralism. See Elmar Lochner, 'Begegnungen ins Innere der Sprachen. Hanns-Josef Ortheils Roman *Hecke*', in Manfred Durzak and Hartmut Steinecke (eds.), *Hanns-Josef Ortheil – Im Innern seiner Texte* (Munich: Piper, 1995), 77-97. On the aspect of the *Zeitroman* see the introduction to my *Der Landvermesser auf der Suche nach der poetischen Heimat. Hanns-Josef Ortheils Romanzyklus* (Stuttgart: Heinz, 1997).

[9] See Manfred Jurgensen, '"...als wollte ich zu mir kommen": Erzählmodelle in den Romanen Hanns-Josef Ortheils', in Durzak and Steinecke (eds.), *Hanns-Joseph Ortheil*, 37-51 (here 44).

immensely high tree-trunks' ('blieb [...] lange verschlossen und war ein kaum zu entzifferndes Geheimnis aus unübersehbar hohen Baumstangen').[10] Only from a bench on a hill, from where the landscape can be kept under surveillance, is she able to take control of the environment. However, only in its *historical* dimension does the landscape turn into a chain of signifiers into which the subject can insert itself; subjective impressions are useless. When Lotta produces an impressionist and idealized version, her father responds that she

> had badly misappropriated the factual. [...] From now on I did no longer see the landscape as a network of lines and knots in which the colours dissolved, but as a context of human intentions [...].

> sich übel am Tatsächlichen vergriffen. [...] Von nun an habe ich die Landschaft nicht mehr gesehen wie ein Netz aus Linien und Flechten, in denen die Farben den Halt verloren, sondern als einen Zusammenhang menschlicher Absichten [...]. (F 133)

The appropriation of landscape as historically grown thus represents an act of mastery that overcomes the insecurity in the face of an environment experienced as unstructured. Lotta's brother Ferdinand manages this appropriation through collecting stones, insects, flowers and leaves, which he catalogues in his room: 'He has put together the landscape once over in his room' ('Er hat die Landschaft in seinem Zimmer noch einmal zusammengesetzt', F 134). In contrast, the protagonist Fermer's emphatic experiences of nature at the beginning of the novel are exposed as an attempt to escape into an impressionist inner space in the face of a society that encloses the individual:

> What he had left were the lonely walks in areas that still were unoccupied by people, [...] the little villages on the river, where the wine-growers lived, the wide plains east of the city, where you could walk for days amongst the golden wheat fields without meeting a single person.

> Ihm aber blieben die einsamen Spaziergänge in Gegenden, die noch menschenleer waren, [...] die kleinen Dörfer am Fluss, in denen die Weinbauern lebten, die weiten Ebenen östlich der Stadt,

---

[10] Hanns-Josef Ortheil, *Fermer* (Munich: Piper, 1991), 128. Referred to in the following as F.

über die man tagelang gehen konnte zwischen den goldgelben
Getreidefeldern, ohne einem Menschen zu begegnen. (F 31)

Fermer, Lotta and Ferdinand only attain a sense of self in relation to their
social environment in the reading of space as historical context. The contrast of
country and city is essential to the appropriation of the environment and the
history that envelops the subject. Only the quietness and immobility of the rural
landscape permits the maintenance of critical distance, whereas the acceleration of
life and the immediacy of the city undermine the possibility of self-location.
Agents, Ortheil's postmodern city novel, describes paradigmatically the
dislocation of the postmodern subject. The idea of the successful appropriation of
the world through collecting is turned on its head. The sister of the protagonist
Maynard moves from the countryside to the city to go to university. Like
Ferdinand in *Fermer*, she collects fragments from her environment. However,
these fragments, debris found on the city streets, do not add up to a meaningful
whole. After her nervous breakdown and a diagnosis as borderline schizophrenic,
Maynard finds in her room

> pickle jars, an indeterminable number, filled to the brim with stuff
> from the street, dirt, leaves, debris. These jars, too, were covered in
> exact coloured signs, with details of location, date and weather
> [...].

> Einweckgläser, eine nicht mehr zu übersehende Zahl, bis oben
> angefüllt mit Zeug von der Straße, Dreck, Blätter, loses Geröll.
> Auch diese Gläser waren exakt mit bunten Zeichen beschriftet, mit
> Angaben von Fundort, Datum und Wetter [...].[11]

Over the course of the novel, the young journalist Maynard progressively loses
the distance to the events in his environment until he is relegated to the fringes of
society. At the end of the novel, he decides to reinstate an experience of distance
by appropriating the pose and gaze of the *flaneur*: 'I would be walking and

---

[11] Hanns-Josef Ortheil, *Agenten* (Munich: Piper, 1989), 316-17. Referred to in the following as A.

gazing, nothing else, for a long time nothing else but this' ('Ich würde gehen und schauen, nicht mehr, für lange Zeit, nicht mehr als nur dies', A 324).[12]

The novel *Fermer* is thus structured paradigmatically around a concept of the modern subject as depending on the ability to maintain a critical distance for the purpose of self-location, while *Agents* deconstructs this distance in the accelerated non-space of the postmodern city.[13] To achieve a sense of self, distance and exact observation are essential. The exact observation of landscape is explicitly related to representational art. Fermer's father is, like Ortheil's own, a land surveyor; his drawings which 'order the landscape' are described as 'the first fragments of art' ('die ersten Bruchstücke der Kunst', F 224).

Ortheil's privileging of the distanced gaze, frequently from an elevated position, is part of the history of seeing, painting and mastering of landscape in modernity. The tradition of realist and perspectival representation of landscape has been subjected to a Foucauldian critique that exposes the 'politics of vision' as centred on a masculine subject that positions itself outside of the picture for the purpose of mastery and control.[14] The development of linear perspectives allows for the organization of represented objects in spatial relation to each other: 'Perspectival art represents a form of visual control, which freezes time and presents things as they empirically appear to be'.[15] However, what is important for Ortheil's narration of spatial experience is the hermeneutic aspect by which the gazing subject begins to experience itself as *part* of the context and history that has produced the current appearance of the environment. Thus, rather than being situated 'objectively' outside the frame, as in perspectival visual representations

---

[12] In this context see Ortheil's 1986 essay 'The Long Good-bye to the *Flaneur*' ('Der lange Abschied vom Flaneur', S 214-33). *Pace* Walter Benjamin, the essay describes the *flaneur* as someone who produces distance by 'bringing things to a standstill through the gaze' ('die Dinge durch den Blick zum Stillstand bringt', S 215).

[13] On the impossibility of critical distance in postmodern cityscape see Fredric Jameson, 'Postmodernism, or The Cultural Logic of Late Capitalism', in *New Left Review*, 146 (1984), 53-92 (here 85-88).

[14] See Julian Thomas, 'The Politics of Vision', in Barbara Bender (ed.), *Landscape and Politics* (Oxford: Berg 1993), 19-47 (here 21ff.). See also Bender's introduction, which describes landscape in the West as 'ego-centred' (1).

[15] Thomas, 'The Politics of Vision', 21

of landscape, Ortheil's characters experience themselves as situated *within* (historical) space, in agreement with recent conceptual developments in archaeology and human geography that articulate the interconnectedness of environment, subjects and power.[16] Fredric Jameson explicitly connects the ability of the subject 'to locate itself, to organize its immediate surroundings perceptually, and cognitively to map its position in a mappable external world' with the subjectivity of the modern subject, based on a hermeneutic experience of self-location.[17]

The subject's relationship to the surrounding space thus participates of the essential dialogicity and preliminary nature of hermeneutics as an 'infinite task'.[18] The principally preliminary nature of hermeneutics as envisaged by Friedrich Schleiermacher appears in *Fermer* in the circulating ways the characters speak about themselves and their experiences:

> He sensed that he would have had to keep on speaking for a long time like this before he could find a single sentence after which he could have stopped.

> Er ahnte, dass er lange hätte so weiterreden müssen, um auch nur einen Satz zu treffen, nach dem er hätte abbrechen können.' (F 129)

If the purpose of philosophical hermeneutics is a deeper understanding of texts, the result of the hermeneutic appropriation of landscape is a deeper understanding of the historical dimension of space and the self within it. Fermer's desire 'to take shape in the single sentence' ('im einzelnen Satz als Gestalt erscheinen', F 238) thus marks an analogy between the subject-constitutive experience of historical space and an emphatic concept of reading space that is tied to a concept of narration and storytelling (*erzählen*) where language yields the 'mirror of one's own story' (Spiegelbild der eigenen Geschichte', F 239).

---

[16] See Thomas, 'The Politics of Vision', 44.
[17] Jameson, 'Postmodernism', 83.
[18] See Jean Grondin, *Einführung in die philosophische Hermeneutik* (Darmstadt: Wissenschaftliche Buchgesellschaft, 2001), 107.

The emphatic concept of storytelling and the reading of space as historically constituted are two aspects of the historical trauma that dominates Ortheil's writing. The historical and spiritual landscapes that Ortheil's novels explore are the landscapes of destruction that were left behind by the Second World War. Fermer only attains an image of himself by understanding himself as part of a history of destruction and forgetting in the post-war period. The novels *Fermer*, *Hedge* and *Farewell to the Combatants* are characterized by a conception of twentieth century history as destructive of experience. National Socialism, war and reconstruction appear as an intensification of the loss of experience in modernity through the experience of traumatic shock. This loss of experience has first to be realized as such:

> After the war [...] they began to put together the ruins again. But the hectic activity lacked calmness and restraint. [...] The activity of reconstructing and repairing served to extinguish the memories. [...] Do you now understand [...] why the people here have lost their memories? The Nazis took advantage of the forgetting that had already begun.

> Nach dem Krieg [...] begann man, die Ruinen zusammenzusetzen. All der hektischen Tätigkeit fehlte es an Ruhe und Zurückhaltung. [...] Das Aufbauen und Reparieren hat herhalten müssen, die Erinnerungen auszulöschen. (F195). [...] Verstehst du jetzt, [...], warum den Menschen hier die Erinnerungen entfallen sind? Die Nazis haben das schon beginnende Vergessen ausgenutzt. (F 201)

The loss of experience through trauma and the reappropriation through topographically oriented storytelling is a theme that pervades Ortheils entire 'post-war' cycle. The figure of the '*storyteller*' (E 56, emphasis in original), who, like the *flaneur* and the collector, is part of Walter Benjamin's typology of modernity, is written into the very fabric of Ortheil's novels; the second novel, *Hedge*, is subtitled 'story' (*Erzählung*), even though it is a novel of 300 pages.[19]

---

[19] Hanns-Josef Ortheil, *Hecke* (Frankfurt a.M.: Fischer, 1983). Referred to in the following as H. See also Ortheil, 'Weiterschreiben'(S 89-103): 'I wanted to *tell stories* at all cost' ('Ich wollte um jeden Preis [...] *erzählen*' (S 100, emphasis in original). See also *The Element of the Elephant*, which mentions the 'figure of the *storyteller*' as ideal (EE 56, emphasis in original).

For Walter Benjamin, the figure of the storyteller is connected to a pre-modern form of experience that is tied to oral tradition: 'Experience which is passed on from mouth to mouth is the source from which all storytellers have drawn'.[20] Due to the specific structure of the story, the storyteller possesses the ability, 'to share experiences':[21] 'The storyteller takes what he tells from experience – his own or that reported by others. And he in turn makes it the experience of those who are listening to his tale'.[22] Benjamin's concept of the story as receptacle of experience is based on a repetition in difference: 'For storytelling is always the art of repeating stories'.[23] Benjamin's original German reads 'weitererzählen', which means handing on to someone else for her to tell the story to a third party. The handing on of the story is a repetition in difference, it is analogous to the work of the artisan who never reproduces the exact object twice. The persona of the storyteller has amalgamated with the story, this is what constitutes the aspect of experience that can be handed on:

> Storytelling [...] submerges the thing into the life of the storyteller in order to bring it out of him again. Thus, traces of the storyteller cling to the story the way the handprints of the potter cling to a clay vessel.[24]

In his theses on the destruction of experience in modernity, Benjamin connected both the shock experience of exact repetition in industrial labour and the traumatic experience of industrial warfare with the loss of experience.[25] For Benjamin, the

---

[20] Walter Benjamin, 'The Storyteller. Observations on the Works of Nikolai Leskow', *Selected Writings, Volume 3, 1935-1938*, ed. by Howard Eiland and Michael W. Jennings (Cambridge/Mass. and London: Belknap Press, 2002), 143-66 (here 144).

[21] Benjamin, 'The Storyteller', 143. Benjamin's original, 'Erfahrungen auszutauschen', also means to exchange experiences.

[22] Benjamin, 'The Storyteller', 146.

[23] Benjamin, 'The Storyteller', 149.

[24] Benjamin, 'The Storyteller', 149. The centrality of this image for Benjamin's theory of experience is evident from Benjamin's word for word repetition of it in the essay 'On Some Motifs in Baudelaire', in *Selected Writings, Volume 4, 1938-1940*, ed. by Howard Eiland and Michael W. Jennings (Cambridge/Mass. and London: Belknap Press, 2003), 313-55 (here 316). The English translation obscures Benjamin's repetition.

[25] 'Wasn't it noticed at the time how many people returned from the front in silence? Not richer but poorer in communicable experience? [...] A generation that had gone to school in horse-drawn streetcars now stood in the open air, amid a landscape in which nothing was the same except the

alienation of the worker of the machine consists not least in the fact that the body movements that the machine forces upon him turn him into an object that is no longer capable of experience, due to the constant exact repetition of movements:

> The hand movement of the worker at the machine has no connection with the preceding gesture for the very reason that it repeats that gesture exactly.

Thus his work is 'sealed off from experience'.[26]

A link can be made between Benjamin's theory of the loss of experience as a result of shock in modernity and theories of trauma. Both the narrator's mother in *Hedge* and the father in *Farewell to the Combatants* display symptoms of Post-Traumatic-Stress-Disorder (PTSD), which, as Susanne Vees-Gulani points out, 'has only been recognized as an independent psychiatric disorder since its inclusion in the 1980 edition of the *Diagnostic and Statistics Manual of Mental Disorders*'.[27] Cathy Caruth describes PTSD as

> a response, sometimes delayed, to an overwhelming event or events, which takes the form of repeated, intrusive hallucinations, dreams, thoughts or behaviours stemming from the event [...] and possibly also increase arousal to (and avoidance of) stimuli recalling the event.

Due to its overwhelming nature, the event 'is not assimilated or experienced fully at the time, but only belatedly, in its repeated *possession* of the one who experiences it'.[28] One of the possible pathologies consists in 'insistent reenactments of the past' which are not so much a form of memory as a sign of 'an experience that is not yet fully owned'.[29]

---

clouds and, at its center, in a force field of destructive torrents and explosions, the tiny, fragile human body.' Walter Benjamin, 'Experience and Poverty', in *Selected Writings, Volume 2, 1927-1934*, ed. by Michael W. Jennings, Howard Eiland, and Gary Smith (Cambridge/Mass. and London: Belknap Press, 1999), 731-6 (here 731-2).

[26] Benjamin, 'On Some Motifs in Baudelaire', 330 and 329.

[27] Susanne Vees-Gulani, *Trauma and Guilt: Literature of Wartime Bombing in Germany* (Berlin and New York: de Gruyter, 2003), 3.

[28] Cathy Caruth, Introduction to the section 'Trauma and Experience', in Caruth (ed.), *Trauma – Explorations in Memory* (Baltimore and London: Johns Hopkins UP, 1995), 3-12 (here 4).

[29] Caruth (ed.), *Trauma – Explorations in Memory*, Introduction to the section 'Recapturing the Past', 151-57 (here 151).

Both the mother in *Hedge* who insists on the exact repetition of her experience of being arrested by the Nazis in 1933, as well as the father in *Farewell to the Combatants*, whose repetitive-compulsive walks westwards reenact his flight from the Red Army, fulfil this pathology. According to the narrator in *Hedge*, the function of the mother's exact repetition of her story is to keep the deeper traumatization by the war at bay: 'My mother forgets by storytelling. But only by telling stories, she masters her forgetting' ('Meine Mutter vergißt, indem sie erzählt; aber nur indem sie erzählt, beherrscht sie ihr Vergessen', H 23). For the son, the mother's stories prove fatal, they force him into the 'prisonhouse of stories' ('Gefängnis der Geschichten', H 280), the 'undergrowth' ('Gestrüpp', H 172), from which he intends to liberate himself by telling his mother's story.

The son's narrative in *Hedge* is an act of storytelling in the emphatic sense, containing an explicit act of handing on of experience. The son leaves his manuscript chronicling his mother's traumatic wartime experience behind for her to find it, with the dedication: 'To whom but you?' ('Wem sonst als dir?', H 316). The son's narrative is thus simultaneously restitution and tradition, an attempt to mend the chain of tradition destroyed by the war by handing on of the experience that the son himself had with the mother's traumatic story. Recalling Benjamin's insights, the proper historical experience of Ortheil's characters consists in their realization of the dimensions of traumatization and destruction of experience in the war. Ortheil's characters in *Fermer*, *Hedge* and *Farewell to the Combatants* experience themselves on the interface of lines that 'reach from the dark into the present' ('aus dem Dunkel in die Gegenwart reich[en]', F 166), as subjects who are determined by an unconscious past that first has to be made conscious. This historical understanding is expressed in *Fermer* in an image that again reminds of Walter Benjamin's theses 'On the Concept of History', an image that represents the complementary shock to the trauma of history:

Maybe these are the stories still worth telling, stories where one
notices *with a start* where everything that has coalesced into an
image comes from and in what way one has been co-opted into it.

Das sind vielleicht auch die Geschichten, die es sich noch zu
erzählen lohnt, Geschichten, in denen man *mit einem Ruck*
bemerkt, woher alles, was zu Bildern geworden ist, herrührt, und
auf welche Weise man hineingezogen worden ist. (F 198, emphasis
in original)[30]

The reading of landscape as historically formed and the concept of
storytelling are thus part of a project of restitution of experience. A prerequisite
for this restitution is the realization of the destruction of experience through
historical trauma. If experience in an emphatic sense is 'a dimension of human
praxis within which relation to self and relation to world are articulated in such a
way that relation to world *becomes articulable* as relation to self and vice versa',
then Ortheil's novels articulate precisely this type of experience.[31] The landscapes
in Ortheil's narratives are thus neither mere 'landscapes of the soul', i.e.
externalized interior, nor mere empirical space. The experience of land- and
cityscape of Ortheil's narrators, all of which after *Fermer* are first-person
narrators, mirrors historical time, which is then re-connected to the history of the
subject and the family: 'Germany consists of [...] nothing but bombed, messed-up
and re-assembled villages' ('Deutschland besteht aus [...] lauter zerbombten,
durcheinandergeratenen, wieder zusammengesetzten Dörfern', AK 92). In this
statement, made by the narrator of *Farewell to the Combatants*, the physiognomy
of the country appears as a correlate of parental traumatization, the physical and
topographical expression of the processes of denial of the era of restoration, in
which the father attempts manically to reconstitute his world that has been
destroyed during the war. Ortheil's 'read' landscapes signify the traumatic

---

[30] See Walter Benjamin, 'On the Concept of History', in *Selected Writings, Volume 4*, 389-400
(here 396): 'Where thinking comes to a stop in a constellation saturated with tensions, it gives that
constellation a shock, by which it is crystallized as a monad'.
[31] See Thomas Weber, 'Erfahrung', in Michael Opitz and Erdmut Wizisla (eds.), *Benjamins
Begriffe*, 2 vols. (Frankfurt a.M.: Suhrkamp, 2000), I, 230-59 (here 236).

experience of German history of the twentieth century, in which the landscape is analogous to the traumatized subject. Ortheil's reading of landscape as iconography of historical trauma is thus informed by Benjamin's idea of reading 'what was never written', which is in turn influenced by the iconographic approach of the art history school of Erwin Panofsky and Aby Warburg and their method of 'reading what we see'.[32]

Metaphors and motifs of space furthermore function as metaphors for the history of the post-war family. In *Hedge*, the intimacy of the motherly protective space, which finds spatial expression in the quietness of the isolated house, increasingly becomes an expression for the 'prisonhouse of stories'. In *Farewell to the Combatants*, the remoteness of the house, situated at a 'trigonometric point' ('trigonometrischen Punkt', AK 215) on a hill, is itself an expression of the traumatized father's desire for mastery and overview. In analogy to the trigonometric point that marks the erection of the parents' post-war house as a mechanism of containment of traumatic disturbance, the death of the brothers and the parents' wartime experiences are described by the narrator as the 'trigonometric point' (AK 411) of his own biography, which is read implicitly as a 'collective biography' of the post-war generations.[33] National, family and personal history are telescoped into each other and are addressed as 'undergrowth', from which the characters have to struggle free. The title *Hedge* has multiple connotations, referring simultaneously to the dark hedges surrounding the terrain of the parental house in the ambiguity between protection and enclosure, the name of the farmstead where the mother loses her three year old son through a shell splinter, and the subtext of the novel, the transgenerational transmission of trauma: *hecken*, in German, means to propagate, to brood.

---

[32] See Walter Benjamin, 'On the Mimetic Faculty', *Selected Writings, Volume 2*, 720-2 (here 722). See also Benjamin, *The Arcades Project* (Cambridge/Mass. and London, Belknap Press, 1999), 464: 'The expression "the book of nature" indicates that one can read the real like a text'.

[33] Jurgensen, "'…als wollte ich zu mir kommen'", 37. On Panofsky's and Warburg's influence on Benjamin see Stephen Daniels and Denis Cosgrove, 'Introduction: Iconography and Landscape', in Daniels and Cosgrove (eds.), *The Iconography of Landscape* (Cambridge: CUP, 1988), 1-10 (here 2-3).

Brian Jarvis has pointed out that space, place and landscape denote 'not a fixed and static object so much as an ongoing process, a spatial praxis', arguing that there is 'no geographical knowledge without historical narrative'.[34] It is significant then, that in Ortheil's novels landscape in its socio-historical dimension occurs significantly tied to the narrative of a collective trauma. Kenneth Robert Olwig has explicitly linked the (scientific) perception and mapping of space to the idea of the nation, suggesting a 'synergistic' connection between the words of landscape, nature, nation and culture linked to 'the very notion of legitimacy'.[35] Susanne Küchler argues that the Western concept of landscape as 'inscribed surface', harbouring assumptions 'about its nature as a record of, or stage for, significant human actions', a surface 'which can be measured, described and depicted', is tied to a concept of landscape as (owned) territory.[36] The symbol of triangulation ties Ortheil's aesthetics of reading historical and psychological space to a concept of 'coming to terms' that has implicit associations of mastery and overcoming and thus to a national project of relating to the National Socialist past. This is explicitly linked to the issue of *Heimat* in *Farewell to the Combatants*, Ortheil's novel which connects the son's successful act of coming to terms with the past to the opening of the Berlin Wall and the end of the Cold War.

In *Farewell to the Combatants*, the father's wartime traumatization is described as a loss of and expulsion from his emphatically regional *Heimat*. The term, which is used in the son's recuperative rendering of the father's life, recurs several times in relation to the regional space of the Rhineland (AK 96) and to his native village ('Heimatdorf', AK 113). The father's concept of *Heimat* is thus emphatically regional and pre-modern, similarly to that to be found in the opening

---

[34] Brian Jarvis, *Postmodern Cartography: The Geographical Imagination in Contemporary American Culture* (London: Pluto, 1998), 3 and 7.

[35] Kenneth Robert Olwig, 'Sexual Cosmology: Nation and Landscape at the Conceptual Interstices of Nature and Culture; Or, What Does Landscape Really Mean?', in Bender, *Landscape and Politics*, 307-43 (here 307-8).

[36] Susanne Küchler, 'Landscape as Memory: The Mapping of Process and Its Representation in a Melanese Society', in Bender, *Landscape and Politics*, 85-196 (here 85-6).

episode of Edgar Reitz's TV series *Heimat I* (1984). Reitz's series is part of the
beginning 'revitalization' of this disgraced term in the late 1970s and 1980s in the
context of the ecological movement.[37] Like Reitz's *Heimat, Farewell to the
Combatants* reads the war as an invasion of modernity (i.e. displacement) into an
agricultural world of order.[38] The splitting of the father's existence as (pre-modern
and pre-war) peasant son and (modern, i.e. war-time and post-war) land surveyor
illustrates the historical rupture. The novel as a whole narrates the son's act of
coming to terms with the family trauma and the subsequent healing of the rift
between the father, who sees himself as a victim of the war, and the son, for
whom the Holocaust has become the paradigmatic signifier of the rupture in the
history of the twentieth century. The healing of the generational conflict that had
dominated post-1968 German memory discourse depends on the son's acceptance
of the legitimacy of the father's experience as a victim. This acceptance is
expressed in an act of imaginary restitution of the destroyed *Heimat* and a peasant
existence to his dead father. In front of Breughel's seasonal paintings, the son,
who after the father's death had fled the country, realizes that these paintings
depict 'simultaneously the images of my *Heimat*' ('zugleich auch die Bilder
meiner Heimat', AK 379). The son's imaginary depiction of his father's *Heimat*
landscape in the manner of Breughel represents a healed landscape:

> Hey, Dad, I have painted you a picture, [...] and the old farm [...]
> is in it and Cologne is in it, Cologne before the war, [...] but the
> war, the war, dad, the war is not in it [...].

> He, Dad, ich habe dir ein Bild gemalt, [...] und der alte Hof, [...]
> auch der ist drauf, und Köln ist drauf, Köln vor dem Krieg, [...]
> aber der Krieg, der Krieg, Dad, der Krieg ist nicht drauf [...]. (AK,
> 391)

---

[37] See David Morley and Kevin Robinson, 'No Place Like *Heimat*: Images of Home(land) in
European Culture', in Erica Carter, James Donald and Judith Squires (eds.), *Space and Place:
Theories of Identity and Location* (London: Lawrence & Wishart, 1993) 3-31 (here 10) and Rachel
Palfreyman, *Edgar Reitz's Heimat: Histories, Traditions, Fictions* (Oxford: Lang, 2000), p. 19.
For a concise summary of the *Heimat* discourse, see Gundolf Hartlieb, *In diesem Ozean von
Erinnerung: Edgar Reitz' Filmroman Heimat* (Siegen: Universitätsverlag Siegen, 2004).
[38] See Heinz-Peter Preußer, 'Eine romantische Synthese und ihr notwendiges Scheitern. Die
filmische Chronik *Heimat 1-3* von Edgar Reitz', *Seminar*, 43.2 (2007), 234-50.

The landscapes that function as ideal-typical model for this restitutive gaze are the landscapes of Breughel's seasonal paintings, which the son reads as an integral and ideal connection between humans and landscape, a peasant existence before the displacement of modernity and the Second World War:

> And thus the people only looked like signs that were part of the landscape, [...] it was a landscape of the world, composed of every imaginable terrain and area [...]. The eye, however, was able to effortlessly assemble these terrains [...]. The most beautiful painting, though, is that of the autumn, where the herd returns home.

> Und so wirkten die Menschen nur wie der Landschaft zugehörige Zeichen, [...] es war eine Weltlandschaft zusammengesetzt aus allen nur erdenklichen Terrains und Zonen [...]. Das Auge aber setzte diese Terrains ohne Mühe zusammen [...]. Das schönste Bild aber ist das vom Herbst, das Bild von der Heimkehr der Herde. (AK 377-79)

The choice of Breughel's paintings for Ortheil's *Heimat* images is indicative. According to Susanne Küchler, Dutch Renaissance landscape painting

> established pictures as record of a great range of knowledge and information about the world. Painted landscapes of the western tradition are thus landscapes of memory, they seize upon and validate personal or social memories [...].[39]

The restitution of the 'healed' space to the dead father in *Farewell to the Combatants* enables the son to accept the destroyed space as heritage and returns the agricultural images of *Heimat* to himself by symbolically integrating the view onto his ancestral farm into Breughel's series of paintings:

> Yes, it was that old view, the view of the parental farm and the inn, the view of the barns and the little rivulet [...] that had not only been my view but also the view of my father.

> Ja, es war dieser alte Blick, der Blick auf den väterlichen Bauernhof und die Gastwirtschaft, der Blick auf die Scheunen und auf das kleine Flüßchen [...], der nicht nur mein Blick, sondern auch der Blick meines Vaters gewesen war. (AK 367)

---

[39] See Küchler, 'Landscape as Memory', 85-6.

Ortheil's attempt to narrate family history as history of collective trauma results in a hegemonic narrative, one that ultimately masters national history by mapping: 'I had seen the landscape in all its details, yet as a single great space where every thing belonged to me.' ('ich hatte die Landschaft in allen ihren Einzelheiten gesehen, und doch wie einen einzigen großen Raum, in dem jedes Ding zu mir gehörte', AK 299). Ortheil's narrator thus integrates himself into 'symbolic geography of patriarchy',[40] the 'most beautiful' painting of the homecoming herd functions as an allegory of the restitution of *Heimat* as a no longer threatening concept, after the successful coming to terms with the legacy of National Socialism and the war: 'All these *Heimat* images that scared you for many years, years during which you were trying to escape the gloomy country' ('All diese Heimatbilder, vor denen dich viele Jahre gegraut hat, Jahre in denen du nur auf der Flucht warst vor dem düsteren Land', AK 300). The acceptance of the images of *Heimat* simultaneously repairs the son's distrust of Germany and images of Germany, which he had inherited from his traumatized mother: '"German" and "Germany" were sinister sounds for mother, sounds of darkness and warning, totally hyper-cathected, gloomy sounds' ('"das Deutsche" und "Deutschland", das waren Dunkellaute für Mutter, Gefahren- und Warnlaute, ganz überbesetzte, düstere Laute', AK 388). Whereas in the father's pre-modern vision, *Heimat* signified merely the place where he was born and raised, in the son's appropriation of the *Heimat* images, *Heimat* functions as a synecdoche, the region signifies the whole country, just as in Reitz's TV series. This personal act of restitution and reattainment of *Heimat* is then mapped onto the opening of the Wall: the end of the division of Germany is simultaneously the overcoming of the traumatic Nazi past.

In conclusion, I would like to remark on two issues. Firstly, that Ortheil's recourse to an emphatic concept of experience in a Benjaminian sense implicitly subscribes to a concept of the subject that Benjamin has declared to be

---

[40] See Jarvis, *Postmodern Cartography*, 9.

incompatible with modernity.[41] To establish the figure of the storyteller one needs precisely the distance that, according to Benjamin, is no longer available to the modern subject. Consequently, all of Ortheil's narrators or protagonists are located on the fringes of society, thus marking the desire for a preservation of subjectivity. Secondly, the issue of mapping and mastery can be reconnected to the ambiguity of the experience of space as protective motherly space and enclosure and open space as both threatening and liberating. The traumatic origin of writing results in a dialectics of closeness and distance, where the threat of the open space is mastered by the production of distance. Like the page, the map thus needs to be filled with signs to manage the threat of the loss of self in unstructured space. As on the Lenox globe from the sixteenth century, in Ortheil white areas mean *here be dragons*:

> The exercise books were the log books of the foreign provinces that had opened up between my mother and myself [...]. Empty pages in my exercise books indicated gaps, I could hardly cope with them.

> Die Hefte waren die Logbücher der fremden Provinzen, die sich zwischen meiner Mutter und mir aufgetan hatten [...]. Leere Seiten in meinen Heften deuteten auf Lücken [...] hin, ich konnte sie schwer ertragen. (EE 85)

The parallelization of Writing and map, and the recurrent spatial metaphors for the act of writing (the winding paths of letters, the crossing of voices, land surveying; three of the five novels of the post-war cycle are variations on the *Odyssey*) correspond to an emphatic concept of the world as text: 'The novel was the landscape set in motion' ('Der Roman war die in Bewegung und Aktion versetzte Landschaft', EE 66-7). The educated bourgeois concept of the subject, however, which this is based on, is always threatened by erosion and tends to order the space to contain its inner turmoil: 'Where I was I needed cleanliness, the things were supposed to be ordered in rank and file' ('Dort, wo

---

[41] See Ortheil's assertion 'I was not a modern storyteller' ('Ich war kein moderner Erzähler, EE 69).

ich mich aufhielt, sollte es sauber sein, die Dinge sollten in Reih und Glied nebeneinander liegen', EE 57). The fear of the 'intrusion of suddenness' originates in the inheritance of trauma. Thus Ortheil's texts of the 1980s and 1990s are still influenced by the desire for peace and security that, according to Norbert Reichel, characterized the philosophical theories of space in the immediate post-war era.[42]

---

[42] Norbert Reichel, *Der erzählte Raum. Zur Verflechtung von sozialem und poetischem Raum in erzählender Literatur* (Darmstadt: Wissenschaftliche Buchgesellschaft, 1987), 16-20.

CHAPTER 2

Projecting the Heterotopia in W. G. Sebald's *Austerlitz*

Dora Osborne

W. G. Sebald's prose is characterized by inter- and intratextual networks, a structural complexity which is also found in densely interconnected narrative topographies. His protagonists are often plagued by feelings of disorientation and isolation, of dispossession and restlessness. In the context of postwar literature, the spatial relations of Sebald's prose have to do with problematic sorts of displacement from the sites of violence, specifically National Socialist violence, to which those at a temporal, generational and cultural remove cannot gain access. The kinds of stories Sebald tells, paradigmatically, those of *The Emigrants* (*Die Ausgewanderten*, 1992), attempt to remember the past, but find sites of memory inaccessible after the event. In his final novel, *Austerlitz* (2001), Sebald constructs elaborate spatial networks, which, I will argue, can be read and viewed in terms of Michel Foucault's 1967 essay 'Of Other Spaces'. I will consider the implications of Foucault's mobilization of the term heterotopia as a means of modelling other spaces for an engagement with the most radically other space of the Holocaust.

Sebald's narrator and protagonist move between different sites in the attempt to recover and reassemble the fragments of a childhood lost when Austerlitz was sent to England on the so-called *Kindertransport*, one of many trains on which children were evacuated from Germany and occupied territories to Britain prior to the Second World War. Part of this ultimately futile work is to find the last traces of Austerlitz's mother, who is believed to have been taken to the ghetto Theresienstadt. Focusing on Sebald's use of the archive, film and the ghetto, I shall consider the significance of his ostensible attempt to make the other space of this traumatic past available through listing, following Foucault's model. I will argue that Sebald's reflection of and on a Foucauldian spatial model exposes the ethical questions asked of a conceptualization of other spaces that works through similarity and interchangeability.

Foucault's 'Of Other Spaces' makes spatial networks its focus, marking a shift away from conceptions of location of places within space:

> Today the site has been substituted for extension which itself had replaced emplacement. [...] Our epoch is one in which space takes the form of relations among sites.[1]

Whilst Foucault draws on the technological and industrial developments of the nineteenth century to show this conceptual change, he does not allude to the radical subversion of their potential in war, and, specifically, in the National Socialist regime. In writing so explicitly about other spaces, the Holocaust remains a notable absence. The railway exemplifies a particularly dense spatial network, but Foucault makes no reference to the misuse of transportation networks in the mobilization of monstrous killing machines. Rather, he goes on to list sites of leisure and resort:

> For example, describing the set of relations that define the sites of transportation, streets, trains (a train is an extraordinary bundle of relations because it is something through which one goes, it is also something by means of which one can go from one point to another, and then it is also something that goes by). One could describe, via the cluster of relations that allows them to be defined, the sites of temporary relaxation – cafes, cinemas, beaches.[2]

Foucault defines the heterotopia in conjunction with, but as different from, utopias, which 'are fundamentally unreal spaces'.[3] Heterotopias, by contrast, 'are outside of all places, even though it may be possible to indicate their location in reality'.[4] In *Austerlitz*, Sebald creates a network of what might be understood as heterotopic spaces in order to show the slippage between the real and fantasy, and to show how memory manifests itself only in this instability. Sebald's networks

---

[1] Michel Foucault, 'Of Other Spaces', trans. Jay Miskowiec, *Diacritics*, 16.1 (1986), 22-27 (here 23).
[2] Foucault, 'Of Other Spaces', 24.
[3] Foucault, 'Of Other Spaces', 24.
[4] Foucault, 'Other Spaces', 24.

are mobilized through the motif of transit and transportation, which finds its excess and perversion in the transportation of Nazi victims to concentration and extermination camps. The particular engagement with Theresienstadt shows the ghetto as a sort of stop on the way to Auschwitz, a *Zwischenstation* which, in turn, figures a terminus or *Endstation*. Sebald's focus on Theresienstadt exposes the problems of modelling other space and of depicting sites of trauma. If the accessibility of the space of the Holocaust is always linked to a deviation, a redirection to other spaces, to what extent does the ghetto, and specifically Theresienstadt in its projection as model village, as spa resort, offer a site of relief from thinking about sites of violence and eradication? The ghetto is made part of a perverse archive practice, adopting an ideal form which is projected as having existed. It becomes a sort of museum settlement which falsely preserves and displays the fantasy of a past utopia. In this sense, the notion of heterotopia in fact avoids the true otherness of these sites, figuring a sort of third space.[5]

I would argue that the significance of Foucault's essay for *Austerlitz* has to do with an engagement with the ideological and ethical concerns of modelling the other space of the Holocaust and, consequently, an evocation of models which look beyond the heterotopia. Where theoretical models are so closely imbricated in and structured through spatial boundaries, it is precisely at the points where the rigid demarcations of internal and external break down, that other spaces find their problematic representation. Such points of rupture follow a logic of Kristevan abjection, that is, the expulsion of that which is so abhorrently foreign and yet familiar to the self in order to construct the 'clean and proper body'.[6] Giorgio Agamben's spatial models consider the implications for the (de)construction of spatial boundaries and the resulting abjection of the subject.

---

[5] In this sense, Foucault's heterotopia might work more as Lefebvre's isotopia. Following this model, the heterotopia is not an interchangeable space, rather a contrasting space. Lefebvre uses the heterotopia as a third space, with which he triangulates the isotopia, and the utopia. Henri Lefebvre, *The Production of Space*, trans. by Donald Nicholson-Smith (Oxford: Blackwell, 1991), 163.

[6] Julia Kristeva, *Powers of Horror: An Essay on Abjection*, trans. Leon S. Roudiez (New York: Columbia University Press, 1982).

Paradigmatic for Agamben's thinking is the site of the camp which, he argues, functioned in a state of exception, concealed within, but exempt from the law, which claimed the right to select and exterminate those who did not fall into its idealized categories.[7] Where Agamben's model deals specifically with spaces which have been rendered invalid, Foucault's treatment of other spaces works notably with examples familiar from everyday life. Foucault's essay works by viewing the heterotopia in terms of the similarities between them, that is, in terms of how other spaces are *like* other spaces. Writing about spatial alterity, Foucault constructs a model which works with notions of proliferation and seriality. The logic of enumeration and similarity used in the essay questions the appropriateness of using its model for thinking the radical otherness and singularity of the Holocaust.

Through the juxtaposition of and slippage between real and fantasy spaces, Sebald's heterotopic networks function as a spatialization of memory, and where this relates to collective memory, of the archive, which, although he does not describe it as such, might figure the heterotopia par excellence for Foucault:

> By contrast, the idea of accumulating everything, of establishing some sort of general archive, the will to enclose in one place all times, all epochs, all forms, all tastes, the idea of constituting a place of all times that is itself outside of time and inaccessible to its ravages, the project of organising in this way a sort of perpetual and indefinite accumulation of time in an immobile place, this whole idea belongs to our modernity. The museum and library are heterotopias that are proper to western culture of the nineteenth century.[8]

However, after 1945, the demands made on the archive exceed the space described. The archive must be thought of in post-catastrophic terms, that is, as a space that can accommodate and acknowledge the scale of the memories that come from a traumatic rupture of history. It is this question that concerns Derrida

---

[7] Giorgio Agamben, *Homo Sacer: Sovereign Power and Bare Life*, trans. Daniel Heller-Roazen (Stanford: Stanford UP, 1998).
[8] Foucault, 'Of Other Spaces', 26.

in *Archive Fever*, where he describes how the burning desire to know about the past threatens to consume its remains. Derrida departs from the etymology of the archive, from its boundedness at once to the home and to the law, to a space of accommodation and a locus of power and appropriation. Elsewhere, Derrida uses ash, the anti-material so closely associated with the Holocaust and, via the ashen poetry of Paul Celan, the attempt to write after the Holocaust, as a paradigm for an irreducible remnant that bears witness to the simultaneous impossibility of destroying and preserving what is past.[9] Where the archive wants to give access to the past there is a sense in which the singularity of the Holocaust repels this attempt and the archive serves instead to elide or circumscribe that to which it claims to bear witness. The archive, as it is exemplified in Sebald's novel, works to displace other sites of testimony, specifically, the ghetto, making it part of an order of display found in displaced forms.

Austerlitz's attempt to re-collect fragments of the past which threaten to dissolve and collapse at every turn echoes the questions Derrida asks of the material status of the archive. Sebald's use of film and photography works paradigmatically for the sorts of anti-materials that haunt the archive. He produces medial networks that work at the limit of visibility and materiality at once to give and refuse Austerlitz access to his lost mother. The peculiar sense of hauntedness exposed in these media finds its archaic form in graveyards or burial sites, which form a key topography for Sebald's work generally, and particularly in *Austerlitz*. Where the latter follows an archaeological methodology crucial to the generation of the archive, the projection of visual media has to do with the exhibition of the archive. I will show how the interconnection, condensation and overlayering of these spaces problematizes the sort of analogous and comparative practice at work in Foucault's essay and marks these other spaces with a spectral trace of the irrepressible and radically other space of the Holocaust.

---

[9] Jacques Derrida, *Acts of Literature*, ed. Derek Attridge (London: Routledge, 1992).

Under the Nazi regime, the erasure of unwanted citizens was, in part, effected initially by their less conspicuous displacement to ghettos. The ghetto ostensibly offered an alternative, autonomously administrated community, but was, in reality, a temporary locus of isolation, marginalization, overcrowding, hunger and disease, before further transportation to extermination camps. It adopts an ideologically liminal position, projected as serving one purpose, but working under the sign of something much more subversive:

> and these people, who before they were sent away had been led to believe some tale about a pleasant resort in Bohemia called Theresienbad, with beautiful gardens, promenades, boarding houses and villas, and many of whom had been persuaded or forced to sign contracts, so-called *Heimeinkaufsverträge*, said Austerlitz, offering them, against deposits of up to eighty thousand Reichsmarks, the right of residence.

> und diese Personen, denen man vor ihrer Verschickung etwas von einem angenehmen böhmischen Luftkurort namens Theresienbad mit schönen Gärten, Spazierwegen, Pensionen und Villen vorgegaukelt und die man in vielen Fällen zur Unterzeichnung von sogenannten Heimeinkaufsverträgen zu Nennwerten bis zu achtzigtausend Reichsmark überredet oder gezwungen hatte.[10]

Theresienstadt in particular came to monumentalize the perverse configuration of depravity and deprivation behind the façade of something more socially creditable. Austerlitz's research reveals how, in anticipation of a Red Cross commission visit in 1944, the ghetto underwent a supposed 'general improvement campaign' ('Verschönerungsaktion', 339; 343), which involved the hurried

---

[10] W. G. Sebald, *Austerlitz*, trans. Anthea Bell (London: Hamish Hamilton, 2003), 335. W. G. Sebald, *Austerlitz* (Frankfurt a.M.: Fischer, 2001), 338-39. In the following, references to *Austerlitz* will appear in parentheses with the page numbers of the English edition listed first, followed by page numbers for the German edition. The shift from Theresienstadt to Theresienbad creates a link to Marienbad, a spa resort where Austerlitz spent a family holiday and where he experiences rare moments of intimacy. The slippage between the two names and the ideological incompatibility of these places is a characteristic part of Sebald's project. The use of Marienbad also refers to Alain Resnais's 1961 film *Last Year at Marienbad*, a meditation on memory and traumatic forgetting. This reference repeats the conflation of heterotopic spaces: the railway station, the resort, the ghetto and the cinema.

construction of various amenities and the dismantling of several prohibitive boundaries:

> the former OREL cinema, which until now had served as a dumping ground for the oldest inmates of the ghetto and where a huge chandelier still hung from the ceiling in the dark space inside, was converted within a few weeks into a concert hall and theatre, [...] not to mention a coffee-house with sun umbrellas and folding chairs outside it to suggest the agreeable atmosphere of a resort inviting all passers-by to linger for a while, and indeed there was no end to the improvements and embellishments.

> das ehemalige Kino OREL, das bislang als Elendsquartier für die ältesten Ghettobewohner gedient hatte und wo noch der riesige Kronleuchter von der Decke herab in den finsteren Raum hing, [wurde] innerhalb weniger Wochen in einen Konzert- und Theatersaal umgebaut [...] sowie ein Kaffeehaus, vor welchem man mit Sonnenschirmen und Klappstühlen eine die Passanten zum Verweilen einladende Kuratmosphäre schuf, und so war der Verbesserungs- und Verschönerungsmaßnahmen kein Ende. (340; 343-44)

This quote comes from the novel's notorious nine-page sentence, and, whilst extracting a section in this way distorts its significance and syntax somewhat, it shows the sort of dense spatial condensation and shifting which structure Sebald's reflections on the arguably heterotopic space of Theresienstadt. He describes how a site of perverse confinement and marginalization is opened out to public scrutiny: where 'some sixty thousand people were crammed together in an area little more than a square kilometre in size' ('an die sechzigtausend Personen auf einer Fläche von kaum mehr als einem Quadratkilometer zusammengezwungen waren'), people are instructed for the purposes of the Red Cross visit to move through the city within a city like *flaneurs* in the projected urban spectacle (331; 335). The description of the ghetto as 'extraterritorial' (331; 335) shows how the location of this real place can only be outside the normal spatial and social order whilst claiming and performing a function which falls within it.

The success of this deceptive staging resulted in the wider dissemination of the myth of the ghetto mobilized through the production of a Nazi propaganda film entitled *The Führer Gives the Gift of a Town to the Jews* (*Der Führer schenkt den Juden eine Stadt*). The gift of *Heimat* was to be made available for nostalgic viewing.[11] Clinging to the hope that in watching these images he might be able to relocate his mother in his memory, Austerlitz tries to procure a copy of the film:

> I found myself unable to cast my mind back to the ghetto and picture my mother Agáta there at the time. I kept thinking that if only the film could be found I might perhaps be able to see or gain some inkling of what it was really like.

> es [ist] mir unmöglich gewesen, mich in das Ghetto zurückzuversetzen und mir vorzustellen, daß Agáta, meine Mutter, damals gewesen sein soll an diesem Ort. Immerzu dachte ich, wenn nur der Film wieder auftauchte, so würde ich vielleicht sehen oder erahnen können, wie es in Wirklichkeit war. (342; 346)

It is, however, only available to him as fragments, which he must watch in the confines of a video booth at the Imperial War Museum. Following Foucault's categorization of the heterotopia, this episode juxtaposes several incompatible spaces in a single real site, blurring the boundary between real and fantasy space; Theresienstadt configures ghetto, spa resort and filmic scenario. The overlayering of heterotopic spaces ruptures the narrative structure that Austerlitz tries to reconstruct in order to relocate his mother. Frustrated at the elusive nature of the footage, he has the fourteen minutes of film extended to an hour in a time-loop copy. As Austerlitz watches and rewatches the film, the materiality of the trace dissolves, leaving only an irreducible remnant, the fact of his mother's mortality.

Whilst Sebald's narrative relay stratifies diegetic spaces, the correspondences between places and their functions or subversions also work to produce linear networks. Austerlitz reports the findings of his research on Theresienstadt on a walk through London with the narrator, a walk which retraces the extensive and compulsive perambulations which he makes to combat

---

[11] For Annette Kuhn, the cinema as heterotopia implies a simultaneous immersion in and consciousness of the fantasy projected. She mobilizes Foucault's concept for thinking about the nostalgic role of cinema and cinema-going in 1930s Britain. Annette Kuhn, *An Everyday Magic: Cinema and Cultural Memory* (London: I.B. Tauris, 2002), 141-47.

insomnia. Beginning at Liverpool Street Station, he reaches Bishopsgate and the old site of Bedlam, where Austerlitz recalls his fascination with the skeletons exhumed there during demolition work. He remembers being told by an archaeologist about the densely packed, make-shift graves: 'on average the skeletons of eight people had been found in every cubic metre of earth removed from the trench' ('in jedem Kubikmeter Abraum, den man aus dieser Grube entfernte, [sind] die Gerippe von durchschnittlich acht Menschen gefunden worden', 184; 188). The accumulation and repeated disinterment of these bodies resulted from the demolition of so-called 'poverty-stricken quarters' ('Elendsquartiere') in the nineteenth century, undertaken in order to make way for the construction of the railway network (186; 190). Where, as shown above, Sebald comes to describe the old OREL cinema as an 'Elendsquartier' and specifies the population density of Theresienstadt, his narrator and protagonist anticipate and condense the ghetto and the sites it configures, that is, ghetto as station, as graveyard, as mental and retirement home, as a space of overcrowding, misery and despair.

The narrative framework of Austerlitz's walk through the city delimits a screen onto which the image of another sort of city can be projected. His speculative descriptions of Bedlam also include references to the cinematic medium and screen which will, in turn, be used by Austerlitz in his attempted reconstructions and rememberings of an inaccessible past:

> I imagined the bleachfields stretching westwards from Bedlam,
> saw the white lengths of linen spread out on the green grass.

> Ich bildete mir auch ein, die Bleichfelder sehen zu können, die sich
> von   Bedlam   westwärts   erstreckten,   sah   die   weißen
> Leinwandbahnen ausgespannt auf dem grünen Gras. (183; 187)

Where the expanse of white sheets prefigures the cinema screen, the resonance being stronger in the German 'Leinwand', the 'Bahnen' again link the cinema, asylum and railway, mobilizing Sebald's network connecting Bedlam and Theresienstadt. Moreover, the use of a white, bleached screen suggests the sorts of coverings and disavowal at work in the heterotopia. The Theresienstadt film is a projection onto a screen that masks a horrible truth and the clean sheets at Bedlam wash away the traces of insanity otherwise contained in the asylum. Beyond the screen, however, is something more real, in a psychoanalytic sense:

> [I saw] on the far side of the bleachfields the places where the dead were buried once the churchyards of London could hold no more.

> [ich] sah jenseits der Bleichfelder die Plätze, auf denen man die Toten beisetzte, seit die Kirchhöfe Londons sie nicht mehr zu fassen vermochten. (184; 187-88)

Where the relay of other spaces might work to defer or disavow the fact of mortality, Sebald's arguably compulsive return to the graveyard seems to show the ultimate failure of this gesture. In Foucault's essay the burial site becomes paradigmatic for the shift in spatial relations, for the dislocation of the dead to other sites:

> The cemeteries then came to constitute, no longer the sacred and immortal heart of the city, but the 'other city', where each family possesses its dark resting place.[12]

Moreover, for Foucault, this shift has to do with the claim to an individual space for the preservation and commemoration of identity. In the ossuary, bodies lost the 'last traces of individuality', but since the nineteenth century everyone has claim to individual burial and 'personal decomposition'.[13] Sebald's engagement with the spaces of burial returns him to the other place of depersonalized, mass burial. Inevitably Austerlitz's attempt to identify his mother in the overcrowded space of the ghetto is marked by this loss of individuality. In the reanimated images of the film, at least, he hopes to be able to find her:

> and then I imagined recognizing Agáta, beyond any possibility of doubt, [...] perhaps among the guests outside the fake coffeehouse, or a saleswoman in the haberdashery shop, taking a fine pair of gloves carefully out of one of the drawers, or singing the part of Olympia in the Tales of Hoffmann.

---

[12] Foucault, 'Of Other Spaces', 25.
[13] Foucault, 'Of Other Spaces', 25.

> und einmal ums andere malte ich mir aus, daß ich Agáta, eine im
> Vergleich zu mir junge Frau, ohne jeden Zweifel erkannte, etwa
> unter den Gästen vor dem falschen Kaffeehaus, als Verkäuferin in
> einem Galanteriewarengeschäft, wo sie gerade ein Paar
> Handschuhe behutsam aus einem der Schubfächer nahm, oder als
> Olympia in dem Bühnenspiel *Hoffffmanns Erzählungen*. (342-43;
> 346)

The *Leinwände* of the bleachfields and the cinema screen offer a surface, onto
which the images of memory and fantasy can be projected. Moreover, they are a
necessary externalization of what, for the protagonist, can no longer be contained
within internal spaces. His compulsive attempts at remembering have broken
down the boundaries between interior and exterior, between past and present.
Whilst recounting his Theresienstadt research, Austerlitz recalls how the journey
he made to Bohemia induced a mental breakdown. Perhaps the asylum Austerlitz
seeks after his attempt to gain access to the ghetto is symptomatic for the way the
other spaces in and of the narrative configure a site of relief from the Holocaust
proper. Austerlitz recalls his time in St Clement's hospital bordering the
graveyard in Tower Hamlets, which forms the present space of narration:

> I wandered [...] up and down the long corridors, staring out for
> hours through one of the dirty windows at the cemetery below,
> where we are standing now, feeling nothing inside my head but the
> four burnt-out walls of my brain.

> [ich] spazierte durchdrinnen [...] in den Gängen herum, blickte
> stundenlang durch eines der trüben Fenster in den Friedhof, in
> welchem wir jetzt stehen, hinab und spürte in meinem Kopf nichts
> als die vier ausgebrannten Wände meines Gehirns. (324; 328)

Once more the spaces of asylum, madness, burial and ghettoization are condensed
through the (dysfunctional) mechanism of Austerlitz's memory.

The ghetto as a heterotopia of incarceration behind a façade of unbounded
leisure configures the dialectic at work between the free space of fantasy and its
boundedness to the material evidence of the archive. Before watching the film
Austerlitz's projection of his mother is one of a carefree *flaneur*, 'among a group

of ghetto residents out for a stroll' ('allein in einer Gruppe von flanierenden Ghettobewohnern', 343; 346). She is divested of the heavy rags more familiar from documentary footage of the Nazi ghettos, and to this extent, perhaps adds a further sense in which the other space of the Holocaust is subject to elision and circumscription: 'I imagined seeing her walking down the street in a summer dress and lightweight gabardine coat, said Austerlitz' ('Auch bildete ich mich ein, sagte Austerlitz, sie auf der Gasse zu sehen in einem Sommerkleid und einem leichten Gabardinemantel', 343; 346). However, the fantasy and memory become a locus of condensation, and the other spaces described start to function in terms of their similarities to each other. The image of his mother is conflated with that of his adoptive mother through the lightness of their clothes, that is, through their anti-materiality: 'I saw [...] a woman in a light gabardine coat' ('eine Frau in einem leichten Gabardinemantel', 193; 197). The site of this vision is subject at once to infinite replication, embedding and dissolution:

> Memories like this came back to me in the disused Ladies'
> Waiting-Room of Liverpool Street station, memories behind and
> within which many things much further back in the past seemed to
> lie, all interlocking like the labyrinthine vaults I saw in the dusty
> grey light, and which seemed to go on and on for ever.

> Erinnerungen wie diese waren es, die mich ankamen in dem
> aufgelassenen Ladies Waiting Room des Bahnhofs von Liverpool
> Street, Erinnerungen, hinter denen und in denen sich viel weiter
> noch zurückreichende Dinge verbargen, immer das eine im andern
> verschachtelt, gerade so wie die labyrinthischen Gewölbe, die ich
> in dem staubgrauen Licht zu erkennen glaubte, sich fortsetzten in
> unendlicher Folge. (192; 196)

The ghetto and station are also linked through the function of Theresienstadt as a sort of *Zwischenstation*, and not for nothing does Austerlitz describe Liverpool Street Station as a simultaneous vision of 'imprisonment and liberation' ('Gefängnis- und Befreiungsvision', 192; 195). The space of the station mobilizes Austerlitz's process of remembering, but he must return to the archive in order to access what he hopes will be material of a more tangible nature.

However, his search for his mother is at once helped and restricted by the archive. It is a source of unlimited associations and links, but ones which may not be usefully extricated, existing only in these relationships and not possessing any integrity as discrete elements. What seems to be an overt reference to Foucault's essay, not least in the condensation of spaces, culminates in Austerlitz's fantasy of a steam liner. The ship is, in fact, the heterotopia *par excellence* for Foucault, but, here, it is evoked on the site of the archive:

> And it was not just of a prison that the archives building in the Karmelitská reminded me, said Austerlitz; it also suggested a monastery, a riding school, an opera house and a lunatic asylum, and all these ideas mingled in my mind as I looked at the twilight coming in from above, and thought that on the rows of galleries I saw a dense crowd of people, some of them wearing hats or handkerchiefs, as passengers on board a steamer used to do when it put out to sea.

> Aber nicht nur an ein Gefängnis erinnerte mich der Innenhof des Archivs in der Karmelitská, sagte Austerlitz, sondern auch an ein Kloster, an eine Reitschule, ein Operntheater und an ein Irrenhaus, und all diese Vorstellungen gingen in mir durcheinander während ich in das aus der Höhe herabsinkende Zwielicht hineinschaute und durch es hindurch auf den Galerierängen eine dichtgedrängte Menschenmenge zu sehen glaubte, in welcher einige Hüte schwenkten oder mit dem Taschentuch winkten, so wie einstmals die Passagiere an Bord eines auslaufenden Dampfers. (205; 209)

Sebald uses the archive to replicate the problematic strategy of enumeration and analogy used by Foucault and projects memory, fantasy and desire into a space of impossible encounter with the past. The archivist, Tereza Ambrosová, 'a pale woman of almost transparent appearance' ('eine blasse, beinahe transparente Frau', 206; 210-11), seems to be as spectral as the figures that appear in the Theresienstadt film:

> The contours of their bodies were blurred and, particularly in the scenes shot out of doors in broad daylight, had dissolved at the edges.

> Die Körperformen waren unscharf geworden und hatten sich, besonders bei den draußen im hellen Tageslicht gedrehten Szenen, an ihren Rändern aufgelöst. (348; 349)

These fragments of the past are so fragile they must be kept in the dark, invisible, in order to preserve them. The archive houses a sort of secret, which must be hidden in order to preserve it, since exposure to the light threatens disintegration:

> The office which we entered straight from this gallery was full of stacks of papers tied up with string, not a few of them discoloured by sunlight and brittle at the edges.

> In dem Bureau, das wir direkt von der Galerie aus betraten, waren überall [...] hohe Stapel spagatverschnürter Faszikel, nicht wenige durch die Lichteinstrahlung gedunkelt und brüchig geworden an ihren Rändern. (207; 211)

Through their transparency and fragility, the archive and its keeper, the film and its actors are bound in a network of other spaces. Arguably, the name of the almost transparent archivist, Tereza, provides another link between the elusive figure of the mother and Theresienstadt (Terezín). The ghetto is projected, via the film, back into the Imperial War Museum, an archival space for preserving memories of Empire, which forms an appropriate, but displaced space for viewing the images of Theresienstadt, named in memory of the Kaiser's mother, Maria Theresia.

Austerlitz's archival encounter attempts to cross the boundary into the other site of the ghetto, and this finds its dramatization in the closeted, other space of the museum video booth:

> I remember very clearly, said Austerlitz, how I sat in one of the museum's video viewing rooms, placed the cassette in the black opening of the recorder with trembling hands.

> Ich weiß noch genau, sagte Austerlitz, wie ich in einer der Videokabinen des Museums die Kassette in die schwarze Öffnung des Recorders hineingeschoben habe mit zitternden Händen. (343; 347)

As a dramatization of the complex relationship of similarity and difference at work in the novel, this episode questions whether an other space can give access to a particular site of otherness, that is, whether the space from which Austerlitz views the ghetto allows him access to the ghetto itself.[14] The restriction of the viewing closet finds its analogy in the lift of the Karmelitská archive:

> As we went up to the third floor in the cramped lift [...] in silence and with a sense of awkwardness because of the unnatural physical proximity into which one is forced in such a box, I saw a gentle pulsation in the curve of a blue vein beneath the skin of her right temple.

> Als wir in dem sehr engen, auf einer Seite gegen den Liftschacht scharrenden Aufzug in das dritte Stockwerk hinauffuhren, stillschweigend und verlegen wegen der unnatürlichen Körpernähe, in die man in so einem Kasten zueinander gezwungen ist, sah ich ein sachtes Klopfen in der Krümmung einer bläulichen Ader unter der Haut ihrer rechten Schläfe. (207; 211)

The pulsating vein works at once as a sign of vitality, which is also, following the x-ray logic derived from Thomas Mann, in which pathologies are projected onto the body's surface, always under the sign of mortality. For Austerlitz this manifests itself in the sort of visual dysfunction that marks the narrative with impenetrable blind spots:

> At first I could get none of these images into my head; they merely flickered before my eyes as the source of continual irritation or vexation.

> Aber nichts von diesen Bildern ging mir zunächst in den Kopf; sondern sie flimmerten mir bloß vor den Augen in einer Art kontinuierlicher Irritation. (344-45; 348)

---

[14] This question can be asked of cinema more generally and has to do with the ethics of aestheticization and replication. Where film tries to represent the events and experiences of the Holocaust, perhaps through the use of archive material, to what extent does this work as an attempt to relocate the audience on the other space it projects? In the case of a film such as Claude Lanzmann's *Shoah* this question is complicated by his strategic avoidance of documentary footage.

Like the uncomfortable proximity experienced in the closeted spaces of the video booth and lift, the distortion resulting from Austerlitz's time-loop copy can only expose the instability of the archive. Precisely in coming so close to these images, in opening out the spaces within the 24 images per second, Austerlitz believes that the transition into another time and space will bring his mother back to him:

> she alone seemed to make straight for me, coming closer with every step, until at last I thought I could sense her stepping out of the frame and passing over into me.

> allein in der Gruppe flanierenden Ghettobewohnern hielt sie genau auf mich zu und kam Schritt für Schritt näher, bis sie zuletzt, wie ich zu spüren meinte, aus dem Film herausgetreten und in mich übergegangen war. (343, 346)[15]

As the pensive spectator described in film critic Laura Mulvey's recent work discovers, the deconstruction of the filmic mechanism exposes the dysfunction of an aging machine, and, for Austerlitz, the breakdown of memory at the point of traumatic separation from the mother.[16] The woman in the Theresienstadt film, who Austerlitz wants to believe is his mother, carries a trace of her existence in time, but always under the sign of erasure. She is an uncanny figure on the threshold of life and death, of archive and memory, of familiarity and strangeness:

> She looks, so I tell myself as I watch, just as I imagined the singer Agáta from my faint memories and the few other clues to her appearance that I now have, and I gaze and gaze at that face, which seems to me both strange and familiar, said Austerlitz, I run the tape back repeatedly, looking at the time indicator in the top left-hand corner of the screen, where the figures covering part of her forehead show the minutes and seconds, from 10:53 to 10:57,

---

[15] Laura Mulvey reads this episode as an uncanny encounter with the body of the mother, where the film has been slowed down to the extent that cinema as a mechanism of disavowal, following a psychoanalytic logic, is exposed as an aging machine and reveals the horror of death/castration that it otherwise serves to screen. Laura Mulvey, *Death 24 x a Second: Stillness and the Moving Image* (London: Reakiton Books, 2006), 39-52.

[16] Mulvey, *Death 24 x a Second*, 52.

while the hundredths of a second flash by so fast that you cannot read and capture them.

Gerade so wie ich nach meinen schwachen Erinnerungen und den wenigen übrigen Anhaltspunkten, die ich heute habe, die Schauspielerin Agáta mir vorstelle, gerade so, denke ich, sieht sie aus, und ich schaue wieder und wieder in dieses mir gleichermaßen fremde und vertraute Gesicht, sagte Austerlitz, lasse das Band zurücklaufen, Mal für Mal, und sehe den Zeitanzeiger in der oberen linken Ecke des Bildschirms, die Zahlen, die einen Teil ihrer Stirn verdecken, die Minuten und die Sekunden, von 10:53 bis 10:57, und die Hundertstelsekunden, die davondrehen, so geschwind, dass man sie nicht entziffern und festhalten kann. (351; 354-55)

Her status as projected, archival image means the woman in the film footage hovers between memory and dissolution. The digital timer adds a temporal dimension to the problem of accessing other spaces and its position over the woman's head arguably brands her with a kind of archival tattoo. The significance of the tattoo carries a particularly heavy load in the post-war and post-Holocaust context, working as a grotesque form of dehumanizing identification and serialization. Whilst the timer shows a minimal temporal difference, these numbers might work as possible permutations of identity, which have been eradicated under the sign of Nazi violence and which, troublingly, have been further obscured by the subsequent mobilizations and appropriations of the archive image. Where there is only one woman in the film, she plays the roles of spectator in the Nazi-Red Cross concert, of Austerlitz's mother for the desperate protagonist and, arguably, for Sebald's project, of an always already lost object of narrative desire.[17] The tattoo is part of an archive, but one always ready to become Derrida's ash. It works as an indelible mark on the body but where bodies turn to ash this last witness to violence is also lost. Moreover, it is the film, the archive material, which projects the tattoo, retroactively, onto the woman, and as such,

---

[17] It is not for nothing that Austerlitz supplements the status of 'Agáta' variously as 'Agáta, my mother' ('Agáta, meine Mutter', 342; 346) and 'the actress Agáta' ('die Schauspielerin Agáta', 351; 355).

asks questions about the extent to which identities are attributed as the constructions and projections of memory where the violence inflicted on the body has overwhelmed any trace of identity.

In conclusion, I would like to return to *Archive Fever*, where Derrida uses Jensen's *Gradiva*, via Freud's reading of the novella, as a sort of emblem for his engagement with a post-catastrophic archive. The walking figure, captured in a bas-relief becomes a fetish object for the peculiar gait she will never be able to reproduce, but which leaves its imprint in the ash of Vesuvius. Sebald also freezes the film image of the women in Theresienstadt and, via the still, returns to the fixed image, to the photograph of another woman. Given the popularity of Sebald's novel and the proliferation of critical interest in his work, there is, perhaps, a sense in which these images, the still and the photograph, work, in excess of their fetishization in the narrative, as critical fetish and, through their acquired recognizability, even iconically. Through the accumulation of associations, it might be argued that the other place from which the film still came has gained an impossible familiarity or knowability. However, one might also understand Sebald's use of an emblematic mode as a means of configuring in one all the spaces that his narrative traverses. In *Austerlitz* the notion of transportation and transit produces a conduit between the other spaces, which relate to the radically other space of the Holocaust, and the use of medial networks reflects this strategy. Arguably the arrestation of this movement between media in the still image, the return to the photograph, via the film, has to do with a return to or re-focusing on the essential material of his narrative after the various detours on which the reader has been taken. The photograph remains, ultimately, despite or because of the nursemaid's emphatic identification of the woman as Agáta, unidentifiable. It is Derrida's 'remainder without remainder'[18] which must be kept, passed on, and perhaps it is the movement of cultural transmission that resists the fetishization of archival material:

---

[18] Derrida, *Acts of Literature*, 370.

Austerlitz gave me an envelope which he had with him and which contained the photograph from the theatrical archives in Prague, as a memento.

[Austerlitz] überreichte mir in einem Couvert, das er bei sich getragen hatte, die Photographie aus dem Prager Theaterarchiv, zum Andenken. (354; 361)

CHAPTER 3

Seeing Strangely:
Migration and Gender in the Work of Birgit Vanderbeke

Emily Jeremiah

The nation is an illusion that relies on forgetfulness. A relatively recent construct, it is nevertheless powerful, inspiring extreme feelings and actions.[1] Those who move between nations are troublesome to those who insist on the purity and fixity of individual national cultures. Migrants to Germany, say, expose that culture's constructedness, relativizing it threateningly. In the German context, where the idea of homeland (*Heimat*), has long been 'at the centre of a [...] moral – and by extension political – discourse about place, belonging, and identity',[2] and where reunification has spelt both optimism and difficulty – as well as a revising of the National Socialist past – the issues of mobility and origin, of identity and difference, are especially tricky and rich.[3]

Writing by migrants to Germany has deservedly received much critical attention.[4] But what of migrants from Germany? Writers who move away from Germany, or who thematize such a move in their work, are engaged in a particularly potent challenge. Departing grants new perspectives; and perhaps more than any other act, leaving Germany questions its status as both a

---

[1] See Benedict Anderson, *Imagined Communities: Reflections on the Origin and Spread of Nationalism* (London: Verso, 1983), 12-5. Craig Calhoun, *Nationalism* (Buckingham: Open University Press, 1997) provides a useful discussion of the phenomenon.

[2] Celia Applegate, *A Nation of Provincials: The German Idea of Heimat* (Berkeley and Los Angeles: U of California P, 1990), 4.

[3] See Frank Brunssen, 'The New Self-Understanding of the Berlin Republic: Readings of Contemporary German History', in Stuart Taberner and Frank Finlay (eds.), *Recasting German Identity: Culture, Politics, and Literature in the Berlin Republic* (Rochester, NY: Camden House, 2002), 19-35. See also Mary Fulbrook, *German National Identity after the Holocaust* (Cambridge: Polity Press, 1999), 19-20.

[4] For example, Mary Howard (ed.), *Interkulturelle Konfigurationen: Zur deutschsprachigen Erzählliteratur von Autoren nichtdeutscher Herkunft* (Munich: Iudicium, 1997).

magnanimous host country and a desirable homeland.[5] Migration also fruitfully raises the issue of identity in postmodernism. If '[h]omes are always made and remade as grounds and conditions [...] change'[6] – an assertion that alludes to and participates in the postmodernist challenge to stable identities and attachments – then the subject is free, or floundering.

For 'nomadism', to refer to Rosi Braidotti's 1994 'figuration', is not necessarily a privileged or favourable condition.[7] And the postmodernist subject is not, cannot be, utterly unfixed. For one thing, she is not alone; her performances are always relational.[8] Sara Ahmed puts forward the idea of 'strange encounters', ethical relationships between embodied subjects. She asserts: 'Identity [...] is constituted in the "more than one" of the encounter: the designation of an "I" or "we" requires an encounter with others'.[9] Ahmed also suggests that qualities traditionally associated with 'femininity' – connectivity, emotionality, bodiliness – can be harnessed in the development of a postmodernist feminist ethics. Such feminine qualities dislodge the universalism of previous moral theories, making 'femininity' a site of critical refusal.[10] An ethical nomadism, then, would involve a 'feminine' relationality.

The female migrant is unsettling. If women in Western culture have traditionally been associated with the private sphere and with passivity, then the figure of the mobile female does not fit. And if 'nation' and 'gender' are constructs that often overlap and support each other in ways that legitimize

---

[5] Emily Jeremiah, 'Shifting Cartographies: Ethical Nomadism and the Poetry of Dorothea Grünzweig', in Marjorie Gelus and Helga Kraft (eds.), *Women in German Yearbook*, 21 (Lincoln, NE: U of Nebraska P, 2005), 241-59 (here 245).

[6] Sara Ahmed et al., 'Introduction', in Ahmed et al. (eds.), *Uprootings/Regroundings: Questions of Home and Migration* (Oxford: Berg, 2003), 1-19 (here 9).

[7] Rosi Braidotti, *Nomadic Subjects: Embodiment and Sexual Difference in Contemporary Feminist Theory* (New York: Columbia UP, 1994). A 'figuration' is 'a politically informed account of an alternative subjectivity' (1). Ahmed et al. point out that mobility does not necessarily connote privilege or freedom; the question 'who can stay at home?' is sometimes more pertinent than the question 'who can travel?' ('Introduction', 7).

[8] Judith Butler, *Undoing Gender* (New York: Routledge, 2004), 1.

[9] Sara Ahmed, *Strange Encounters: Embodied Others in Post-Coloniality* (London: Routledge, 2000), 7.

[10] Sara Ahmed, *Differences That Matter: Feminist Theory and Postmodernism* (Cambridge: Cambridge University Press, 1998), 54.

masculinist hegemony,[11] the female border-crosser is even more disruptive. Thus, 'strange encounters' could dislodge not only postmodernist ideals of disembodied, free-floating subjects; but also masculinist models of nation.

Birgit Vanderbeke is a writer who challenges both Germanness and gender, as we will see. She was born in 1956 in Dahme/Mark in the GDR, and moved with her family to West Germany in 1961. She was brought up in Frankfurt am Main, where she later studied Law and French. Her first novella, *The Mussel Dinner* (*Das Muschelessen*) was published in 1990 and was awarded the Ingeborg Bachmann Prize. In 1993, Vanderbeke moved to the South of France. She is the author of eleven subsequent novellas, a cookbook, and a travel guide. A volume of essays, interviews, and reviews concerned with Vanderbeke was published in Germany in 2001.[12] In Anglo-American German Studies, however, her work has been little discussed.[13]

'If everyone believes it, it means it's working' ('Wenn alle daran glauben, heißt es, es funktioniert').[14] This wry assertion, in Vanderbeke's *Your Money or Your Life* (*Geld oder Leben*), illuminates the writer's scepticism with regard to dominant discourses, and her awareness of the operations of power. Her works deal caustically with consumerism and capitalism, family and gender, the media and advertising. Their mode is typically satire or irony. Vanderbeke is a postmodernist writer *par excellence*: self-reflexive, playful, parodic. But Vanderbeke is also interested in community and commitment: notions that have been viewed by postmodernist theorists as outdated.[15] Vanderbeke can be read as usefully questioning this assumption, as will be shown.

---

[11] Nira Yuval-Davis, *Gender and Nation* (London: Sage, 1997), 4 and 7.

[12] Richard Wagner (ed.), *"Ich hatte ein bißchen Kraft drüber": Zum Werk von Birgit Vanderbeke* (Frankfurt a.M.: Fischer Taschenbuch, 2001).

[13] But see Alison Lewis, 'The Agonies of Choice: Gender, the Family, and Individualization in Birgit Vanderbeke's *Das Muschelessen*', *Seminar*, 40.3 (2004), 221-35; Special edition: 'Beyond 'Ostalgie': East and West German Identity in Contemporary German Culture', ed. by David Clarke and Bill Niven.

[14] Birgit Vanderbeke, *Geld oder Leben* (Frankfurt a.M.: Fischer Taschenbuch, 2005), 7. All translations from German are mine.

[15] See Ahmed, *Differences*, 45.

This chapter is concerned with the novellas *I Spy with My Little Eye* (*Ich sehe was, was du nicht siehst*) (1999) and *The Strange Career of Mrs Choi* (*Die sonderbare Karriere der Frau Choi*) (2007), although it draws on other of Vanderbeke's works where appropriate. It traces a development in the writer's thinking about the questions of migration and identity, to argue that Vanderbeke moves from a conception of subjectivity as embodied, relational, and in process ('nomadic'), to a feminist, ethical slant on this condition, comparable to that of Ahmed.

I Spy tells of the narrator's decision to move from Germany to the South of France, and of her and her son's attempt to establish a new life there. I will look firstly at how Germany and Germanness are depicted here, then at how the central themes of representation and perception are handled, and finally at the text's understanding of identity and community.

The unnamed first-person narrator of *I Spy* views daily life in Germany as dull and monotonous; she claims that in every German town there are primary-school teachers called Gaby, streets named after Gustav Heinemann, and squares after Konrad Adenauer. She notes irritations such as the postman's unwillingness to deliver parcels to her door, and the unsafeness of parks for women at night. When 'Gaby' instructs the narrator's child to fabricate a 'mother' using cardboard, this seems to the narrator the final straw. These random details are offered as reasons for the decision to move away, although there are also practical and financial factors.[16] The absurdity of the analysis suggests that motivation is not clear, rational, or noble; the narrator assures us that her decision has nothing to do with courage (IS 13).

Dominant debates in Germany are parodied and undermined. The narrator summarizes the contents of the evening news; they include 'health insurance reform and only then the other wars' ('Krankenkassenreform und dann erst die anderen Kriege', IS 31). In France, the narrator imagines talking with her friends

---

[16] Birgit Vanderbeke, *Ich sehe was, was du nicht siehst* (Frankfurt a.M.: Fischer Taschenbuch, 2001), 7-14. Referred to in the following as IS.

in Germany about 'the East and the West and the health insurance reform' ('den Osten und den Westen und die Krankenkassenreform', IS 102). Such repetition – typical of Vanderbeke – serves a mocking function. The reference to East and West harks back to an earlier passage in the novella, where the narrator comments satirically on post-unification Germany:

> and that was the East, and now the East is the West, and it's anarchy. The East always wanted to be the West, and then it was it, and when it was it, it suddenly didn't want to be it any more, because of rents and unemployed people, and the West didn't want to have the East because of the health insurance reform and the taxes and because of the funny shopping bags they just keep on using....

> und dies war der Osten, und jetzt ist der Osten der Westen, und das ist die Anarchie. Immer wollte der Osten der Westen sein, und dann war er es, und als er es war, wollte er es nun plötzlich doch nicht sein wegen der Mieten und Arbeitslosen, und der Westen mochte den Osten nicht haben wegen der Krankenkassenreform und der Steuern und wegen der komischen Einkaufsbeutel, die sie dort einfach weiterbenutzen.... (IS 8-9)[17]

This flatly funny diagnosis both points up the tensions within the Berlin Republic – elsewhere, the narrator sees the country as acutely afflicted with paranoia (IS 87) – and derides the surrounding debates as facile. Through observations about her new home country, the narrator implies further criticism; she notes, for example, that France is permissive and relaxed (IS 100). While German children are not allowed to drink Coca-Cola, French children are (IS 93).[18] German culture thus appears prohibitive and joyless.

And the Germans who come to France as tourists are thoroughly lampooned, particularly by means of the ghastly figure of Mechthild. This loud and tactless woman bears comparison with the ever-dissatisfied Hildebrand in Vanderbeke's *The South of France: A User's Guide* (*Gebrauchsanweisung für*

---

[17] On the tensions and promises of the Berlin Republic, compare Brunssen, 'New Self-Understanding', 26.
[18] Compare Birgit Vanderbeke, *The South of France: A User's Guide* (*Gebrauchsanweisung für Südfrankreich*) (Munich: Piper, 2002), 137. Referred to in the following as G.

Südfrankreich), the female companion of the male reader to whom the text is addressed. Mechthild and her fellow German holidaymakers live in fear of 'indigenous thieves, gypsies and other riff-raff' ('einheimische Dieber, Zigeuner und sonstiges Gesindel'), complain about the inferiority of the local beer, and manifest a greedy paranoia (IS 74, 75 and 77). The visitors from Germany who invade the narrator's house buy yoghurts from Aldi, deck themselves in lurid cycling gear, and make crass comments on ways to improve the house (IS 40-9). Germanness is associated with avarice and insensitivity.

Germany is again and again relativized by the new country: by others' views of it or by their total lack of interest in it (IS 70-1).[19] Such continual relativization is, as Vanderbeke notes in an interview, both exhilarating and exhausting.[20] It involves a questioning of the dominance and desirability of the homeland. One of the narrator's friends in *I Spy* tells her that she is mad to go away, 'from the centre of culture' ('mitten aus der Kultur', IS 16). The narrator herself views the centre as relative. Vanderbeke challenges the notion of centrality, then, and the concept of a dominant culture (*Leitkultur*).[21]

The narrator's new life is not idealized, it should be noted; her house is cold and uncomfortable. France, the host country, is not homogeneous – Paris is a world away – and not ideal. Despite one character's claim that the narrator is living in a paradise, and despite the (satirized) fantasies of escape nurtured by other Germans (IS 88 and 120), this is a complex and alien culture, which unfolds only gradually, and never entirely, to the narrator.

Vanderbeke's style, here and in other works, involves complex and teasing patterns of assertion and withdrawal; it thereby reflects and enacts her texts' interest in the instability of reality and the risks of representation. The narrator of *I Spy* is writing a series of radio programmes for children about prominent painters.

---

[19] In *The South of France*, Vanderbeke notes a lack of awareness on the part of the natives of the outside world (G 82).

[20] Birgit Vanderbeke, 'Himmelfahrt und Happy-End: Birgit Vanderbeke im Gespräch mit Hans Ulrich Probst', in Wagner (ed.), *"Ich hatte ein bißchen Kraft drüber"*, 142-55 (here 153).

[21] On the notion of *Leitkultur*, see Stuart Taberner, 'Introduction', in Taberner and Finlay, *Recasting German Identity*, 1-15 (here 1).

The title of the series, the same as that of the novella, points to the problem of subjective perception.

The narrator's move to France brings about freshness of vision (IS 50, 56 and 64) or a new way of seeing. In the context of postmodernism, where nothing is new (IS 21), this is to be welcomed. But perception is shifting, potentially falsifying. Colours are experienced subjectively and hard to label; the narrator and her partner debate the colour of the stars. In paintings, colours change over time (IS 88-90). The narrator refuses to attempt a programme about van Gogh, whose work is felt to be too intense, too demanding. However, at the end of the novella it is suggested that perhaps she will undertake the task after all, with the help of her partner – a decision that points, perhaps, to the unavoidability of interpretation (IS 90, 110 and 121). Communication is also thematized and problematized in the text; the narrator finds it impossible to convey her experiences to those back in Germany (IS 45 and 67).

The narrator's partner René is an expert in the forgery of paintings: a detail that raises the issue of authenticity. He notes: 'It's strange [...] that you can see things without perceiving them' ('Es ist sonderbar [...] daß man Dinge sehen kann, ohne sie wahrzunehmen', IS 95). Sight, 'a privileged sense in the discourse of subjectivity and knowledge in Western modernity',[22] is thus decentralized here. The issues of sight and recognition are bound up with the questions of strangeness and familiarity; the work of Paul Klee becomes 'strange' to the narrator, for example (IS 101). Such strangeness, or 'difference', is frightening, and causes a crisis. During a sleepless night, the narrator reflects:

> how different everything was from how I thought it would be. It was so different that I didn't really know any more how I thought it would be. How it was, I didn't really know either.
>
> wie anders alles geworden war, als ich es mir gedacht hatte. Es war so anders geworden, daß ich gar nicht mehr richtig wußte, wie ich

---

[22] Caren Kaplan, 'Transporting the Subject: Technologies of Mobility and Location in an Era of Globalization', in Ahmed et al. (eds.), *Uprootings*, 207-23 (here 212).

mir gedacht hatte, daß es werden würde. Wie es geworden war,
wußte ich auch nicht so richtig. (IS 68)

The notions of 'difference' and of 'knowing' are problematized in a way that
recalls Ahmed, who asks: 'How do you know a stranger?' – that is, how is
strangeness knowable?[23] The narrator also reports on not understanding what is
being said to her in France (although she understands literally what the words
mean): 'I can't choose what I think about' ('Ich kann mir nicht aussuchen, woran
ich denke', IS 38), she concludes. This worrying uncontrollability is the source of
the fear that takes hold of her later, and which can be read as a fear of the shifting
signifier, and the fluid self.

'[T]he self is always somewhere,' Caren Kaplan remarks; it is not possible
to transcend locatedness.[24] In Vanderbeke, leave-taking is not a single, simple act,
but a lengthy and ambivalent process, whereby the old self is not simply erased,
but disturbingly persistent (IS 50). The narrator's decision to remain in France is
accompanied by an 'uncanny' ('unheimlich') feeling – this recalls Homi Bhabha's
concern with postmodern 'unhomeliness' – and by a 'cold feeling of
groundlessness' ('kaltes Gefühl von bodenlos', IS 87). The narrator identifies the
source of this feeling: her departure, and the fact that she does not now know
where she is.[25] Knowing is again a problem. But later the narrator reports a phone
conversation: 'I couldn't say exactly [to my mother] how it was here, but I noticed
that I was beginning to sense it' ('Ich hätte ihr nicht genau sagen können, wie es
hier ist, aber ich merkte, daß ich anfing, es zu ahnen', IS 117). Seeing has given
way to sensing, as a mode of knowing.

Sensuality is key to Vanderbeke's notion of the self. Her writings about
food, in her guidebook and cookbook, stress physicality, materiality; she opposes
these to a bland and consumerist plasticity she perceives as dominant in

---

[23] Ahmed, *Strange Encounters*, 55.
[24] Kaplan, 'Transporting the Subject', 210.
[25] On 'unhomeliness' see Homi K. Bhabha, *The Location of Culture* (London: Routledge, 1994),
13.

Germany.[26] The narrator of *I Spy* admires the way people shop in France, feeling every individual item (IS 82). She also experiences a beneficial fusion of technology and tradition. As René puts it: 'what a strange life, there are computers in every room of the house, and we're going to gather wood in the forest' ('was für ein komisches Leben, zu Hause stehen in jedem Zimmer Computer, und wir gehen zum Holzsammeln in den Wald', IS 84). Culture and nature are enmeshed in a way that is refreshing and fulfilling. Keeping a cat and growing plants serve to root the narrator.

Vanderbeke avoids romanticization by exploring the difficulty and anxiety involved in being an acceptable subject. The narrator recalls moving to the West from the GDR as a child, and being a misfit. She fears that her own child will face similar experiences of alienation and isolation (although these fears are not borne out) (IS 19, 21 and 70).[27] The anxiety about not doing things right is suggested when the narrator plans to procure a book about *apéritifs*, in order to do things correctly (IS 91). Vanderbeke does not buy into facile discourses around globalization, whose patness she mocks; she cites satirically the assumption that 'the world is just a little global village, you only need a couple of computers' ('die Welt is doch nichts als ein klein globales Nest, du brauchst bloß ein paar Computer', IS 118). As Kaplan notes: 'the rhetoric of cyberspace and information technologies relies heavily on the hyperbole of unlimited power through disembodied mobility'.[28] Vanderbeke's stress on the body and on nature undermines this illusion.

I Spy charts a gradual (delicate, difficult) formation of contacts, of community. The narrator reports that previously she had not been bothered by

---

[26] Vanderbeke links her emigration to food: 'I tortured myself a while longer in the diaspora, until I gave up and left the country, henceforth to be able to eat taboo-free horsemeat-sausage with our neighbours in France – as often and as much as I wanted' ('Ich quälte mich noch eine Weile in der Diaspora, bis ich aufgab und das Land verließ, um fortan bei den Nachbarn in Frankreich tabufreie Pferdewurst essen zu können, so oft und so viel ich nur mochte'). Birgit Vanderbeke, 'Billiges Fleisch', in Wagner (ed.), *"Ich hatte ein bißchen Kraft drüber"*, 48-59 (here 58).

[27] A chilling example of exclusion is given in an earlier short story – a deft and devastating critique of (German) insularity and ignorance. Birgit Vanderbeke, 'Irina', in Wagner (ed.), *"Ich hatte ein bißchen Kraft drüber"*, 38-47.

[28] Kaplan, 'Transporting the Subject', 210.

being alone, but that now she is, and she is relieved by this development (IS 65). When the child starts school, both he and his mother are wrenched out of 'no man's land' ('Niemandsland', IS 69). German urban isolation is contrasted with French rural community (e.g. IS 81). The French are portrayed here as cordial and respectful; in her guidebook, Vanderbeke attributes to them 'politeness, warmth and charm' ('Höflichkeit, Wärme und Charme', G 10). The French extended family is also highlighted and celebrated (IS 63; see also G 155-56).

Vanderbeke does not idealize family or relationships in general; many of her works conduct a shrewd deconstruction of the family and of heterosexual romance. Relationality, it is acknowledged in *I Spy*, is a process, something that must be constantly maintained (IS 72). And yet, relationships are upheld as key to mental health. The narrator asks René about his experiences of being foreign in the United States. René reports feeling mad sometimes: 'And what did you do then, I said, and he said, somehow found company' ('Und was hast du dann gemacht, sagte ich, und er sagte, irgendwie unter Leute', IS 91). The final line of the text tells us that the narrator and her family went for a picnic with their neighbours: an apparently throwaway conclusion that points to the importance of community. As we will see, Vanderbeke will later take up the issue of (transnational) community, gendering it mischievously.

The Strange Career of Mrs Choi is a fable that recounts the changing fortunes of a village in the South of France, 'M**', thanks to the arrival there of a Korean woman, Mrs Choi. The novella begins with a description of this arrival seventeen years ago. We learn that Mrs Choi is now famous 'far beyond the borders' ('weit uber die Grenzen hinaus').[29] The book opens, then, with a border-crossing that will eventually challenge and blur boundaries, as we will see. I will look firstly at the question of strangeness in the novella, then at the issues of narration and gender, then at Vanderbeke's concern with 'glocalization', a term that will be explored, and with feminine space.

---

[29] Birgit Vanderbeke, *Die sonderbare Karriere der Frau Choi* (Fischer: Frankfurt a.M., 2007), 5. Referred to in the following as FC.

The strangeness of the encounter between the inhabitants of M** and Mrs Choi is immediately established; it is labelled 'astonishing' ('erstaunlich', FC 5). Meeting a resident named Yolande, Mrs Choi smiles in a 'strange' ('seltsam', FC 9) way. She and her son Piet present a striking ('auffällig', FC 12) sight in the village. Mrs Choi is described, later, as 'a wondrous vision' ('eine wundersame Erscheinung', FC 80). Such risky Orientalism, or 'stranger fetishism',[30] is tempered by Vanderbeke's understanding of strangeness as both universal and relative. Early on, it is observed: 'Actually, she [Mrs Choi] suits M**. The people in M** are a bit odd' ('Eigentlich paßt sie ganz gut nach M**. Die Leute in M** sind ein bißchen merkwürdig', FC 9). Mrs Choi claims that people from Gwangju, her place of origin, are 'peculiar' ('eigen'); but the narrator tells us that Mathilde, a resident of M**, is also 'eigen' (FC 18-9).

This is not a tale of assimilation of the Other by the host culture; for example, Piet's habit of addressing his mother in the third person is soon adopted by the local children. Reactions to Mrs Choi include admiration for her hard work and practicality. Mrs Choi gradually establishes connections, friendships, and status. Despite the traditional insularity of the residents of M** – a detail that calls to mind *I Spy* and *The South of France* – Mrs Choi's food is well received. Her business is highly successful and her activities lead to the regeneration of the whole area.

Here again, the host culture is not presented as ideal or as homogeneous. The village is the site of corruption and backwardness. Yolande herself is an outsider, having moved to the village from elsewhere in France. She and her husband Yves once yearned for escape from M**, but were unable to leave because of practical and familial concerns. The narrator notes that 'everyone dreams of the Caribbean' ('jeder träumt von der Karibik', FC 11); escapist fantasies are again mocked. France is again understood as a complex, divided place, with Paris seeming like another world (FC 25).

---

[30] Edward W. Said, *Orientalism: Western Conceptions of the Orient* (Harmondsworth: Penguin, 1985), 2-3; Ahmed, *Strange Encounters*, 4-6.

In contrast to Vanderbeke's previous works, the narrator here is not the story's protagonist, so that the taut, monologic quality of those texts is absent.[31] *Mrs Choi*'s narration is characterized by shifting points of view, and sudden jumps in location and time. The effect is one of elusiveness. Uncertainty characterizes the description of Mrs Choi's first meeting with Yolande; we are told that 'perhaps' ('vielleicht') Mrs Choi commented on the weather, or similar (FC 7-8). The narrator's situation and stance are unclear. She also appears to have little access to Mrs Choi's motivation and thought processes. This dislocation and opacity contribute to the text's challenge to fixed viewpoints and stable identities. They raise the questions of knowing and strangeness, recalling Ahmed's description of identity formation as 'the sliding across of subjects in their meetings with others.'[32]

Another striking feature of the text is the fact that the narrator occasionally addresses remarks to the reader, who is imagined here (as in *The South of France*) as a German man. The narrator's tone is often mocking; she asserts her superior knowledge of the area, which is out of the way and not favoured by tourists. She assumes the reader will not have visited Mrs Choi's restaurant, given that holidaymakers could not cope with two kinds of foreignness at once (FC 49 and 99). The fact of a Korean restaurant existing in rural France indeed gives rise to mirth among a group of *Strasbourgeois*: a comical moment that also implies the violence of rigid definitions of the Other (FC 91).

The reader is positioned as a sceptic with regard to Mrs Choi's plans to start her business (FC 15), and as sceptical, too, about the Korean woman's healing skills, which will be discussed shortly (FC 55). His position is assumed to be that of a (Western, masculine) rationalist; and it is seriously questioned, as we will see. As before, Germanness is relativized. The narrator helpfully 'translates' events into the German context, asking the reader to imagine such goings-on as

---

[31] But compare Birgit Vanderbeke, *Sweet Sixteen* (Frankfurt a.M.: Fischer Taschenbuch, 2007). *Alberta Receives a Lover* (*Alberta empfängt einen Liebhaber*) (Frankfurt a.M.: Fischer Taschenbuch, 1999) plays elegantly with narrative perspective.
[32] Ahmed, *Strange Encounters*, 7.

those in M** taking place at his local Greek or Italian restaurant (FC 55). This appeal to ordinary German reality highlights the existence of German Others. The German reader is himself othered; he is informed he would not be privy to discussions in M**, being an outsider (FC 112).

Where the narrator of *The South of France* is clearly on the side of the open-minded, easy-going male – as opposed to the petty and complaining female – this male reader is under threat. When the mayor of M** becomes ill, the narrator comments: 'You know yourself how flu feels' ('Sie wissen ja selbst, wie sich Grippe anfühlt', FC 41). In fact, the mayor has likely been dispatched by foul means. The reader is also apparently aware of how rage feels, like the insane stalker Marc, who is also dispatched (FC 66). These interpellations read as joky threats; the menacing effect reaches its culmination at the end of the work, when the male reader is explicitly warned that he may be the target of a feminist-motivated murder.

Mrs Choi is a fantastical, feminist tale. Mrs Choi forms friendships with women and enables their professional and personal growth. A sketchy character herself, she is a catalyst for the development of others. Her project has to do with the valorization of feminine knowledge and skills. In this way, it can be linked to Ahmed's concern with 'strange encounters', especially between women, and with her celebration of values traditionally defined as 'feminine'.

The text is interested, for example, in women's story-telling. As in *The South of France*, Vanderbeke is concerned here with the folk tales and superstitions of her adopted homeland (FC 163-66). 'Werewolves and White Ladies' ('Werwölfe und Weiße Frauen', FC 6) have traditionally haunted the imaginations of the local people; this phrase becomes a leitmotif of the novella. Yolande has compiled a book of tales told by women. Mysteriously, her book begins now to sell in great numbers, and is to be reissued by her publisher. Female achievement is also affirmed by the mention of Maria Sibylla Merian (1647–1717), a naturalist and scientific illustrator. Ariane, the mycologist, wishes to see

Merian's work publicized and acknowledged, believing that it has been unfairly overlooked.

Mrs Choi is a kind of fairy, or witch. One of Yolande's informants alludes to women 'who could help' ('die helfen konnten', FC 52), and who used snakes to make medicine (FC 55); Mrs Choi, similarly, is rumoured to have cured a young boy of migraines with the aid of snake powder (FC 54). She is linked to food – important for Vanderbeke, as we have seen – and to health; she runs courses in *kimchi*, a type of Korean cuisine with great health benefits. She practises alternative medicine, as mentioned. The local doctor is ineffectual in comparison: a critique, perhaps, of the male-dominated medical establishment, which has traditionally sidelined women's knowledge and skills.

Mrs Choi also disposes of hostile or violent men, as suggested. The mayor dies in mysterious circumstances, and is succeeded by a woman. It later becomes clear that his widow has befriended Mrs Choi; the two women exchange looks at a public event. This gesture is read by the narrator as confirming their friendship: an example of the speculative, slippery nature of this text. The gesture itself bespeaks a silent intimacy (FC 47). A supportive community of women gradually takes shape. Mathilde's daughter Marie-Ange returns to the village and begins work at Mrs Choi's restaurant. The women are joined by Ariane. Thus, a transnational feminist community is formed.[33]

Despite Vanderbeke's claim in *The South of France* that there is no 'battle of the sexes' ('Geschlechterkrieg', G 150) in the region, this work does suggest that French law is patriarchal. When Marie-Ange's violent ex-boyfriend Marc pursues her aggressively, the law apparently offers her no protection. Marc dismisses his ex's complaints to the police with the conspiratorial explanation 'hysteria' ('Hysterie', FC 68). Violence lurks under the surface of the everyday. The mayor's wife realizes that there is 'another M**' ('ein anderes M**', FC 37) underneath the visible one, and it is shadowy and dangerous. Reflecting on her husband's inadequacies, she declares: 'Enough now [...] Her voice sounds strange

---

[33] See Ahmed, *Strange Encounters*, 178.

to herself' ('Jetzt ist es genug [...] Ihre Stimme klingt ihr selbst fremd', FC 37).
Strangeness is associated with a (feminist, or queer) challenge to the status quo.

But while traditional masculinity is criticized in the text, individual men –
those sympathetic to female achievement – are treated more favourably. Yves is
shown to be receptive and understanding (FC 52); he is later helped by Frau
Choi's innovative and beneficial business advice (FC 57). Piet uses his IT skills to
assist his mother and holds computer classes for women, enabling them to use
technology for their own advancement (FC 113).

Mrs Choi is a text that is explicitly concerned with globalization and
transnationalism. At the time of Mrs Choi's arrival, M** is cut off from the world.
It is 'exposed to an overdose of nature' ('einer Überdosis Natur ausgeliefert', FC
6), and out of range of mobiles. But even at this stage, M** has 'become Europe'
('Europa geworden', FC 17): an allusion to European integration. M** becomes
ever more linked to the wider world; it receives an internet connection (FC 108),
and a European flag joins the French one in front of the camping site (FC 74). The
narrator asserts early on that these are no longer the times of werewolves and
White Ladies, but rather of 'mass media and global play [*sic*]' ('Massenmedien
und global play', FC 15). As before, Vanderbeke cites such discourses with irony;
but technology is indeed shown to be enabling here, as implied.

Tradition and modernity – issues raised in *I Spy* – are also concerns in this
text. The two are brought together in Mrs Choi's restaurant, the new female
mayor claims (FC 46). The building has been constructed using typical local
materials, but in a radically different style (FC 80-1). The under-floor heating
technology it employs is thousands of years old, 'and at the same time the most
modern thing in the world' ('zugleich weltweit das Modernste, was es gibt'), Mrs
Choi states (FC 57). Notions of tradition and modernity are thus relativized and
confused; the narrator, significantly, notes that the dawning of the new
millennium means that the world cannot decide whether it is going forward or
backwards (FC 107-8).

Mrs Choi can be seen as an illustration of and a participant in 'glocalization', 'the interpenetration of the global and the local resulting in unique outcomes in different geographic areas'.[34] Mrs Choi asserts repeatedly that being from Gwangju, she needs everything that is in Gwangju, and in her garden she cultivates the necessary plants and vegetables. A rare butterfly is found there by Yolande; it contributes to the regeneration of the village, enticing more visitors. The butterfly is typically found in Korea; it thus links Mrs Choi to her country of origin, while also suggesting mobility and transformation.

Mrs Choi's emphasis on her origins in Gwangju is significant in terms of contemporary debates about postmodernism and place. Mrs Choi begins running her *kimchi* courses at the same time as the first *kimchi* festival is held in Gwangju (FC 104). The latter coincides with the World Cup, for which the slogan '[t]hink global, act local' ('Global denken, lokal handeln', FC 105) is chosen. Mrs Choi takes this slogan to heart. Towards the end of the text, we are told that while Mrs Choi is now famous, if you wish to take advantage of her services, you will need to go personally to M** (FC 117). Mrs Choi has reflected 'globally' ('global') on the fact that she will 'act [...] locally' ('lokal [...] handeln', FC 108). She thus challenges the view that '[g]lobalization [...] is delocalization'.[35]

This text affirms the importance of local community. The mayor, who rigs elections to ensure his own victory, plans to sell off land to a supermarket chain or to the military (FC 18-9). He does not see, or does not wish to see, how elements of the community are interrelated, and how if one business suffers, all the others will: an appeal, perhaps, for a more holistic view of local communities (FC 27). The reference to the 'international security situation' ('international[e] Sicherheitslage', FC 25), which would justify using the land in M** for military purposes, calls to mind broader debates regarding terrorism and the 'war' against it. M** indeed becomes a centre for anti-globalization, anti-capitalist, pacifist

---

[34] George Ritzer, 'Art, McDonaldization and the Globalization of Nothing', in Samir Dasgupta and Ray Kiely (eds.), *Globalization and After* (New Delhi: Sage, 2006), 228-40 (here 239).
[35] See Leslie Sklair, 'Capitalist Globalization and the Anti-Globalization Movement', in Dasgupta and Kiely (eds.), *Globalization and After*, 293-319 (here 307).

activism, with large numbers of protestors setting up camp there (FC 38). Vanderbeke thus raises issues of militarism and opposition in ways suggestive from a feminist point of view.

The migrant Mrs Choi deliberately and determinedly creates her own space, working with a locally-based architect (with a German name: Eric Halbwachs) to design a restaurant inspired by the work of a Japanese architect (FC 33). For the people of Gwangju, she claims, it is important that one room ('Raum') is empty: 'When a room is full, no presence can unfold in it' ('Wenn ein Raum voll ist, kann sich darin keine Anwesenheit entfalten', FC 35). The idea of space recurs later, and is gendered. When Marc invades Marie-Ange's flat, the latter registers that the man and the empty room ('Raum') do not belong together (FC 71). Ariane, the scientist mocked and thwarted by an embittered male colleague, says that she finds this man's presence in the room ('im Raum') unbearable (FC 118). In the light of these suggestive echoes, Mrs Choi's space can be seen as a specifically feminine one; and as mentioned, her project has to do with female agency and community.

To conclude, then: Vanderbeke's relationship to feminism is ambivalent. The character of Katrin in *Missing Parts* (*Fehlende Teile*) is self-absorbed and shallow, drawing on feminist ideas for her own convenience. But in the same work, the figure of Lila serves as a biting exposé of the constructedness of femininity. And *The Mussel Dinner*, for example, relates the 'toppling of the family patriarch'.[36] Vanderbeke's work is thus teasing and interesting from a feminist point of view. In *I Spy*, as we have seen, Vanderbeke presents a female migratory subject engaged in a process of uprooting and regrounding. This involves the formation of connections with other subjects, and is implicated in the nature, culture, and technology. 'Place' here is dynamic – a shifting site of identification and differentiation – but it is also salient, intractable. The self is embodied and embedded: enmeshed with other selves and with locality. It is also gendered, as *Mrs Choi* implies. In this text, Vanderbeke charts the formation of a

---

[36] Lewis, 'The Agonies of Choice', 224.

transnational feminist community, in which difference is acknowledged and celebrated, and identities become instituted 'through encounters with others that surprise, that shift the boundaries of the familiar, of what we assume that we know'.[37] Through this strange narrative, then, Vanderbeke promotes strange encounters, proffering, finally, a sly but delighted feminism.

---

[37] Ahmed, *Strange Encounters*, 7.

CHAPTER 4

Berlin as Space and Place in Wolfgang Koeppen's Later Texts

Simon Ward

The surfeit of recent investigations into Berlin and memory, instigated principally by Brian Ladd's study of *The Ghosts of Berlin* (1997), has paid a tremendous degree of attention to the material 'sites of memory', but less close scrutiny has been afforded to the forms of mediation which are required to activate that memory. On the one hand, the medialization of memory has to be problematized in a more rigorous fashion, and not simply assigned to a pre-linguistic, pre-mediated state as asserted by Dolores Hayden, that Berlin is 'a repository of environmental memory far richer than every verbal code'.[1] On the other, a certain narrative of memory in and of Berlin has become paradigmatic, which sees the first post-war decades as an era of 'repression and forgetting', and which reads the remembrance of an earlier Berlin in the post-unification era as a new phenomenon. Central to this analysis is a reading of the Berlin that predated National Socialism, as this city is invoked as a kind of 'prelapsarian urban utopia' in, for example, the works of Wim Wenders, or the exhibition 'Mythos Berlin' ('The Myth of Berlin') from 1986, to mention two examples which predate the undoubted post-unification fascination with the Weimar era.

Wolfgang Koeppen too was fascinated with Weimar Berlin, but the case of Koeppen is, in many ways, unique, and this is to a large extent due to his unusual autobiography. Wolfgang Koeppen's life and prose centre around Berlin, but always in an eccentric fashion. Koeppen's biographical details were always sketchy, but he did work for a Berlin newspaper in the early 1930s, until he voluntarily left Germany for Holland in 1934. He also worked in Berlin from 1938 onwards within the film industry, as recent biographical research has firmly

---

[1] Cited in Andreas Huyssen, *Present Pasts: Urban Palimpsests and the Politics of Memory* (Stanford: Stanford UP, 2003), 227.

established, despite his many prevarications in interview. After the war, Koeppen lived and wrote in Munich. The setting of his first post-war novel, *Pigeons on the Grass* (*Tauben im Gras*, 1951) is modelled on the Bavarian city, and while Berlin does appear in that book, it is only through the haunted memories of the Jewish actress Henriette. Berlin lies in ruins, and with it the idea of a German-Jewish cultural tradition. Berlin also appears in his 1953 novel, *The Hothouse* (*Das Treibhaus*), but, with the exception of one example to be discussed below, only through the main character Keetenheuve's recollections of his times at the *Volksblatt* newspaper. Berlin functions as a kind of 'identity anchor' in uncertain post-war times in these works, and indeed Koeppen's post-war writings are, as I have suggested elsewhere, shaped by a remembrance of Weimar Berlin and of the cultural tradition associated with that time.[2] It is only in Koeppen's later (shorter) prose, however, that the city comes to the fore, and while Koeppen's search for a lost self is frequently mediated through a meditation on his childhood in Masuria and Greifswald, a key role is played by Berlin. Since a fundamental given of Koeppen's project is the ultimate inaccessibility of this 'lost self', which is only to be rendered through the masquerading performance of the fictionalizing act, then past Berlin played off against contemporary Berlin is a key strategy: past Berlin, invoked by the spatial markers of a cosmopolitan modernity and modernism, being inaccessible due to the passage of time, the traumas of history; present Berlin being dominated by the spatial structures of the administered world of instrumental reason, which Koeppen, throughout his post-war work, criticizes in a manner informed by Adorno and Horkheimer's *Dialectic of Enlightenment*.[3] As Koeppen is one of few post-war German writers to have experienced the 'Weimar Berlin' of the 1920s and 1930s, and to have been shaped by literary modernism and influenced by the modernist climate of the city in those years, his memory of

---

[2] Simon Ward, *Negotiating Positions: Literature, Identity and Social Critique in the Works of Wolfgang Koeppen* (Amsterdam: Rodopi, 2001), 99-129.
[3] See Otto Lorenz, *Die Öffentlichkeit der Literatur: Fallstudien zu Produktionskontexten und Publikationsstrategien: Wolfgang Koeppen, Peter Handke, Horst-Eberhard Richter* (Tübingen: Niemeyer, 1998).

Berlin is mediated through his own peculiar literary method, informed by a modernist critique of the dogmas of modernity, suspicious of the technocratic homogenization inscribed in modernity as it was analysed by Siegfried Kracauer in his essays, particularly on 'The Mass Ornament' (1926), and indebted to the modernist critiques of modernity composed by Baudelaire and interpreted by Walter Benjamin in the 1930s. This method manifests itself in a particular sensitivity towards urban space, and the interstitial spaces of the urban environment which seemed to provide a place for re-writing the prescriptions of the subject imposed by objective culture and space.

In Koeppen's *The Hothouse* there is a telling scene soon after Keetenheuve, the central character, arrives in the new, provisional capital, Bonn.

> A traffic policeman was playacting at being a traffic policeman in the Potsdamer Platz in Berlin. He waved the traffic on down the Bonner Strasse. It swarmed and buzzed and squeaked and honked. [...] What was the scene at the real Potsdamer Platz? A wire enclosure, a new international frontier, the end of the world, the Iron Curtain [...].

> Ein Schutzmann spielte Schutzmann in Berlin am Potsdamer Platz. Er gab die Bonner Straße frei. Es wimmelte, es schwirrte, quietschte, klingelte. [...] Was war am wirklichen Potsdamer Platz? Ein Drahtverhau, eine neue und recht kräftige Grenze, ein Weltende, der Eiserne Vorhang.[4]

Bonn, the novel's eponymous artificial hothouse, is only playing at the memory of what it means to be a capital, just as Koeppen's prose recalls, for a sentence, what it means to use the stylistic devices of the 'big city' novel. The reality of Berlin is very different, the Potsdamer Platz already, as it would be for the next forty years, the marker of abstract division not just in Germany, but in the world. Already captured in this brief passage is Koeppen's engagement with the abstract space of

---

[4] Wolfgang Koeppen, *The Hothouse*, trans. Michael Hofmann (London: Granta, 2001), 64. Wolfgang Koeppen, *Gesammelte Werke*, 6 vols. (Frankfurt a. M.: Suhrkamp, 1996), II, 257. All further references to Koeppen's *Gesammelte Werke* (*Collected Works*) appear as GW. All translations, unless noted otherwise, are my own.

Berlin after 1945, a melancholic recollection of the topographical (and literary) motifs of the Weimar era played off against the frosty realities of the Cold War.

In my earlier work on Wolfgang Koeppen, I demonstrated how his 'non-conformist' protagonists' sense of self is primarily produced through a continual, if elusive negotiation with public contexts rather than trying to escape from them. Koeppen's protagonists find an 'anti-structural' location in a liminal space between discourses.[5] The city of Berlin as a site of discourse figures as a liminal space particularly in Koeppen's later texts. To work with a distinction made by Marc Augé, neither the 'place' of Berlin past nor the abstract 'non-place' of Cold War Berlin's present can be inhabited, with the result that the protagonist's sense of self is generated out of the dialogue between past and present, but also situated in the interstitial spaces of Cold War Berlin itself.[6] In the following analysis of key examples from Koeppen's oft-neglected post-trilogy prose, I investigate how he plays the image of Berlin as an abstract space off against Berlin imagined as a place, whereby the idea of place is also firmly connected to a historical period now vanished and fundamentally irrecoverable other than through literary fiction. While the act of remembering Berlin past is Koeppen's primary tactic for undercutting the dominant spatial reality of the present, the act of moving between the regulated spaces of both East and West Berlin is a parallel device for locating the self. Koeppen's protagonists are between both structures of time and space in Berlin. Strategies of literary fictionalization are the means to elude structure.

In the course of Koeppen's rail journey to Russia, recorded in his first book of travel prose from 1958, *To Russia and Elsewhere* (*Nach Russland und anderswohin*), the author has to pass through Berlin. This provides him with the opportunity to reflect on the effects of war and rebuilding:

> What remained of Zoo Station, what of the square on Hardenbergstrasse, Kurfürstendamm, Tauentzienstrasse? What

---

[5] Ward, *Negotiating Positions*, 1-72.
[6] Marc Augé, *Non-places: Introduction to an Anthropology of Supermodernity*, trans. John Howe (London: Verso, 1995).

remained of Pompeii? The new buildings look like they have been
erected after an earthquake.

Was blieb vom Bahnhof Zoo, was von dem Square
Hardenbergstrasse, Kurfürstendamm, Tauentzienstraße? Was blieb
von Pompeji? Die neuen Bauten sehen wie nach einem Erdbeben
errichtet aus. (GW IV, 105)

Koeppen is keen to note the ways in which Americanization (an early form
of globalization, perhaps) has affected the spatial practice and experience of the
city, at the same time equating such influences with the spread of global capital
and the construction of empty homogeneous space:

The waiter directed me, in English, to a seat; there were American
breakfast dishes and overseas newspapers, and the men, who ate
these dishes and read these newspapers, looked as if they had built
the earthquake-proof buildings in the city and now wanted to see
what return they were getting on their investment.

Der Kellner wies mir auf Englisch einen Platz an; es gab
amerikanische Frühstücksspeisen und überseeische Zeitungen, und
die Männer, die diese Speisen aßen und diese Zeitungen lasen,
sahen aus, als ob sie die erdbebensicheren Bauten in der Stadt
errichtet hätten und nun nach ihrem Gewinn sehen wollten. (GW
IV, 106)

The buses, as Koeppen notes, used to run to the 'City', a 'City' that no
longer exists as the bus line ends at the Potsdamer Platz. Koeppen, though,
acknowledges the presence of a regulated world on both sides of the divide (not
yet the Wall): 'Policemen over here, policemen over there'. Yet, in the midst of
this administered world, there is the potential of the interstitial space:

The weeds in the middle – a fragment of truth or a chimera? In the
burnt-out hall of the Anhalter Station grass is growing and children
are screeching: the children shot at one another with water pistols
and fell down dead.

Das Unkraut in der Mitte – ein Stück der Wahrheit oder der
Chimäre? In der ausgebrannten Halle des Anhalter Bahnhofs
wächst Gras und lärmen Kinder; die Kinder schossen mit
Wasserpistolen aufeinander und fielen tot um. (GW IV, 106)

The space between the regulated spaces is one of truth and illusion, a space of play and nature amidst ruins, whose potential romanticism Koeppen undercuts with his vision of the kinds of games the children (re)play.

Koeppen's next published piece of writing on Berlin appeared in 1965 in a fascinating volume, *Atlas*, edited by Klaus Wagenbach, and containing short pieces by forty-three German authors including Peter Weiss, Günter Kunert and Günter Grass. Koeppen's contribution was entitled 'A Coffeehouse' ('Ein Kaffeehaus'), although it subsequently appeared as 'Romanic Café' ('Romanisches Café') in the prose collection of the same name, returning to its original title in Koeppen's *Collected Works*.

'A Coffeehouse' is the first text to concern itself specifically with the earlier period of Koeppen's life, and it is a text in which Koeppen is primarily concerned with searching for the Berlin that has been lost. It is a memory of a place, the site of the bohemian Romanic Café near the Gedächtniskirche in Berlin. The text, which covers three and a half sides in the *Collected Works*, is one long sentence, suggesting the correlation and seamless progression of all events. It narrates the story of the place from the day when the church was built through to the darkest days of the Second World War. What appears to be third-person narration shifts halfway through to reveal a first-person protagonist. The text is not primarily a personal act of recollection, but a detailing of the effects of history and culture on a place, with its concomitant effects on the subject. It recalls the 'gold and iron' which formed the Wilhelmine Reich; the Protestant Prussian militarism; the end of the Great War; the November Revolution; the bohemian set which congregated in the inter-war years; the arrival of the Third Reich and, finally, the destruction of Berlin in the air-raids.

It is during the air-raid described in the text that the narrator meets a publisher in the underground tunnel which is functioning as a shelter:

> we were in the purgatory between Wittenbergplatz and the
> Zoological Garden, a publisher stumbled over gravel and sleepers
> and said, you will write this, and I thought, I will write this, and
> knew that I died, in this era, in these years, even if I was not

hanged or beaten to death or cremated, above the city blazed, the firestorm raged, I climbed out of the shaft, the tower of the church was shattered, and the Romanic House with the Romanic Café was glowing, as if in victory the Oriflamme of a secret fatherland were alight.

wir waren im Purgatorium zwischen Wittenbergplatz und Zoologischer Garten, ein Verleger stolperte über Schotter und Schwellen und sagte, Sie werden das schreiben, und ich dachte, ich werde es schreiben, und wußte, daß ich starb, in dieser Zeit, in diesen Jahren, auch wenn ich nicht gehenkt würde oder erschlagen oder verbrannt, über uns loderte die Stadt, brauste der Feuersturm, ich stieg aus dem Schacht, der Turm der Kirche war zerschmettert, und das romanische Haus mit dem Romanischen Café glühte, als leuchtete im Sieg die Oriflamme eines geheimen Vaterlandes. (GW III, 168)

The narrator understands himself to be inextricably linked to the fate of the victims around him.[7] He is witnessing the end of a culture, a culture which he saw flourishing in the Romanic Café, and it is the end of a culture with which he could identify. 'A Coffeehouse' takes up a project that was always at least implicit and often explicit in the post-war novels. Whereas Philipp in *Pigeons on the Grass* is lost in the present and unable to access the past, in this purgatory (a liminal space *par excellence*) a future of sorts is implied. It is the future of 1965, when the narrator must question why he survived. Thus he fulfils his promise to write, to access the past and to maintain a cultural memory.

What are the consequences for a self which knows that it 'died' between 1933 and 1945? Where is there left for it to go? The narrator escapes purgatory and is left standing in a ruined and fiery landscape. Yet there is a possible positive note. The fire which consumes the Romanic Café may be the purgatorial fire which will cleanse and provide redemption. The task of the 'I' is to carry the

---

[7] The moral ambiguities of Koeppen, who was never explicitly a victim, taking up such a position have been discussed with reference to *Jakob Littner's Notes from a Hole in the Ground* (*Jakob Littners Aufzeichnungen aus einem Erdloch*, 1992) by David Basker. Basker, *Chaos, Control and Consistency: The Narrative Vision of Wolfgang Koeppen* (Berne: Peter Lang, 1993), 328. It is a mistake, however, to read this first-person as primarily autobiographical. It is first and foremost culturally representative, as the quotation suggests.

'Oriflamme' (the banner or ensign which is the rallying-point for a struggle) for the secret 'fatherland' (GW III, 168).[8] Through its resolution, this spectator 'I' is implicitly linked with the narrator 'I', who then does tell the story of the coffeehouse. Those texts which follow on from 'A Coffeehouse' demonstrate the interdependence of these two positions. Writing becomes the act of memory by which a sense of self can be narrated, and Berlin is frequently the place where that self is performed.

Koeppen's 'autobiographical fragment' or 'fragmentary autobiography', *Youth (Jugend)* was published in 1976. The perspective of the young man in *Youth* predates the experiences of Philipp and Keetenheuve in the post-war trilogy. He has yet to experience their feelings of impotence, their sense of being trapped on the stage of history. When he leaves his hometown, however, he does indeed find it more difficult to locate such an Archimedean point, unable to find a basis for a career in either directing or acting. The metropolis is a more complex place than his hometown. While this text illustrates all the typical role-playing that one might expect of a Koeppen protagonist, its function within the trajectory of Koeppen's work being told here is to ground the formative significance of pre-1933 Berlin. Whereas the texts before and after *Youth* play off the difference between that Berlin and the disciplined post-war Berlin, here Koeppen summons up some archetypal images of Berlin between the wars that owe as much to literary, artistic and cinematic depictions of the city as to any notional 'recollection' around which the text is structured:

> It was snowing. Berlin lay covered in snow. The Empire lay in snow. The Stettin Station was a cavern of wind and soot and the sounds of grand movement. It was Babylon; a place to leave behind. I liked the taste of the air. I chewed freedom. They stood on every street corner, stood leant against the walls, they froze, they went hungry, they were unemployed, disqualified, homeless, they were the revolution. [...] The police came. They jumped down from the green car. They swarmed about. There were whistles. The

---

[8] The implications of this invocation of 'fatherland' for the presentation of nation in Koeppen's post-war texts are considered in Chapter Five of my monograph, *Negotiating Positions*.

policemen raised their truncheons. They drove us apart. I ran with the others.

My heart quivered. It beat fast. This was it now, I had found it, what I wanted to show, the moral institution, the unfettered theatre [...]. I staged the drama *Masses and Man* by Ernst Toller against a sublime, dark backdrop. The Schlesian Station too was a hollow cavern of wind and soot and noise. It was not Babylon. It was a hell for the poor, who had nowhere else to go.

Es schneite. Berlin lag im Schnee. Das Reich lag im Schnee. Der Stettiner Bahnhof war eine Höhle aus Wind und Ruß und den Geräuschen großer Bewegung. Es war Babylon; ein Ort, um aufzubrechen. Mir schmeckte die Luft. Ich kaute Freiheit. Sie standen auf allen Straßen, sie standen gegen die Mauern gelehnt, sie froren, sie hungerten, sie waren Arbeitslose, Ausgesteuerte, ohne Obdach, sie waren die Revolution. [...] Es kam Polizei. Die Schupos sprangen vom Deck ihrer grünen Wagen. Sie schwärmten aus. Pfiffe gellten. Die Polizisten hoben ihre Knüppel. Sie zerstreuten uns. Ich rannte mit den anderen.

Mein Herz bebte. Es schlug hoch. Das war es nun, ich hatte es gefunden, das wollte ich zeigen, die moralische Anstalt, das entfesselte Theater [...] Ich stellte das Drama *Masse Mensch* von Ernst Toller in erhabene, düstere Kulissen. Auch der Schlesische Bahnhof war eine Höhle aus Wind und Ruß und Gekreisch. Es war nicht Babylon. Es war eine Hölle der Armen, die nicht wußten, wohin. (GW III, 91)

This brief section illustrates the young man's education about the city, not as a mythical Babylon, but as a place of real poverty, but this education is tempered by the fact that it is still (transformed into) an aesthetic performance. *Youth* passes briefly through Berlin, but another text that Koeppen apparently worked on throughout the 1970s, the unfinished novel, *Into the Dust with All the Enemies of Brandenburg* (*In Staub mit allen Feinden Brandenburgs*) is set more firmly there. One excerpt, which was first published in 1978 under the title 'A Beginning an End' ('Ein Anfang ein Ende'), tells another story of a different young boy growing up in the early thirties in and around Berlin, and gives us a sense of the context in which other fragments of that project, which I shall examine in more detail, are to be read.

One such fragment is the piece 'Tiergarten', referring to a large green space at the heart of Berlin. Here Koeppen reuses the model of 'A Coffeehouse' to tell the history of a location, albeit from a much longer perspective on this occasion. Koeppen establishes the Tiergarten as 'a forest, a swamp region on the Spree, a beaver settlement' ('ein Wald, ein Sumpfgebiet an der Spree, eine Bibersiedlung'),[9] it is the development of nature ('islands formed in the stream, extended themselves', T, 549) that leads to the arrival of 'fishermen and sailors', and with human intervention (reclaiming the land), we see settlement, the arrival of 'merchants' and the establishment of a feudal social order. It is the nobility which now clearly becomes the active agent in the space, as Koeppen provides a series of verbs to describe their engagement with and production of the space ('protected, dominated, assisted and exerted pressure, established guards, an army, organized, built earldoms'; 'schirmte, herrschte, förderte und drückte, stellte Wachen auf, ein Heer, rodete, exerzierte, richtete aus, baute Markgrafen', T, 549). Ultimately, but still within the same sentence, 'the forest became a game park'; Prussia's 'strict social order' is mirrored in the built environment, 'the broad road to Charlottenburg, did he desire parades, goosesteps and flags?' ('die breite Straße nach Charlottenburg, wünschte er Paraden, Stechschritt und Fahnen?', T, 549), already betraying a post-National Socialist awareness of history on the part of the narrator. As with 'Romanic Café', the ruler (here Frederick the Great) orders his architect (Knobelsdorff) to produce representative space ('a Versailles'), but also to create a Romantic ideal of nature in the Tierpark with its 'Rousseauinsel' (AP 549). In line with the political dimension of Romanticism which informs Koeppen's invocation of the period in *Into the Dust with All the Enemies of Brandenburg*, we now see the rise of a politicized bourgeoisie in Berlin, again linked to the spaces and spatial development of the city: 'Unrest came into the city, passionate spirits discussed in the avenues, a bohemian scene was formed, a great city arose' ('Unruhe kam in die Stadt, Schwarmgeister diskutierten in den

---

[9] Wolfgang Koeppen, 'Tiergarten', in *Auf dem Phantasieross* (Frankfurt a.M.: Suhrkamp, 2001), 549-552, 549. All subsequent references to this volume appear as AP.

Alleen, Boheme bildete sich, eine Großstadt entstand', AP 549). This is reflected in the spatial order of the city: 'the court barouches made way for the traffic order of the coaches of the bankers and factory owners' ('die Kaleschen des Hofes fügten sich der Verkehrsordnung der Kutschen der Bankiers und der Fabrikanten', AP 550). The technocratic bourgeoisie, figured in Koeppen's narrative by the 'moneyman' 'Herrn Bleichröder', conjoin with the aristocracy to give the Tiergarten 'its final, bourgeois, definition' (AP 550).

The Tiergarten, the second, and concluding paragraph tells us, was never a public park ('Volkspark'). The sentences are now shorter, as the narrator, again as in the model of 'Romanic Café', now enters the story as a schoolchild, subjected to the tales of his schoolteacher's visit to the Imperial capital and receiving a counter version from his architect uncle, Theodor, who calls the Siegesallee 'a merely decorative piece of work' ('eines Zuckerbäckers Werk', AP 551). The schoolchild, now a student in Berlin, views the avenue for the first time and finds it boring, reading the city monuments as a literary *lieu de memoire* through his recollections of Heinrich Mann's *Man of Straw* (*Der Untertan*, 1918). He recalls that Liebknecht and Luxemburg had been murdered in the Tiergarten, their bodies thrown into the Landwehrkanal. He observes the noble houses, 'somewhat shabby in their facades' ('etwas verfallen im Verputz', AP 551), with their social-spatial order for admission; he rents a furnished room, and sees the statue of Bismarck on his wobbly pedestal. This second paragraph concludes with Noske and Ebert followed by a watchful von Seeckt. 'When he set them in the saddle, he had won' ('Als er sie in den Sattel setzte, hatte er gewonnen', AP 552).

According to Pierre Nora, almost anything can be a 'site of memory': a history book or a memoir of the Tour de France, anywhere where 'memory crystallizes and secretes itself'.[10] That memory studies have been so concerned with material places is perhaps due to the apparent ease with which, as Brian Ladd rather poetically suggests, 'memories often cleave to the physical settings of

---

[10] Pierre Nora, 'Between Memory and History: *Les Lieux de Memoires*', *Representations*, 26 (1989), 7-24.

events'.[11] Wolfgang Koeppen's heightened literary anamnesis means that his texts, from 1934's *A Sad Affair* (*Eine unglückliche Liebe*) onwards, often read like patchworks of quotations that tickle the literary memory muscle and flatter the ego of the well-read reader. I think it is productive to think of these quotations as referring to literary texts as 'sites of memory', creating a coherent lineage of the literary and cultural tradition into which Koeppen's texts are embedded, and which is staged here with the reference to Mann's *Man of Straw*. The short text 'Tiergarten' thus refers to a topographical location in Berlin and is a history/memory of that site (objective to subjective), but also refers to a 'topographical text', a section in Walter Benjamin's *Berlin Childhood Around 1900* (*Berliner Kindheit um 1900*, 1940). That text situates the autobiographical persona in the context of Benjamin's analysis of the Wilhelminian bourgeoisie, and it is to the gentrification of the natural space of the Tiergarten that Koeppen's narrative leads, all the way from wilderness to this display of the political order that will lead ultimately to the National Socialist dictatorship, already foreshadowed in the reference to Speer's architecture of domination.

'Tiergarten' remains in the period that is maintained (until its final section) by *Youth*, and does not invoke the back and forth between past and present that we see in other Koeppen texts from the late period of his career. The text 'Dawn' ('Morgenrot'), subtitled 'Beginning of a Tale', does engage in this mixing of time/space coordinates, but also begins in Munich, and only towards the end do we suddenly find the narrator in a room with day breaking through 'thin curtains, printed with a modern pattern' (GW III, 264), and the narrator looking out at a landscape that he has not seen before. We learn that he is in Berlin, 'but how should I believe it, when I stood in the open air, in front of a grand nature, wide open and unprotected from everything' ('aber wie sollte ich es glauben, wenn ich im Freien stand, vor einer großen Natur, schutzlos allem ausgeliefert', GW III, 264). This narrator clearly equates Berlin with an urbanity that is strongly

---

[11] Brian Ladd, *The Ghosts of Berlin* (Chicago: U of Chicago P, 1997), 1.

contrasted with nature (though this nature is the Wannsee, as we later learn); this narrator does not like 'excursions from a city that had been my great adventure' ('Ausflüge aus einer Stadt, die mein großer Ausflug gewesen war', GW III, 264). The usual biography is established: he left Berlin, 'then it had undergone its downfall' ('dann war es untergegangen', GW III, 264), and the typically unrecoverable past is established through the interplay of space and time: 'the place which one leaves, does not stand still in time, but becomes more distant, hurries away in the other direction, one can never retrieve the city from which one came' ('der Ort, den man verläßt, nicht stehenbleibt in der Zeit, auch er entfernt sich, enteilt in die andere Richtung, nie kann man wiederfinden die Stadt, aus der man kam', GW III, 264). As in earlier texts, the post-war changes in the city are noted, with a nod towards a Proustian recovery of spatial practice: 'I knew the city, I had lived here, on every corner lay the lost time, but rebuilt by others for whom I had made way' ('Ich kannte die Stadt, ich hatte hier gelebt, an jeder Ecke lag die verlorene Zeit, doch umbaut von anderen, denen ich Platz gemacht hatte', GW III, 264).

In typical Koeppen fashion, the narrator celebrates the potential of the in-between space, the 'non-place' of the airports, which he likes to visit: 'One sits amidst great possibilities. The world is a pleasure. Even time can be twisted and turned' ('Man sitzt inmitten großer Möglichkeiten. Die Welt ist ein Vergnügen. Selbst an der Zeit läßt sich drehen', GW III, 264). The liminal space allows for negotiation with both space and time: 'I can choose: in New York for night, in Siberia for dawn' ('Ich kann wählen: in New York die Nacht, in Sibirien das Morgenrot', GW III, 265).

As in Koeppen's post-war novels, however, there is no escape from history, only a negotiation via the liminal space, and his journey via the urban railway leads him through a city he does not recognize:

> They had cut broad urban clearways through the city, where the bombs, or Hitler's architect, had done their preparation [...]. [T]hese were connecting routes, not in my sense, however, no boulevard, no coffeehouse, petrol stations where with the petrol

one sold lemonade, poisonously coloured fizzy stuff, one drank in the neon light, treated ulcers, out of rubble, destruction, piles of rubbish, allotments high tower blocks raised their heads, there were illuminated dead windows […] in all spaces the artificial light, no-one is there, no-one awaits you, you stray through the corridors […].

Sie hatten breite Schnellstraßen in die Stadt geschnitten, wo die Bomben vorgearbeitet hatten oder Hitlers Architekt [...]. [E]s waren Verbindungswege, nicht in meinem Sinn, kein Boulevard, kein Kaffeehaus, Tankstellen, wo man zum Benzin Limonade ausschenkte, giftfarbene Sprudel, man soff das Neonlicht, pflegte Geschwüre, aus Schutt, Zerstörungen, Müllfeldern, Schrebergärten ragten hohe Blöcke auf, erleuchtete tote Fenster [...] in allen Räumen das künstliche Licht, niemand ist da, keiner erwartet dich, du irrst durch die Gänge [...]. (GW III, 266)

This is an archetypal modernist critique of the empty homogeneous space of the modern city, the irony being that the older 'spatial practices of connection' to which Koeppen alludes – the boulevard and the coffeehouse – are also archetypal for the modern city (as constructed by Baron Haussmann, or analysed by Jürgen Habermas); it is just that the narrator remembers these as the 'lost' Berlin of the 1920s, which is also the location for his own 'lost' spatial practices.

The narrator then imagines a career as a speculator in the city, which comes to an end as he finds himself in a taxi back to the city. As he is driven along the Avus, he looks left: 'To my right, in shadow lay the forest, stood the pines, was sand, Fontane's Walks through the Brandenburg Marches' ('Rechts im Schatten lag Wald, standen die Kiefern, war der Sand, Fontanes Wanderungen in der Mark Brandenburg', GW III, 267). As in 'Tiergarten', the site of memory is as much a literary text as a material place.

The taxi brings the narrator to the Kurfürstendamm, and, as usual, the past and present intermingle in this specific location. He thinks of the good red Bordeaux at Mampe's, 'which the dead friends had drunk. I had not known the dead friends. I had stood outside and gazed through the window. When they committed suicide, I was not there' ('den die toten Freunde getrunken hatten. Ich hatte die toten Freunde nicht gekannt. Ich hatte draußen gestanden und durch das Fenster geblickt. Als sie sich umbrachten, war ich nicht da', GW III, 268). As elsewhere in the story, the narrator stylizes himself as an outsider in the past; in that sense, the idea of a 'past home' is doubly negated; it is irretrievable, and was not a home for the narrator in the first place.

The short text 'Bless Our Exit, Our Entrance Also Bless' ('Unsern Ausgang segne, unsern Eingang gleichermaßen'), published in 1979 and also an excerpt from *Into the Dust with All the Enemies of Brandenburg*, is set in *the* post-war liminal city of Berlin. I want to look at some of the narrative strategies by which the text deals with the multiple boundaries which confront Koeppen's narrator, for not only are there two geographically-divided cities in one, but also the present city and the remembered capital from the 1930s. This text chooses the ideal arena for its meditation on identity and memory. Where *Youth*'s spectating narrator was a passive observer and commentator, the narrator of this text is an active traveller. His position is established in the opening sentences of the story:

> My first journey to the capital of the German Democratic Republic was undertaken on a Sunday. It was a Sunday before Christmas. The sky above Berlin was boundlessly grey. Perhaps snow, perhaps rain, the grand Advent.

> Meine erste Reise in die Hauptstadt der Deutschen Demokratischen Republik unternahm ich an einem Sonntag. Es war ein Sonntag vor Weihnachten. Der Himmel über Berlin war grenzenlos grau. Vielleicht Schnee, vielleicht Regen, der große Advent. (GW III, 297)

This opening allows us to connect this story to another fragment of prose from the Brandenburg project, 'Advent', published in Koeppen's posthumous volume *On the Horse of Fantasy* (*Auf dem Phantasieross*, 2000). It traces a narrator's recollections of an Advent Sunday in Berlin shortly after 1933 (SA-men are carrying collecting boxes 'for the Führer, for the future), which then carry over into a present-day narration set 'in Berlin, divided by the Wall, in old cowed Brandenburg' ('im mauergetrennten Berlin, im alten geduckten Brandenburg', AP

547), where the protagonist relates a search for Kleist's grave that had ended at a railway station, 'the terminal destination of lines, which only led back into the past, guilt, failure, loss' ('die Endstation von Gleisen, die nur zurückführten, in die Vergangenheit, die Schuld, das Versäumnis, das Verlorene', AP 547), presumably pointing towards the relationship between the location Wannsee, where the Final Solution was planned. That first text, which leaves the narrator on the urban railway travelling eastwards to Friedrichstraße Station, is not constricted by the boundaries of time, and neither is its published partner piece. The capacity to move across borders is already suggested by the boundless grey of the Berlin sky. As in *Youth*, time shifts are provoked by association, so that the mention of Advent sends the narrator back into mixed memories of a Wilhelmine childhood of Christmas trees, nuts and a benevolent authoritarianism. The second paragraph of the story enacts a time shift without actually shifting in location:

> In the West I had taken part in an end of life sale. The Christmas markets were selling the oldest illusions. If I remember, I travelled with the urban railway to the Stock Exchange Station. Young years. The young man embarked, he disembarked. He fleetingly greeted the monument to Schlemihl, or Schlemihl's father. The urban railway stops now at Friedrichstraße Station, and the Stock Market, I heard, no longer exists.

> Ich hatte im Westen an einem Lebensschlußverkauf teilgenommen. Die Weihnachtsmärkte handelten die ältesten Illusionen. Wenn ich mich erinnerte, reiste ich mit der Stadtbahn zum Bahnhof Börse. Junge Jahre. Der junge Mann stieg ein, er stieg aus. Er grüßte flüchtig das Denkmal des Schlemihl oder des Schlemihls Vater. Die Stadtbahn endet nun schon am Bahnhof Friedrichstraße, und die Börse, hörte ich, gibt es nicht mehr. (GW III, 297-98)

With the introduction of the present tense, there is the incontrovertible difference of the historical present (of 1979): the train now stops at Friedrichstraße, the Stock Exchange is no longer there. While these are fairly banal observations, there are more subtle aspects to this passage which reflect on the processes of memory and identity, such as the remarkable phrase 'Lebensschlußverkauf' (an 'end-of-life sale') and the 'oldest illusions' which could well be read as a critique, reminding us of the dangers of a sepia-tinted, senile nostalgia. The reference to 'Schlemihl, or Schlemihl's father' has at least two connotations for the text. First it suggests the close relationship between fictional characters and their authors. Second, Chamisso's story of Peter Schlemihl concerns a man who lost his shadow and went on a journey around the world. The relevance of this story for a narrator in search of his lost self is undeniable.

The text then turns its attention to the physical border which cuts across Berlin. The narrator imagines in great detail what it would be like to cross the border in a tourist bus as 'a foreigner twice over, set behind glass, distanced from any reality' ('ein doppelt Fremder, hinter Glas, jeder Wirklichkeit entlaufen', GW III, 298). As with all of Koeppen's travellers, this narrator does not want to emphasize his tourist-spectator status, and rather than maintaining his distance, he seeks to enjoy that solitude in the crowd. On the one hand, his destination is a personal one – to visit the Pergamon Altar 'at which my uncle died' ('an dem mein Onkel gestorben war', GW III, 298). On the other hand, he wants to mix with the local inhabitants, and so travels with the urban railway.

> But I travelled with the urban railways. [...] In the history to which time petrifies, today again, now, in an instant, the time in which I live, this is an historical moment, for me, par excellence, a border-crossing of a particular kind. The red house of the Charité hospital, death, over, over, I do not know wherefrom and whereto, and there they speak and write of worlds in competition with one another [...].

> Ich reiste aber mit der Stadtbahn. [...] In der Geschichte, zu der die Zeit versteint, heute wieder, jetzt, im Nu, die Zeit, in der ich lebe, ist dies ein historischer Augenblick, für mich, par excellence, ein Grenzübertritt besonderer Art. Das rote Haus der Charité, der Tod, vorbei, vorbei, ich weiß nicht woher und wohin, da sprechen und schreiben sie von miteinander konkurrierenden Welten [...]. (GW III, 298)

In its short breathless phrases the text tries to capture the moment of presence, the moment at which the 'I' is alive in the present tense, the moment of a 'special kind' of 'border-crossing' before time becomes history again. Where Friedrich merely crossed the border into his 'alien and familiar' environment, the narrators of the late texts attempt to capture the moment of *being* between-states. Once the moment has passed ('over, over'), the sight of the Charité hospital on the eastern side of the border is equated with the return of history, of petrifaction ('versteint') and death.

Although the previous excerpt would seem to suggest that the narrator has crossed the border, we in fact discover that he is standing on the platform at Bellevue Castle, waiting for the urban railway and observing the station attendant. Indeed, we have now had two imaginary border-crossings, but the text has not actually progressed beyond its opening sentences:

> I spoke to Sonja, asked advice of Sonja, whom I called Sonja after Dostoyevsky and Raskolinikov [...], Sonja on the platform of Bellevue Station, at the mercy of my gaze and my dreams, [...] Sonja [...] with a red Soviet military cap over the boyish haircut of a young girl who like girls, Sonja, who carried out in cheeky fashion what once serious royal Prussian officials had carried out in earnest fashion, sending trains in east and west directions, unpolitical when she took off the clothes of the State once work was over and was perhaps naked, only a girl from Berlin [...]. Yet on the platform Sonja held the rod of command in her fur-gloved hand and could the rod of command not have been the marshal staff for Sonja with her Russian and Prussian director's cap? In a brain tortured by history the Convention of Tauroggen. German and Russian generals against Napoleon. Did Napoleon denote the West?

> Ich sprach Sonja an, fragte Sonja um Rat, die ich Sonja nannte, nach Dostojewski und Raskolnikow, den erhebenden Mustern falschen Verhaltens, Sonja auf dem Perron des Bahnhofs Bellevue meiner Beobachtung und meinen Träumen ausgesetzt, [...] Sonja [...] mit einer roten Mütze sowjetisch militärischen Schnitts auf dem bubenhaft geschorenen Haar eines Mädchens, das Mädchen mag, Sonja, die mürrisch tat, was einmal ernste königlich preußische Beamte ernst vollzogen hatten, Züge abfahren zu lassen nach West und Ost, Sonja von der Reichsbahn eingestellt und eingekleidet und wohnhaft in Berlin West, unpolitisch, wenn sie den Staat auszog nach dem Dienst und vielleicht nackt war, nur eine Berlinerin [...]. Doch auf dem Bahnsteig hielt Sonja den

> Befehlsstab in der pelzbehandschuhten Hand, und hätte der
> Befehlsstab nicht der Marschallstab sein können für Sonja mit der
> russischen und preußischen Vorstandsmütze? Im historisch
> gequälten Gehirn die Konvention von Tauroggen. Deutsche und
> russische Generäle gegen Napoleon. War Bonaparte der Westen?
> (GW III, 299-300)

The railway platform at Bellevue Castle, ostensibly an ultra-administered space of the Cold War world, is transformed by Koeppen's narrator into a space for dreams and invention. The narrator stresses the fact that Sonja's name is one he has given to her, a name derived from literature (again, as with the reference to Peter Schlemihl, the text plays with the conflation of author and protagonist).[12] Nor does he attempt to conceal the fact that he is imposing his inventions upon her: on the platform she is opened up by the male gaze to demonstrate the complexities and ironies of German history. Sonja is androgynous, possibly lesbian, and divided too in the sense that she works for the East, but lives in the West. There is a sense of erotic play (and possibly subversion of the 'serious Prussian officials') in the phallic 'rod of command' which she holds in her 'fur-gloved' hand.

Hers is not the mind 'tortured by history', however: that is the privilege of the narrator. On the railway platform, historical past and present are conjoined in the image of Sonja: she recalls Prussia but also Soviet Russia, and even further back to the convention of Tauroggen. This was concluded on 30th December 1812, when the Prussian rebellion against Napoleon began (thus presumably aiding the Russian army). Thus the question of East and West is further complicated: does Napoleon represent Western Enlightenment or just another form of repression? Where does Prussia stand? Sonja, with her ambivalent sexuality, uniform and national identity, can also be seen as a projection of the confusion of German identities which are present in the narrator, with his

---

[12] In an ostensibly comic interlude in *The Hothouse*, another novel indebted to *Crime and Punishment*, we are told that Keetenheuve has a former girlfriend by the name of Sonja Busen (Sonja Bust!), whose sexual demands Keetenheuve tries to deflect by suggesting they read the works of Marx together (GW II, 303).

memories of Masuria and Weimar Berlin, and his current status as a citizen of the Federal Republic.[13]

The railway platform is an imaginative environment in which past and present can be kaleidoscopically refracted. The narrator's arrival in the East is a nightmarish daydream about losing his day-pass (and therefore the assurance of his identity), and being on the run from the authorities, hoping 'to find the back door, the mouse hole which is after all everywhere' ('die Hintertür zu finden, das Mäuseloch, das es schließlich überall gibt', GW III, 302). He does find an exit:

> Where was the narrow gate here? With those who had come with presents for long-lost relatives, I went down over grey concrete steps into a narrow shaft.

> Wo war die enge Pforte hier? Ich stieg mit ihnen, die gekommen waren, fremd gewordene Verwandte zu beschenken, über graue Betonstufen in einen engen Schacht hinab. (GW III, 302)

Koeppen's sentences walk a tightrope between the concrete situation (the arrival of West Berliners at Christmas with presents for their relatives in the GDR) and the metaphorical resonances of the situation for his narrator. His own 'long-lost relative' ('fremd gewordene Verwandter') is his Weimar self. At the same time, the narrow tunnel reverses the conclusion of Koeppen's earlier Berlin text, 'A Coffeehouse', where he came out of the underground shaft to witness the destruction of the city. For the narrator of 'Bless Our Exit', the only exit out of the liminal space where history and identity are fragmentary and fragile is disappearance into a narrow tunnel. It is death.

The 'secret fatherland' of 'A Coffeehouse' is the enigmatic 'collective' which is present throughout the latter part of Koeppen's post-war career, the site of memory where the personal identity of the self and a broader collective are conjoined. It is not a lost organic community, but the memory of the

---

[13] The reference to Tauroggen and the Prussian rebellion might well explain the significance of the references to Chamisso, who wrote *Peter Schlemihl* (*Peter Schlemihls wundersame Geschichte*) in August/September 1813, while living in Kunersdorf in Oderbruch, where he had retreated during the popular uprising against the Napoleonic occupying forces.

cosmopolitan, yet German, modern metropolis that was pre-1933 Berlin, imagined after its death. The tendency of modernity towards homogenization, already identified by the likes of Kracauer at the time, is not part of that memory, but is rather identified in the rebuilding and reorganization of the city in the post-war era. Berlin becomes a site of the literary self through the ways in which literature can cut across time and space in its forms of representation. It is striking that Koeppen seeks the 'in-between spaces' of the city to locate that literary self: the interstitial spaces of the urban environment seem to provide a place for re-writing the prescriptions of the subject imposed by objective culture and space. Koeppen's literary memorialization gives concrete form to Karen Till's rather literary observation that

> [places] are fluid mosaics and moments of memory, matter, metaphor, scene and experience that create and mediate social spaces and temporalities. Through place making, people mark social spaces as haunted sites where they can return, make contact with their loss, contain unwanted presences or confront past injustices.[14]

If we look to theoretical perspectives, rather than such poetic positions to elucidate Koeppen's interstitial space, then the work of Edward Soja on 'Thirdspace' seems most apposite. Soja defines 'Thirdspace' as a 'real-and-imaged' space, a space 'other' that undermines and deconstructs ossified polarizations by introducing 'a critical "other-than" that speaks and critiques through its otherness'.[15]

---

[14] Karen Till, *New Berlin: Memory, Politics, Place* (Minneapolis: U of Minnesota P, 2005), 8.
[15] Edward W. Soja, *Thirdspace: Journeys to Los Angeles and Other Real-and-Imaged Places* (Cambridge: Blackwells, 1996), 61.

CHAPTER 5

Berlin: A Topographical Case History

Andrew Webber

This chapter considers what might be called the psychotopography of the city of
Berlin, a place that perhaps more than any other has a recent history that can be
understood as case history.[1] It is a city that, following its belated and over-
accelerated maturity at the end of the nineteenth century, became a centre for
expansionism and megalomania in the first decades of the twentieth century and
for the massive violence and trauma that followed from this, was then subject to a
grievous splitting, and is now host to the after-effects of that historical experience.
The chapter is partly devoted to assessing the theoretical possibility of describing
such a fraught and haunted urban history in psychopathological terms, drawing on
the work of Freud. In order to test the theory, it also considers episodes from the
conjectural case history in the form of literary texts written on the city at different
historical stages: *ancien régime* Berlin at the end of the nineteenth century, West
Berlin in the post-war era of the economic miracle, and the contemporary, post-
unification capital. The essay begins with the first of these, dwelling on a
historical moment that seems distant from the terrain of this volume. But this
anachronistic move seeks to show that the post-war case history of Berlin, with its
arresting psychotopographical symptoms, also has a prehistory to which the
category of 'post-war writing' can all too easily be blind.

Fontane's *Delusions, Confusions* (*Irrungen, Wirrungen*, 1888) provides an
approach to the twentieth-century city from its edges, in the form of an 'everyday
Berlin story' ('Berliner Alltagsgeschichte').[2] The novel is set in a borderline
space, both topographically and historically. It is a narrative on the cusp of

---

[1] The essay is substantially drawn from my book: *Berlin in the Twentieth Century: A Cultural
Topography* (Cambridge: CUP, 2008).
[2] The novel was given this generic classification when published in the *Vossische Zeitung*.

metropolitan modernity, split between anachronistic social structures and fantasies and the looming realities of a new urban order. The text's title is, at one level, about the confusions of the heart, but it also points towards a different kind of programme, towards disorientation at the gates of the modern city and in the spaces around and within it. By setting the establishing section of the text in this suburban hinterland, in the liminal space where the city is cast as village, Fontane sets up a distanced perspective on what has been called 'Fontanopolis',[3] a version of the city that is always divided between real and poetic, centre and margins. Berlin-Fontanopolis is constructed here under the topographical figure of the boundary, with past time and para-urban space configured as – to follow Bakhtin – a chronotopical alternative reality.[4]

In its introduction to this chronotope, or time-space constellation, the opening section of the text functions as a highly theatrical *mise-en-scène*. The novel enters the modern city by way of a topographical time-warp. Its object is not the new building projects or the burgeoning industrialization of late nineteenth-century Berlin, but rather anachronistic scenery that has been displaced by those developments, its impermanence marked by the passing 'still' ('noch') of the opening sentence.[5] This setting on the edge of the city, which was 'still there' in the 1870s, is only available to nostalgia at the time of writing. The opening sentence of the novel sets this out in its hypotactic clause structures, at once achieving a topographical location and marking it out with processes of retraction and transition. At the topographical crossing-point between Kurfürstendamm and Kurfürstenstraße, when the great arteries of the Imperial city still disperse into open fields, and where natural and cultural growth converge (in the zoo and the

---

[3] For an account of 'Fontanopolis', see Charlotte Jolles, '"Berlin wird Weltstadt": Theodor Fontane und der Berliner Roman seiner Zeit', in Derek Glass et al. (eds.), *Berlin: Literary Images of a City* (Berlin: Erich Schmidt, 1989), 50-69.

[4] For Bakhtin on the chronotopical, see Pam Morris (ed.), *The Bakhtin Reader: Selected Writings of Bakhtin, Medvedev and Voloshinov* (London: Edward Arnold, 1994), 184.

[5] Theodor Fontane, *Delusions, Confusions*, in *Delusions, Confusions and the Poggenpuhl Family*, ed. by Peter Demetz (London: Continuum, 1997), 3. Theodor Fontane, *Irrungen, Wirrungen*, in *Werke, Schriften und Briefe*, 20 vols., ed. by Walter Keitel and Helmuth Nürnberger (Munich: Carl Hanser Verlag, 1962-97), I.2, 319.

nursery), the narrative at once asserts its scene and takes it away through the repetition of 'zurück' ('back') and the description of the street as 'vorübergehend' ('passing'). This is a site at once of temporal transience and of spatial transition.

The second, no less elaborately constructed sentence accordingly dismantles the moment of recognition with which the first ends, for what really matters is concealed by what is apparent as if by a theatre set. This is a scene-setting that works towards confusion, where the organization of space seems designed to disorientate the reader-traveller. It constructs a scene that mediates between the city and its surroundings, with a theatrical façade that might act as the face of the city to one approaching it, or its last outpost to one leaving it. In either case, this façade is a cover that – albeit without apparent intention – dissimulates. As the outward face of the city, it is not hard to see that this rambling, Romantic construction, with barely a sign of life, and cast in a sequence of disarming diminutives, dissembles. For the Berlin of 1870, never mind that of 1887 when the novel first appeared, was already a bustling Imperial capital with around a million inhabitants. In 1875, before which the 'still' of the opening line is probably to be located, the Kurfürstendamm was transformed under Bismarck's orders from a sandy bridle path into a boulevard to compete with the Champs Elysées, the royal road of Paris as capital of the nineteenth century.

This Berlin novel settles in a time-locked scene at the city's margins in an elaborate performance of evasion, for which the opening section can be seen as emblematic. The novel's subsequent plot takes it both into and out of the city, and its story of love lost is charted through its negotiation of space, always marked by a sense of errancy and passage. While the programmatic 'Irrungen' (suggesting at once errant understanding and movement) of the title are principally traced in the borderline territory of the opening scene, it also charts the often wayward movements of its protagonists into the city proper. Both Lene and Botho are made to feel their loss through encounters with the metropolitan topography. For Botho, this is in the form of a virtual traffic accident, when his carriage is suddenly held up in the heavy traffic on the way to the cemetery. The mass collision of the carriages ahead is then felt by him with delay, in a stalled fashion that is characteristic of traumatic experience. Making the proverbial connection between the fragility of happiness and glass, he catches sight of a load of broken glass in the cart in front, and is made to feel the pain of his breakage and loss, as he has the sense that the shards are cutting into every finger-tip.

Lene suffers a street 'accident' of her own, when she almost bumps into Botho and his new bride on a busy thoroughfare. The girl from the edge of town is first transfixed by the bustle of the market at the Magdeburger Platz, then shaken out of this as a fire engine rushes by. She hurries on down the Lützowstraße, only to meet her own version of postponed accident: the shocking alarm of the fire bells has prepared the way for personal collision and injury. While Lene just manages to avoid Botho and Käthe by turning towards a shop-window, the missed encounter, in the nick of time, is rife with symptoms of traumatic impact. She finds herself standing on what is taken to be the cover for an opening into the cellar, which trembles precariously under her feet. The glass before her, taking up the 'happiness and glass' motif, is protected by a vertical brass bar, and she senses that in her broken state she will need to take hold of this for her own protection. She feels her way along the fronts of the houses, borne along without consciousness of her surroundings or sense of orientation. Only when she gets beyond the Zoo and the edge of the city does she pause to struggle for breath, and she returns to the house in a state between life and death, the leitmotif of the narrative.

While *Delusions, Confusions* is a novel with a nostalgic attachment to a time and place *before* the city, to the territory of the '*Vor*stadt' or suburbs, it thus also engages in a painful negotiation of it as presence. That the two scenes described here should operate under the sign of the virtual accident is symptomatic for a narrative always out of joint in its spatio-temporal dimensions. The traumatic failure of love at the borderline of social arrangements is brought to bear in these chance events. That the accident is, in each case, only virtual, a near miss, only serves to emphasize the psychical pain that is sustained after the event.

The façade of the first page turns out to be a cover for the traumatic experience involved in passage from the romantic to the real, from the apparently enchanted space of the boundary into the time-bound space of the modern city. It can thereby also be viewed as an exemplary, ambivalent entrance into the twentieth-century case history of Berlin: a city between freedom and constraint, conjunction and division, vitality and morbidity.

The psychotopographical scenes highlighted here are constructed as accidents of human or vehicular traffic, their impact felt on the level of psychosomatic distress. Freedom of movement around the city is blocked as the traumatic afterlife of a failed relationship is brought to bear. When Lene is caught before the shop-window, it seems that an underground space is ready to open up. The cellar with its trembling cover is a corollary of the quicksand-like 'Schloon' as symbolically laden subterranean threat in the liminal space between land and sea in *Effi Briest* (1895). Berlin, too, is built both actually and allegorically on sand, and this is a recurrent feature of its psychocultural topography over the twentieth century.

For Effi the topography of Berlin becomes a site of projection for the ghosts that haunted her outside the city. The constellations from the Berlin of *Delusions, Confusions* return here. The view of the city from the apartment that Effi takes presents the life of the modern city and its transportation system, but this against the backdrop of the Matthäikirchhof, sustaining her morbid attachment to cemeteries. Mortality and mobility are intermeshed here. Hence the return of the 'mortal terror' ('Todesangst') from Effi's past when she has a chance encounter with her daughter Annie on a tram.[6] It seems that there are ghosts in the urban machinery. The Berlin of the last decade of the nineteenth century is still that of E. T. A. Hoffmann and the uncanny habitation of his 'The Deserted House' ('Das öde Haus', 1817) on Unter den Linden, and already suggesting that of the different types of ghosts that will come to haunt it in the new century, those

---

[6] Theodor Fontane, *Effi Briest*, trans. Hugh Rorrison and Helen Chambers (Harmondsworth: Penguin, 2000), 197. Theodor Fontane, *Effi Briest*, in *Werke, Schriften und Briefe*, I.4, 268.

phantoms of history that Ladd describes in his *Ghosts of Berlin*,[7] and others besides. Thus the view from Effi's window is recalled at the end of Peter Weiss's *The Aesthetics of Resistance* (*Die Ästhetik des Widerstands*, 1975-81), this time from one of the key sites of the topography of terror which he exposes there, the building in the Prinz Albrecht Straße that housed the Gestapo cells.[8]

The subterranean void beneath the feet of Fontane's Lene is understandable as a living grave. The façade that opens *Delusions, Confusions* with its effects of concealment recurs in Lene's scene before the shop-window in the form of a cover for what has been repressed and comes over the subject with such convulsion that she seems on the point of collapsing into it. This finds its counterpart in a series of underground networks, closed off or subject to investigation, that run through Berlin's modern cultural history, functioning not least as a space for unacknowledged memories. While the psychotopographical disorientations and divagations of the protagonists of *Delusions, Confusions* are personally motivated, it is a principle of Fontane's texts that the personalized surface of the love story, and the topography that it negotiates, is itself a cover for the political, concealed and dangerous ('das versteckt und gefährlich Politische').[9] What overwhelms and injures the ex-lovers is not only their personal loss, but a more psycho-social sense of damage that arises out of the failures of a moribund order. The psychotopographical experiences of personal narratives also contribute to a psychotopography that operates on a more general, socio-political level. The movements of individuals around the city intersect with those of groups, sometimes running in concert and sometimes at odds with them, and both invest Berlin with their desires and anxieties.

The danger from her personal history encountered by Lene on and under the street in the Berlin of the 1870s can be associated with the sorts of concealed

---

[7] Brian Ladd, *The Ghosts of Berlin: Confronting German History in the Urban Landscape* (Chicago and London: U of Chicago P, 1997).
[8] Peter Weiss, *Die Ästhetik des Widerstands*, 3 vols. (Frankfurt a.M.: Suhrkamp, 1983), III, 211.
[9] In a letter of 2 July 1894 to Friedrich Stephany, in Fontane, *Werke, Schriften und Briefe*, IV.4, 370.

danger from collective history that is still felt in and under the topography of the city over a century later. The false start made by Fontane's novel is also true to what follows. The theatre walls in place of a city wall, opening up uncertain perspectives into the city one way, and across the fields the other, look forward, in particular, to the summation of the 'open field' of Berlin in the twentieth century that Günter Grass would construct in his millennial version of Fontanopolis. The errancies of Fontane's novel lead to the wandering topographical explorations of Grass's *Too Far Afield* (*Ein weites Feld*, 1995). They extend not least to the fields – no man's land, nature reserve,[10] and killing field – that came to be incorporated into the city after the building out of place, at its centre, of another kind of false city-wall.

Grass's Berlin fields open out in their turn to foreign fields, specifically occupied France, given that his protagonist's 'inner geography' has the Spree flow into the Rhône. And this also opens up an intertextual cross-flow with the predicaments of *Delusions, Confusions* in the shape of historical 'confusion' ('Wirrnisse') that leads 'astray' on errant paths ('Irrwege'), not only 'in the field of politics'.[11] Personal delusions and confusions and their dangerous secrets are bound up with those of political history. The lost love of Lene with her ashen hair here becomes an intertextual complex, organizing a more general sense of the recycling of loss through history in the city of Berlin. And, beyond Grass's intertext, the dialectic between surface appearance and hidden truths, as mediated by such symptomatic scenes as that of Lene at the shop-window, is in evidence across the field of cultural production at the start of a new millennium. Like the hysteric in Freud's account, of which Lene and Effi are contemporaries, Berlin

---

[10] This is how the Potsdamer Platz, once the 'navel of the world', now no man's land in the shadow of the Wall, is ironically charted in Sarah Kirsch's poem 'Nature Reserve' (Naturschutzgebiet', 1982). Sarah Kirsch, *Erdreich* (Stuttgart: Deutsche Verlags-Anstalt, 1982), 48.

[11] Günter Grass, *Too Far Afield*, trans. Krishna Winston (London: Faber, 2000), 346. Günter Grass, *Ein weites Feld* (Göttingen: Steidl, 1995), 415.

suffers from reminiscences, from memories that take displaced forms, as confused and deluded as they are compulsive.

In the summer of 2005 the *Literaturhäuser* or Literature Houses in Berlin and other cities mounted a poster campaign as a prelude to the 2006 soccer World Cup, bringing poetry-reading into the city. One of the texts they used was a playful anti-poem by Elfriede Jelinek, a notorious exposer of cultural-geographical duplicities and repressions. The poem consists of a series of variations on the football adage: 'Die Wahrheit liegt auf dem Platz' ('the truth lies on the pitch/ground', i.e. is there for all to see).

> The truth is lying on the ground.
> The truth is lying under the ground.
> The truth is after all bought.
> The truth has been displaced under the ground.
> The truth is left to consort with criminals.
> The truth has been left out.
> The truth has left off markedly.
> The truth has done the unimaginable.
> The truth sparks emotions through two curious penalties.
> The truth: very risky! Life on a cash high.
> It can happen.

> Die Wahrheit liegt auf dem Platz.
> Die Wahrheit liegt unter dem Platz.
> Die Wahrheit ist doch gekauft.
> Die Wahrheit ist unter den Platz verschoben worden.
> Die Wahrheit hat sich mit Kriminellen eingelassen.
> Die Wahrheit wurde ausgelassen.
> Die Wahrheit hat stark nachgelassen.
> Die Wahrheit hat das Unvorstellbare getan,
> Die Wahrheit erregt die Gemüter durch zwei merkwürdige Elfmeter.
> Die Wahrheit hochriskant! Ein Leben im Rausch der Kohle.
> So etwas passiert.

In German, 'Platz' can also mean place or a square, and the second line of the poem immediately turns this commonplace on its head, turning the 'place' over and revealing its false ground: the truth, we now learn, lies under the 'Platz'. The poster hung, for example, in the entrance to the under- and over-ground station at

Bundesplatz, and might well have provoked passers-by to consider the disposition of that square with the exemplary name (Federal Square) and its underground. It is apt to question the toponymic regime of the city.

If the place, square, or ground of this poem, number five in a formation of such texts and printed on a stylized football jersey set against a green background, is to be understood as sports' ground, then we might most obviously think of the Berlin Olympic Stadium, elegantly refurbished for the World Cup but with a historically laden substructure that speaks of other kinds of dreams of world championship. But Jelinek likes to see sport and its duplicities as a paradigm for contemporary culture in general. In this light, it is no less clear that the place in question could equally be the Heldenplatz of Jelinek's, or indeed Thomas Bernhard's, Vienna – annexed, as it were, to National Socialist Berlin. Or it could extend to a whole series of public spaces in Berlin: the Potsdamer Platz as the symbolic place of the excavation, covering over, and rebuilding of a walled and bunkered history, or the Bebelplatz, scene of the Nazi book-burning and now housing Micha Ullman's *Library* (*Bibliothek,* 1995), an underground memorial to the burning of the books. The easily missed void of Ullman's monument to destruction acts as a counter-monument in the sense developed by James Young, at once provoking acts of remembrance and representing the lacunary condition of 'memory lapse', a gap in the city's narrative of itself.[12] It is, in this sense, performative, rather than simply constative, of the elision and repression that constitute the city's 'case history'. This sort of memorial in negative form and space opens up the underground history of the city, projecting a historical spectacle on the 'Platz' into an inaccessible crypt beneath it, the sort of subliminal spaces of which Berlin over the last century is full. It is set to evoke the same sort of uncanny sense of the city's topographical underground as the opening in the pavement did for Fontane's Lene.

---

[12] James Young, 'The Counter-Monument: Memory against Itself in Germany Today', in W. J. T. Mitchell (ed.), *Art and the Public Sphere* (Chicago and London: Chicago UP, 1992), 49-78 (here 69).

The call to reading that is publicized in the poster campaign is thus as much directed at the places and spaces of the city as at literary texts. Jelinek's literary publicity text works, however, to question the reliability of that extended type of urban reading. Its apparent form as an apodictic series of statements in the style of sports headlines proceeds ironically to undermine and displace the truth that it purports to locate. The variant that locates truth 'under the ground' suggests the place of the past, the site of 'Geschichte' (history) as 'Ge-schichte', a spatio-temporal 'layering' of past experience. The urban memory of a city like Berlin is at once in evidence in both intentional and accidental forms above ground and, as the poem has it, 'displaced' ('verschoben') under the 'Platz'. This displacement suggests a psychoanalytic reading of the layered fabric of the city-text. For Freud, *Verschiebung* or displacement is a constitutional function in the work of the unconscious, in its scenic and narrative regime as exemplified in dreams. And this extends to the sort of understanding that psychoanalysis might have of the city through analogy with the psyche, as a place of both individual and more collective psychotopographies. In Jelinek's formulation, 'verschoben' resonates with this kind of psychical displacement.

For Freud, psychical truth lies at once underground, with the unconscious cast as the space below, and over-ground, but in forms that are necessarily dissembled, subject to both displacement and condensation. He thus attempts in the famous image from the beginning of *Civilization and Its Discontents* (*Das Unbehagen in der Kultur*), to engineer his understanding of the relations between personal and collective histories through the figure of the psyche as city. For this he chooses the 'eternal city' of Rome, where the archaeological layers of successive architectural and topographical orders are perhaps uniquely convergent. The elaborately constructed fantasy of the psycho-city fails because of the ultimate impossibility of representing the hypothesis of psychical simultaneity in spatial dimensions: the remainders of past eras may still be in evidence, but they can only ever be virtually coextensive with each other and the constructions of the present: the cityscape follows the spatial principle of contiguity, and this in turn can only support a conception of psychical time as historical succession. Freud manages to salvage a certain purchase on psychical truth from his broken model, a provisional one that arises out of dialectical contradiction, the glimpse of what the psycho-city might indeed be that is afforded, paradoxically, by the 'striking contrast' that undermines the analogical process.[13]

The mapping of psyche onto city is a recurrent feature of Freud's work, be it in the Little Hans case history, the essay on Jensen's novella *Gradiva*, or the reading of E. T. A. Hoffmann's *The Sandman* (*Der Sandmann*) in *The Uncanny* (*Das Unheimliche*). His psycho-topographical conjecture occurs in these works under categories with a particular bearing on the case of Berlin: topophobia, archaeology, and uncanny returns. In his *Analysis of a Phobia in a Five-year-old Boy* (*Analyse der Phobie eines fünfjährigen Knaben*), the fantasies and anxieties of Little Hans's nursery are transposed, or transported, onto the urban topography of Vienna and its transport systems. Hans's phobic condition 'derives its imagery from' (or, literally, is 'under the sign of') traffic, whereby the fantasies of the exposure of parental intercourse ('Verkehr'), the sexual trafficking associated with the primal scene, are relayed into the child's negotiation of urban space and networks of traffic ('Verkehr').[14] Freud understands the city street as the site for the return of the repressed, an unsettled archaeological site. That is, Little Hans's psychical truth lies upon the 'Platz' in the form of his psycho-topographical anxieties, but also beneath it in terms of what motivates these. The child's 'Platzangst', so to speak, the 'fear of place' as a scene for fantasies of collapse and collision, is graphically represented by the sketched street-plans. The sort of

---

[13] Sigmund Freud, *Civilization and Its Discontents*, in *Standard Edition of the Complete Psychological Works of Sigmund Freud*, trans. and ed. by James Strachey et al., 24 vols. (London: Hogarth, 1953-74), XXI, 71. Sigmund Freud, *Das Unbehagen in der Kultur*, in *Gesammelte Werke*, ed. by Anna Freud et al., 18 vols. (Frankfurt a.M.: Fischer, 1999), XIV, 429.
[14] Sigmund Freud, *Analysis of a Phobia in a Five-year-old Boy*, in *Standard Edition*, X, 84. Sigmund Freud, *Analyse der Phobie eines fünfjährigen Knaben*, in *Gesammelte Werke*, VII, 319.

accidental encounters that we witnessed in *Delusions, Confusions* are evidence of this kind of urban 'Platzangst' or topophobia.

In Freud's *Delusions and Dreams in Jensen's 'Gradiva'* (*Der Wahn und die Träume in W. Jensens 'Gradiva'*), the protagonist's dreamlike experience of a ruined city and its fissured topography arises out of catastrophe on a grand, historical scale: the eruption of Vesuvius. The ghosts of this traumatic catastrophe visit the city and at the same time become vehicles for the visitation upon the protagonist of repressed desires from the psychical household of his childhood. The post-catastrophic city is a stage for a drama of the return of the repressed: childhood and adult experience, Munich and Pompeii, are transposed into an uncanny psycho-topographical double-ground, as the archaeology of an undead love moves about the ruined city. While Little Hans's catastrophic fantasies are mobilized by the everyday life of the modern city, here the traumatic impact of mass destruction – and with it the 'psyche' in ruins of a once great city – is aligned with the disasters of the personal psyche, a case history of repressed desire that recalls that of Lene and Botho.

Hoffmann's *Sandman* too is a sort of case history of personal trauma and lost love, albeit within a more Gothic framework. The uncanny here has its roots in private catastrophe (the death of the father in an explosion in the family home) and the ultimately fatal interference of the Sandman figure, as anti-father, in the psychical household and landscape of the protagonist. The experiences of the home, and its *un-heimlich* secrets, are projected into the topographical space of the hometown, as organized by the Sandman as uncanny visitant and guide (providing eye-glasses for the protagonist to view the city and its attractions). This text full of projective fantasies ends with a final projection of the pathological psyche into urban space. The town hall tower serves here as a kind of optical instrument, enabling the apparently recovered protagonist to take a view of his home town and the mountains in the distance, which are perceived in their turn as

a 'giant city' ('Riesenstadt').[15] And on the square he perceives the repressed
psychical truth as embodied by the return of the Sandman.

If the Sandman rises 'gigantic' ('riesengroß') above the assembled
spectators,[16] then he is identified at once with the mountains as 'Riesenstadt' and
with the town hall tower with its 'gigantic shadow' ('Riesenschatten'),[17] as a
construction within a monstrously enlarged urban and para-urban architecture.
The uncanny visitation of the subject by this gigantic topography is under the sign
of *Entstellung*, standardly translated as 'distortion', but with particular resonances
of physical disfigurement, the fundamental principle of dream- and other
psychical work in Freud's account. On the one hand, the Sandman is perceived as
a monstrously overreaching building, and, on the other, by virtue of his distinctive
bushy grey eyebrows, as described earlier in the text, a mobile, grey bush: a
topographical figure of distortion or disfigurement, at once condensed and
displaced in form. The uncanny revenant is a particularly drastic form of psycho-
topographical figure or 'disfigure'. He returns, or re-turns,[18] upon the home town,
casting its topography into uncanny motion, and projecting into it the sort of
experience of urban circulation that Freud describes elsewhere in the essay in his
recursive wandering through an Italian town.

Following Freud's understanding of *Entstellung*, the Sandman's morphing
and mobile shape embodies both a principle of corporeal disfigurement (the sort
of drastic change of shape that comes with catastrophe) and one of removal: the
propulsion of the subject into another scene. This psycho-topographical projection
gives some sense of the sort of truth that Freud looks to find, less upon the 'Platz'
than the more reclusive ground of the 'other scene', the 'andere Schauplatz', of
the unconscious. The uncannily transformed topography of the square at the end

---

[15] E. T. A. Hoffmann, *The Sandman*, in *The Golden Pot and Other Tales*, ed. and trans. by Ritchie
Robertson (Oxford: OUP, 2000), 117. E. T. A. Hoffmann, *Der Sandmann*, in *Sämtliche Werke*, 6
vols., ed. by Wulf Segebrecht et al. (Frankfurt a.M: Deutscher Klassiker Verlag, 1985), III, 48.
[16] Hoffmann, *The Sandman*, 118. Hoffmann, *Der Sandmann*, 49.
[17] Hoffmann, *The Sandman*, 117. Hoffmann, *Der Sandmann*, 48.
[18] For a discussion of the vicious circularity of the return of the Sandman, see my *The
Doppelgänger: Double Visions in German Literature* (Oxford: Clarendon, 1996), 121-48.

of *The Sandman* seems to follow the design principles of just such an other scene as 'Schau-platz' (literally, 'show-place'). *Entstellung* always follows this sort of model for Freud: at once a disturbing alteration, through internal condensations and displacements, of the psycho-corporeal figure, and an 'Ent-stellung' ('displacement') as removal to another place. It is a process that at once disguises psychical truth and embodies it in an encrypted form.

Freud mobilizes this double grounding in his study *Moses and Monotheism* (*Der Mann Moses*), a work on myth and memory, origin and migration, identity and non-identity, accident and trauma.[19] Here the exegetic, topographical, and ethnographical tracing back of the identity of Moses proceeds by means of what Freud calls 'Entstellungen' in the texts, disfiguring transpositions that evince the truth of the case as 'ent-stellt' or dis-placed (he emphasizes this 'double meaning').[20] The analyst, working as criminologist, biographer, and cartographer is charged with relocating and refiguring that truth, putting it back into shape and place. A correlation is made between space and body as elements of the scene of the crime: the body as *corpus delictus*, whose disfigurements are also clues as to the violence done, is always also understood in its relationship to surrounding space.

The bodily *Entstellungen* that might follow from acts of violence, whether by human agency or natural catastrophe, can thus be projected into the topographical 'body' of the city. The eyebrows of the uncanny Sandman, as metonymically embodied in the bush on the square, prefigure the more drastic *Entstellung* of the protagonist after his suicidal leap as he lies smashed on that same place, providing an acute example of the disfigurement of body into city-body. While, the model of *Moses and Monotheism* suggests that the analyst is equipped to read that disfigurement back into a true sense of identity, Freud's

---

[19] For an account of how the rhetorical structuration of *Moses and Monotheism* places the 'Fall', or case, on the traumatic side of 'Unfall', or accident, see Cathy Caruth, *Unclaimed Experience: Trauma, Narrative, and History* (Baltimore and London: Johns Hopkins UP, 1996), 22.

[20] Sigmund Freud, *Moses and Monotheism*, in *Standard Edition*, XXIII, 43. Sigmund Freud, *Der Mann Moses und die monotheistische Religion*, in *Gesammelte Werke*, XVI, 144.

acknowledgement that the act of recognition will not always be an easy thing serves a cautionary purpose. The recognition of figure and ground, of the body and where it properly belongs, is always fraught with uncertainties and speculations. The psychotopography of individuals, cities, or cultures, the way in which the psychical identity of each of these is inscribed into place, works on ambiguous ground, and this has implications in turn for their proper placement in memory, be it in the individual case history or collective cultural history.

The *artes memoriae* or arts of memory famously originate in topography, leading scholars of urban history to return repeatedly to the originating scene, as described in the life of Simonides of Keos. What is less often discussed is that this primal scene of memorative technique is also brought about through catastrophe. Place as the carrier of clues for memory only becomes so under the impact of violent catastrophe. And what is here enacted in a room that collapses is certainly extendable to urban topography under the impact of history. In the story of Simonides, as related by Cicero and Quintilian, the poet is called upon to provide a panegyric for the wrestler Scopas on the occasion of a banquet. He duly praises his host, but also angers him by turning his praise to Castor and Pollux. The poet is called away from the feast to speak to two young strangers at the door (presumed to be the dioscuri), and in his absence, the banquet hall collapses and buries all present. The corpses are so terribly disfigured that they cannot be identified and thus appropriately buried, but Simonides is able to identify them by remembering where each sat at the banquet table. He thus invents the arts of memory by vesting mnemotechnics in spatial order. The mnemonic process is, in a literal sense, topographically conceived, as a writing or marking of space or place. Thus, Cicero, in his *De oratore*, compares the method to the act of writing, whereby the spatial disposition of the figures that are to be committed to memory is modelled upon the wax tablet.

For Simonides the truth is indeed to be found 'upon the place': the location of the disfigured body provides its true identity. But for Freud, as we have seen, psychical disfigurement always also implies spatial removal. The figure that suffers disfigurement appears not only otherwise, but also in another place. Freud implicitly takes up the model of Simonides and develops it in a more psycho-topographical direction when he sets out his version of the arts of memory in the introduction to his 'A Note upon the "Mystic Writing-Pad"' ('Notiz über den "Wunderblock"'). He writes here of annotations on a writing tablet or paper that can be called upon in aid of failing memory in order to avoid its constitutional 'distortions', its 'Entstellungen'.[21] For Freud, Simonides' wax tablet, the topographical framework for memory, is not a dependable or stable place. Memory is recognized as always subject to *Entstellung*, not only in its objects but also in its processes.

The psychoanalytic *artes memoriae* are inscribed in a different form of wax tablet: the 'Wunderblock'. For Freud, the psyche as memory-ground works in the fashion of a palimpsest. The 'Wunderblock' is a place of writing that is, we might say, *geschichtet*, 'layered' with its recording history ('Geschichte'). Its inscriptions are complex and elusive. The memory machine of the 'Wunderblock' is a memory block in more senses than one, and this should be borne in mind as we transfer this model onto the psycho-topographical systems of Berlin, the city that is, according to Andreas Huyssen in his account of the voids of Berlin, 'part palimpsest, part *Wunderblock*'.[22] If the city is to be understood as an archaeological text or texture, then the analysis of the layers beneath the current surface, of surfaces that have gone underground as 'Geschichte', will always be complicated for the psychotopographer by the sorts of processes of *Entstellung* that have been set out here.

Grass's monumental memorialization of Fontane and Fontanopolis in the 'Wunderblock' of his *Too Far Afield* is thus also marked by the more disfigured and displaced aspects of the 'case history' of Berlin over the twentieth century, by counter-monumental elisions. The grand-daughter of Grass's memory-working

---

[21] Sigmund Freud, 'A Note upon the "Mystic Writing-Pad"', in *Standard Edition*, XIX, 227. Sigmund Freud, 'Notiz über den "Wunderblock"', in *Gesammelte Werke*, XIV, 3.
[22] Andreas Huyssen, *Present Pasts: Urban Palimpsests and the Politics of Memory* (Stanford: Stanford UP, 2003), 52.

protagonist, Fonty, can recite 'to this day' ('Jetzt noch') the opening lines of *Delusions, Confusions*.[23] But memorative recall, whether in Fontane's narrative of a bygone Berlin or Grass's revival of it, is shadowed by the 'noch' of Fontane's first sentence, signifying in passing that which has past. Not for nothing does Fonty proceed to ask his grand-daughter whether Perrache station and the Café de la Paix are still ('noch') in existence in Lyon, and then – anxiously – about the fate of the woman, her grandmother, he left behind there.[24] He needs help with his personal memory work. She replies that the station is still functioning but that the – symbolically named – Café de la Paix has been closed after trouble with the authorities and the illness and subsequent death of the owner, and then tells of her grandmother's victimization at the end of the war for consorting with the enemy. The urban field of memory – public and personal – is an irregular terrain, at once continuous and discontinuous, painful and pleasurable, dead and alive, still able to yield truths but also characterized by confusions and delusions.

Another of the topographical memories woven into *Too Far Afield* is that of a renovated 'wartime ruin' where another ash blond woman, Ingeborg Bachmann, lived when in Berlin in 1963.[25] Fonty laments his missed encounter with her, but sees her unhappy presence at the address in question as lending it the sort of immortality that is a leitmotif of the novel, always with ironic shading. Here, it is in tension with the implications of the intertextual reference to Bachmann's poetry collection *Mortgaged Time* (*Die gestundete Zeit*). This leads us to another example of the principle of case-historical *Entstellung*, laden with the traumatic after-effects of the post-war city. Bachmann's *A Place for Coincidences* (*Ein Ort für Zufälle*, 1964) explores the Berlin of the early 1960s as a place at once of coincidence and of collapse, of 'zufallen' as 'falling to'.[26] The text, for which Grass provided illustrations, foresees the buildings of the restored

---

[23] Grass, *Too Far Afield*, 352. Grass, *Ein weites Feld*, 422.
[24] Grass, *Too Far Afield*, 352-53. Grass, *Ein weites Feld*, 422-23.
[25] Grass, *Too Far Afield*, 214. Grass, *Ein weites Feld*, 258.
[26] For a more extended reading of this text, see my 'The Worst of All Possible Worlds? Ingeborg Bachmann's *Ein Ort für Zufälle*', *Austrian Studies*, 15.1 (2007), 112-29.

city as being accelerated back in history, collapsing under the weight of what has 'coincidentally' happened there before, and reduced once more to the ruins out of and upon which they are uncannily constructed. The rise of the city is collapsed back into its fall. In this light, the erstwhile wartime ruin described in *Too Far Afield* remains a ruined structure for the writer's habitation, undermining its ostensible immortality. For Bachmann, the glossy Berlin of the German economic miracle is, in more than one sense, 'geschichtet':[27] it is a city layered in the collapsed heap of its historical fabric. Berlin is thus a place designed at once to provoke and to outdo the archaeological investigations of the urban psychotopographer. And in the capital city of trauma, wrought in psychopathic fashion and leaving an epidemic of psychical disorder in its wake, psychotopography is always ready to collapse into psychopathography.

The 'Zufälle' of Bachmann's programmatic title are turned, by a trick of etymological coincidence, into a trope that can take on an exemplary character for the representability of Berlin. The 'place for coincidences' ('Ort für Zufälle') is in the first instance a *topos*, 'place' as a figure of location in space, and Bachmann's text teases away at the work of identifying a proper sense of place in the city. But the mobilization of 'coincidence' ('Zufall') involves a move from *topos* to *tropos*, the turning of a spatial location into a figure of movement. Topography is, in other words, turned here towards tropography. At the same time, 'coincidence' enacts a movement, a figurative turn, which is false: it is an anti-trope. Rather than extending the terrain of the city into new dimensions, it suggests a collapsing ('Zufallen') of it back into the inescapable place of its foundations. Berlin is, in these terms, a fallen city, one that enacts in drastic form the sort of catastrophic fall that always haunts the fantasy life of cities. It is, to invoke a twinning that is a recurrent feature of the city's imaginary, especially in the Weimar years, Berlin Babylon.

---

[27] Ingeborg Bachmann, *Ein Ort für Zufälle*, in *Werke*, 4 vols., ed. by Christine Koschel et al. (Munich and Zurich: Piper, 1993), IV, 287.

This figure, or anti-figure, of falling is a recurrent feature of the case of Berlin. This case might indeed be glossed, following the title of an early post-war film – *Der Fall von Berlin* (*The Fall of Berlin*, 1949) – as fall. 'Fall' in German is readable in both ways, serving to collapse the two terms. While the end of the Second World War is the most drastic historical embodiment of the fall of Berlin, the case of Fontane's *Delusions, Confusions* (the projected falling of the protagonist before buildings) has already shown that it reverberates in other forms before as well as after that event. A more recent example would be the falling to the ground of Arthur Daane, the melancholic topographer in Dutch author Cees Nooteboom's ghostly narrative of post-Wall Berlin, *All Souls' Day* (*Allerseelen*, 1999), as he returns to film the scene of an accident he had witnessed on the Potsdamer Platz construction site. As he falls, so a photo of his son, who had been killed in a plane crash, also falls from his pocket, and he sees this visitation of the dead and the doubling of accidents and acts of falling as no coincidence, no mere 'Zufall'.[28] If it were to be seen as 'Zufall', then this would be understood in the fraught, uncanny sense developed by Bachmann for Berlin as 'place of coincidences', where things and people 'happen' to collapse, to fall to and together.

Both the collapsing of individuals and the tumbling of buildings or other structures in response to ideological or other pressures are a constant feature of twentieth-century Berlin. Such personal stories of falling in Berlin as those of Lene Nimptsch or Arthur Daane are always also informed by the political, in 'concealed and dangerous' form. Falling becomes, of course, in particular the dominant trope of a later event of world historical import: the dismantling of the Wall as its 'fall', where the collapsing of a monumental, totalitarian architecture is understood as creating new building ground for a reconstructed capital, falling turned into a rising moment. The collapse of Nooteboom's melancholically inclined protagonist appears to be an ironic personal counterpart to that

---

[28] Cees Nooteboom, *All Souls' Day*, trans. Susan Masotty (London: Picador, 2001), 108. Cees Nooteboom, *Allerseelen*, trans. Helga van Beuningen (Frankfurt a.M.: Suhrkamp, 2000), 147.

monumental moment of falling, and the Babylonian reconstruction of the haunted ground of the Potsdamer Platz to which it led.[29] The psychotopography of Berlin over the long twentieth century encompasses the mania, the trauma, the uncanniness, and the melancholy that characterize the personal and public effects of these different forms of falling. Such is its extraordinary case history, or what German would call its 'Fallgeschichte'.

---

[29] In an interview for Gaby Imhof-Weber's documentary film *Architecture of the Millennium: Berlin* (*Architektur der Jahrtausendwende: Berlin*, 2001), architect Rienzo Piano described the Potsdamer Platz as a ghostly site for his building work.

CHAPTER 6

Landscape as an Interpretational Model: The Function and Tradition of Landscape Imagery in GDR Literature

Thomas Möbius

The preference for landscape imagery based on the experience of concrete places is characteristic of the literature of the German Democratic Republic. Authors appropriate places and their history for their own purposes and form them into literary landscapes, which serve as an interpretational model for reflections on history, the relationship of human beings to nature and social utopias. They become a medium through which to make visible historical experiences, which are inscribed in the landscape as text. The most prominent characteristic of these literary landscapes is their historicity: they are as much a way of thinking about the social production of landscape as they are a means for considering the relationship of humans to it. Nothing could be further removed from these landscapes than the portrayal of an idyllic and eternal nature as an escape from social reality.

This is apparent, for example, in the landscapes in texts by Wolfgang Hilbig and Angela Krauß.[1] The concrete observation of the area around Leipzig and its industry serves as the starting point for a reflection on the question as to whether work can (still) offer a site of individual or social emancipation.

The description of Dresden as a landscape in poetry after 1945 clearly offers another interpretational model. In the manner of a palimpsest, Karl Mickel, Volker Braun, Heinz Czechowski, Durs Grünbein and others overwrite the mythologized image of Dresden as a city of culture with images of the destruction of Dresden in February 1945, taking the drawings of Wilhelm Rudolph as their reference point.[2] Within this historical landscape of Dresden they locate their own

---

[1] See Ute Wölfel's contribution to the current volume.
[2] Wilhelm Rudolph, *Das zerstörte Dresden. 65 Zeichnungen* (Leipzig: Reclam, 1988).

experiences of the city and its history. In so doing, they configure Dresden as a moral landscape of remembrance and a memorial to the causes and consequences of National Socialism, to the destruction of humanism.

Yet this notion of landscape as an interpretational model is equally valid for descriptions of landscape that are closer to nature, for example in Kerstin Hensel's miniatures of the Erzgebirge mountains. In these texts, Hensel describes landscapes whose characteristics are rooted in a concrete region and whose sensual presence expands into language itself. By rooting these landscapes in the local, Hensel develops the question of the constitution of *Heimat* and its meaning in the construction of identities.

A further significant example of a literary landscape of this kind in the literature of the GDR are images of Lusatia and the mythical space of the *Wendische* in the work of writers of the New Regionalism.[3] From the 1930s, Peter Huchel's poetry formed what he called the *Wendische* into a poetic landscape, which drew on a reservoir of images of Lusatia, without however becoming mere photographic description. The landscape, history, the local variations and names of plants and animals 'create in his poetry an emblematic series of images which stand for a meaningful and centred existence amongst nature'.[4] The landscape, according to Huchel in a commentary on his volume *The Boy's Pond* (*Der Knabenteich*), is not naively celebrated by him in his poetry, which instead

> seeks to overcome the mere idyll [...] [I]t is not so much [...] the return to nature that wants to express itself in the poems, but rather it is nature as actor, entering people and drawing them into itself. [...] That which links people and the landscape: our face, our feeling melts into it.[5]

---

[3] On New Regionalism in GDR literature, see Ursula Heukenkamp, 'Lo que queda. El discurso sobre patria y región en la literatura de la República Democrática Alemana', in León E. Bieber (ed.), *Regionalismo y federalismo. Aspectos históricos y desafíos actuales en México, Alemania y otros países europeos* (México, D.F.: El Colegio de México, 2004), 275-90; also, on the gesture of resistance typical of the development of New Regionalism in contemporary Sorbian literature, see Peter Barker, '"The Pain of a Dying Species" or the "New Waters" of a Bicultural Literature: Sorbian Literature since 1990', *Neohelicon*, 33.2 (2006), 89-101.

[4] Heukenkamp, 'Lo que queda', 282.

[5] Peter Huchel, 'Selbstanzeige zum Gedichtband „Der Knabenteich"', in *Gesammelte Werke*, ed. by Axel Vieregg (Frankfurt a.M.: Suhrkamp, 1984), II: *Vermischte Schriften*, 242-51 (here 248-49).

In the middle of the 1960s, authors who felt a strong connection to Lusatia, such as Kito Lorenc, Benedikt Dyrlich, Jurij Brězan, Hanns Cibulka, but also Heinz Czechowski, took up Huchel's 'invention of the Wendland' and the critique of civilisation formulated in it as an interpretational model. They turned the decision for the regional into a position of resistance. The landscape of Lusatia becomes in their poetry an alternative space, which has taken on individual contours through Sorbian history, culture, language, its way of life and economy. It was from here that they criticize the destruction of nature and the landscape by industrial pollution and open-cast lignite mining as well as the imposition of uniformity by the demands of centralizing political power: for example, by using poetry as a space for collecting and preserving local plants and animals threatened with forgetting or extinction. Their purpose is not to create a warning environmental poetry; what they seek instead is an interpretational model for the relationship between human beings and nature, in opposition to history and progress.

The literary construction of landscape described above is based on a tradition of the experience and description of landscape characterized by the sensual presence of the landscape and by the claim that landscape does not exhaust itself in the contemplation of the beauty of nature, but that it rather allows the making visible of ideas of society and the philosophy of history. With the modern landscape garden, such as the parks at Dessau-Wörlitz and Bad Muskau in the eastern regions of today's Germany, this tradition found a form of expression that goes beyond the landscape imagery of literature and painting.[6] These landscape gardens, both created by reform-minded princes, are an attempt to form nature into a representation of an ideal society. They reflect utopian notions, originating in the concept of the English landscape garden, of the noble savage, who reclaims an 'unspoiled' state of nature where he can be free and find

---

[6] [The Park of the Palace of Wörlitz in Saxony-Anhalt and the Park at Muskau, which now straddles the German-Polish border, are two of the finest examples of the English-style landscape garden built in Germany in the eighteenth and nineteenth centuries respectively. Tr.]

his true calling.[7] These traditions of forming the landscape are clearly taken up again in, for example, projects to clean up and recultivate eastern Germany's open-cast lignite mines. These do not return to the utopia of the noble savage, of course, but they do return to that equally utopian claim to find an aesthetic mediation between human activity and nature, as well as seeking to construct social meaning and identities through the formation of landscape. Landscape is appropriated here as a space capable of reflecting historical processes, such as industrialization and deindustrialization, as well as social discourses.[8]

In the following, I will show how the Harz Mountains have, in their literary representation, become an interpretational model, and how GDR literature contributed to this process. My theoretical starting-point is the assumption that landscape is something which is not a natural given, but that it is rather a particular way of seeing: 'Landscape is not found ready made in the world, instead the world is transformed into landscape as soon as it offers itself for aesthetic experience'.[9] My second basic assumption is that, to adapt Hans Blumenberg's of 'working on myth', landscape only becomes an interpretational model by means of a 'working on the landscape' which continuously refashions it.[10] In other words, the goal of the following is not a complete enumeration of the literary themes and meanings ascribed to the Harz Mountains. The aim is to examine the motivated gaze that creates landscape: with what motivations do authors perceive 'the sphere of the passive pre-given' (Husserl) and how does the literary appropriation of landscape result from this?

The literary representation of the Harz is conditioned by the tension between its perception as an example of natural beauty, its association with figures from folklore, themselves linked to nature, and its status as a symbol of

---

[7] See Eva-Maria Seng, 'Die Wörlitzer Anlagen zwischen Englischem Landschaftsgarten und Bon-Sauvage-Utopie?', in Richard Saage und Eva-Maria Seng (eds.), *Von der Geometrie zur Naturalisierung. Utopisches Denken im 18. Jahrhundert zwischen literarischer Fiktion und frühneuzeitlicher Gartenkunst* (Tübingen: Niemeyer, 1999), 117-50.

[8] See *Berliner Debatte Initial*, 13.4 (2002); Special issue: 'Überall Landschaft'.

[9] Eckhard Lobsien, *Landschaft in Texten. Zur Geschichte und Phänomenologie der literarischen Beschreibung*, (Stuttgart: Metzler, 1981), 1.

[10] Hans Blumenberg, *Arbeit am Mythos* (Frankfurt a.M.: Suhrkamp, 1979).

national unity. In these variously overlaid meanings it becomes clear that the Harz Mountains as a literary landscape have their origins in a tradition dating back to the beginning of the experience of landscape in German literature in the eighteenth century, and whose images and significations constantly overwrite each other in the manner of a palimpsest.

The beginning of the modern experience of landscape in the context of European literature is represented by Petrarch's account of his journey on foot over Mont Ventoux in Provence in April 1336. Petrarch's text amounts to nothing less than a literary description of nature from an exclusively aesthetic perspective. It is a contemplation free of all economic, theological and scientific approaches to nature. This unmotivated contemplation is the condition for an experience of nature as landscape. The turn towards a pleasurable contemplation of nature without a practical purpose changes the face of nature. What had previously been ignored as useless wasteland or seen as an environment hostile to human beings becomes the sublime and beautiful,[11] which one seeks to be near in order to have access to what is proclaimed to be the liberating character of nature.

In German literature, the literary experience of landscape also begins with the view from the mountain. The poets of the eighteenth century placed themselves consciously in the tradition of Petrarch when they began to seek out the mountains (preferably in the Harz, the Thuringian Forest or the Alps) with the one sole aim: to look. This move to a contemplation of nature as landscape can be seen paradigmatically in Goethe's poem 'Ilmenau, 3 September 1783':

> How often did I return with changing fortune,
> Sublime mountain, to your foot.
> O let me see today on your gentle heights
> A youthful new Eden!
> [...]
> Let me forget that here the world
> Keeps many a creature in the bonds of the earth,
> [...]
> The miner seeks meagre bread in the chasms.

---

[11] See Joachim Ritter, *Landschaft. Zur Funktion des Ästhetischen in der modernen Gesellschaft* (Münster: Aschendorff, 1963), 18.

Wie kehrt ich oft mit wechselndem Geschicke,
Erhabner Berg an deinen Fuß zurücke.
O laß mich heut an deinen sachten Höhn
Ein jugendlich ein neues Eden sehn!
[...]
Laßt mich vergessen, daß auch hier die Welt
So manch Geschöpf in Erde-Fesseln hält,
[...]
Der Knappe karges Brot in Klüften sucht[12]

Here Goethe deliberately overlooks the oppressive qualities of nature, from which
the basic means of survival must be wrested. He is interested only in the
immediate aesthetic experience of a nature, which is felt to be liberating and
beautiful. The aesthetic perspective covers over and represses the (still present)
experience of nature as a source of deprivation and compulsion.

The Harz Mountains already appear as a landscape created by the act of
seeing in 1570 in a poem by the Thuringian poet Wendelin von Helbach:

From deep within the mountain forest emerges the great peak of
                                            the Harz, [...]
The countryside sees him from far and wide, and thus he is aptly
                                    know as 'Proculus':
'Looker-into-the-world' the language of the Latium rightly calls
                                                    him.
For along with the Thuringians, the Saxons and the Hessians also
                                            see his brow;
Further the Eichsfeld sees him from its own territory.

Tief aus dem Bergwald raget des Harzes gewaltiger Gipfel, [...]
Weithin sieht ihn das Land, drum 'Proculus' sinnig bedeutsam:
'Weithinschauer' mit Recht Latiums Sprache ihn nennt.
Denn mit den Thüringer siehet den Scheitel der Sachse, der Hesse;
Ferner das Eichsfeld auch sieht ihn auf heimischer Flur.[13]

Helbach, however, does not yet see the landscape quality of the Brocken,
the Harz's tallest mountain, in the feeling of freedom that the view produces, but

---

[12] Johann Wolfgang Goethe, 'Ilmenau, am 3. September 1783', in *Sämtliche Werke nach Epochen
seines Schaffens*, ed. by Karl Richter et al., 20 vols. (Munich and Vienna: Carl Hanser, 1985-), II.1,
ed. by Hartmut Reinhardt (1987), 82-7, here 82-3.
[13] Quoted in Friedrich Günther, *Der Harz in Geschichts-, Kultur- und Landschaftsbildern*,
(Hannover: Meyer, 1888), 478.

rather in the mountain's distinguished visibility: it can be seen from afar and this has in itself an aesthetic quality. Only when in the eighteenth century it becomes usual to walk through the Harz Mountains onto the Brocken itself does the perspective change. Now it is the view from the Brocken which determines the view of the Harz as landscape: on the one hand, the view from the top of the Brocken onto the surrounding landscape and, on the other hand, the changing natural scenes on the way to the summit. Initiated by literary descriptions, there begins what Thomas Wieke refers to sarcastically as 'the gradual production of the Harz whilst travelling':[14] In search of sublime nature, one walks through the Harz. Just two hundred years after Helbach, walking tours in the Harz and literary memoirs of them were so in fashion that a touristic infrastructure began to be constructed in order to allow even less sturdy walkers to participate in the contemplation of nature as landscape. The criteria for this were extracted from literary descriptions of landscape: one walked and observed for preference along those paths created by literary models.

If it had only offered natural beauty, however, the Harz would soon have fallen prey to a combination of hackneyed literary enthusiasm for nature and local colour. What proved to be decisive for the definition of the Harz as a literary landscape was the fact that the mountains were already 'occupied'. In folkloric tales, the Harz is occupied by mythical beings: witches, devils and nature spirits. Tales of witches are particularly characteristic of the literary landscape of the Harz, and are more significant than a mere natural idyll or local folk stories. Early on the Harz Mountains were regarded as a national meeting point for witches for the Walpurgis Night celebrations of 30 April: the first written reference to witches on the Brocken was in 906, and the Witches' Circle was first mentioned at the end

---

[14] Thomas Wieke, 'Über die allmähliche Verfertigung des Harzes beim Reisen oder Was wollte Harry Heine eigentlich im Harz?', *Konturen. Magazin für Sprache, Literatur und Landschaft*, 2 (1999), 5-16. [The pun here is on the title of Heinrich von Kleist's essay 'On the Gradual Production of Thoughts whilst Speaking'. See Heinrich von Kleist, *On the Gradual Production of Thoughts Whilst Speaking*. Ed. and trans. by David Constantine. (Indianapolis: Hackett, 2004). Tr.]

of the thirteenth century in relation to Walpurgis Night.[15] At this point, however, the nature spirits of folklore were not yet incorporated into the image of the Harz Mountains as a landscape. This happened only when the notion of landscape developed at the beginning of the modern period and also especially as a consequence of its extension during the Romantic period: alongside the contemplation of free nature Romanticism placed the folkloric aspects, in particular the folk tales as an expression of a folk understanding of history and nature. The understanding of landscape expanded from an aesthetically mediated experience of nature to a concept of a historically developed cultural landscape.

What the Harz Mountains mean as a literary landscape can again be seen with Goethe, in this case in his *Faust* (1808): here a rivalry develops between the Harz as a natural landscape and the Harz as figured in folk mythology. During the ascent to the Brocken on Walpurgis Night, Mephisto suggests imitating the witches and flying up to the Brocken on a broom-stick; it is, he says, more comfortable and quicker. Faust, on the other hand, insists on climbing up through the mountains on foot, in other words insisting on the sensual experience of nature whilst walking:

> What gain have we in shortening our ways?
> I love to thread the giant valley's maze,
> Then climb the fell from whose majestic height
> The torrent falls in ceaseless silvery flight:
> Thus beauty gives the zest to travelling days.
>
> Was hilft's, daß man den Weg verkürzt! –
> Im Labyrinth der Täler hinzuschleichen,
> Dann diesen Felsen zu ersteigen,
> Von dem der Quell sich ewig sprudelnd stürzt,
> Das ist die Luft, die solche Pfade würzt![16]

The ascent of the Brocken is described by Faust in the classical imagery of landscape experience: as a contemplation of sublime nature. Yet this

---

[15] See Günther, *Der Harz*, p. 90. [The Witches' Circle, or *Hexentanzplatz* – literally 'witches' dancing place' – is one of the sites of the Walpurgis Night celebrations, situated above the town of Thale. Tr.]

[16] Johann Wolfgang Goethe, *Faust Part One*, trans. Philip Wayne (Harmondsworth: Penguin, 1949), 167. *Faust I*, in *Sämtliche Werke*, VI.1, ed. by Viktor Lange (1986), 535-673 (here 648).

contemplation of nature increasingly mingles with figures from folk mythology: a bride of the wind, witches, spirits hidden in the rock. Nature itself seems to be an expression of mythical forces. This emergence of the mythological into nature, overwriting it, is often taken up and emphasized in illustrations for *Faust*; for example, in the illustrations by Moritz Retzsch (1812) (see Illustration 1), praised by Goethe, by Eugène Delacroix for the French edition of 1828, again by Max Slevogt (1925), and in Hermann Hendrich's paintings for the Walpurgis Hall in the Harz (1901).

In the perception of the Harz Mountains these images of beautiful nature and figures from folk mythology thus overlay each other. Subsequently, the Harz is unimaginable without witches, dwarves, and water and mountain spirits. They become, as Fontane observes in *Cécile* (1886), a primary characteristic of the Harz Mountains and subordinate the experience of the beautiful and the sublime in nature in the context of the perception and description of the Harz:

> Here the witches are [...] a local product and grow like red foxgloves all around the mountains. [...] [T]he landscape is so drenched in such stuff that it finally gains a real power over us, and, as for me, I have to admit: as I was recently passing the Bode Valley, cast in shadow, with the crescent moon in the sky, it seemed to me as if a witch were looking out from behind every alder trunk.

> Die Hexen sind hier [...] Landesprodukt und wachsen wie der rote Fingerhut überall auf den Bergen umher. [...] die Landschaft ist hier so gesättigt mit derlei Stoff, daß die Sache schließlich eine reelle Gewalt über uns gewinnt, und was mich persönlich angeht, nun so darf ich nicht verschweigen: als ich neulich, die Mondsichel am Himmel, das im Schatten liegende Bodetal passierte, war mir's, als ob hinter jedem Erlenstamm eine Hexe hervorsähe.[17]

With the formulation 'witches as a local product', Fontane is indicating that these are more than figures of a naive folk understanding of nature and history. They are products of a folkloristic image of the landscape, to whose creation and propagation literature and art have been central. As such they have lost any sense

---

[17] Theodor Fontane, *Cécile*, in *Werke, Schriften und Briefe*, ed. by Walter Keitel and Helmuth Nürnberger (Munich and Vienna: Hanser, 1990), I.2, 165.

of threat or compulsion. The fright and the impression of the uncanny which they produce are part of an aesthetic play; they are sought out for the sake of entertainment. The compelling element of this landscape or the experience of it now lies rather in the folkloric omnipresence of the witches and their like. When Fontane writes that the landscape is so drenched in them that they seem to possess a 'real power', this can be understood as a reference to the fact that the images of the Harz that have been handed down in literary description can no longer be ignored. The only way to escape them is through irony.

As Heinrich Heine had already observed in his *The Harz Journey* (*Die Harzreise*, 1824), faced with the power of literary tradition, the Harz can no longer be looked upon naively and without preconceptions, and certainly not as natural beauty:

> In fact, when we ascend the upper half of the Brocken, no one can well help thinking of the attractive legends of the Blocksberg, and especially of the great mystical German national tragedy of Doctor Faust.

> In der Tat, wenn man die obere Hälfte des Brockens besteigt, kann man sich nicht erwehren, an die ergötzlichen Blocksberg-geschichten zu denken, und besonders an die große, mystische, deutsche Nationaltragödie vom Doktor Faust.[18]

The image of the Harz, defined by Goethe's *Faust* and Retzsch's illustrations, as a place of witches and elementary spirits, as Heine calls the dwarves and water and mountain spirits, is so present that it covers over his own perception and his experience of nature. Heine's solution, in order to make clear the dominance of existing literary models and, in doing so, to overcome them, is irony: through ironic exaggeration these literary models can be broken open. The result is a representation of the Harz that continues the tradition both of folk

---

[18] Heinrich Heine, *The Hartz Journey*, in *The Sword and the Flame: Selections from the Prose of Heinrich Heine*, ed. by Alfred Werner (New York and London: Yoseloff, 1960), 236-97, here 273. Heinrich Heine, *Reisebilder: Erster Teil. Die Harzreise*, in *Historisch-kritische Gesamtausgabe der Werke*, ed. by Manfred Windfuhr, 16 vols. (Hamburg: Hoffmann und Campe, 1973-1997), VI, 81-138 (here 116).

myths and the lyrical contemplation of nature, whilst at the same time relativizing their claim to authenticity through the use of irony.

Heine's strategy of calling upon traditional images and breaking them with irony itself founded a tradition in the literary description of the Harz, as the example of Fontane shows: a tradition which continues with Thomas Rosenlöcher's *The Rediscovery of Walking whilst Hiking* (*Die Wiederentdeckung des Gehens beim Wandern*, 1991). With this development, the Harz as a landscape gains not only ambivalence and multidimensionality, but above all a self-reflexivity which makes visible the historicity of the landscape imagery and significations in question. This allows the Harz Mountains, that is to say their literary expressions as a landscape, to become an interpretational model with which political myths drawing on the imagery of the Harz can be called into question and deconstructed.

In the nineeteenth century, the Harz Mountains became a symbol of the efforts to achieve German national unity. The images associated with this political symbolism were primarily configured and propagated in literature. The first motif of the Harz as a symbol of national unity can already be found in Helbach's poem of 1570: the view of the Brocken, which is visible from Thuringia just as it is from Hessia and Saxony, has supposedly a unifying effect and thus creates a sense of national solidarity. The legends about the witches could also be pressed into the service as a symbol of national unity. As the site of the witches' Walpurgis Night celebrations, the Brocken achieved the status of a ritual and cultural site, whose national status was emphasized not least by the Walpurgis Night episode in *Faust*. The decisive basis for the political symbolism of the Harz Mountains was provided, however, by the legend of Barbarossa. According to this legend, Hohenstaufen Emporer Frederick I Barbarossa (1152-1190) was sitting in a cave in the Kyffhäuser Mountains on the southern edge of the Harz, waiting for the German states to unite into a single empire. In the course of the liberation and nationalist movements of the beginning of the nineteenth century, the legend of Barbarossa was taken up and linked to political demands for a German nation state.[19] The most well-known literary adaptation of the saga at the time was Friedrich Rückert's poem *Old Barbarossa* (*Der alte Barbarossa*, 1817). As compulsory reading in schools, it made a significant contribution to the popularization of the motif throughout the nation. With the building of the Kyffhäuser Monument (1890-1896) the legend of Barbarossa achieved the status of a national founding myth. The series of pictures that Bruno Schmitz created for an annexe conceived as a national monument to Emperor Wilhelm I shows the Emperor as the saviour of Frederick I as he waits for national unity, thus legitimizing the Empire of 1871 as the heir to the medieval Holy Roman Empire of the German Nation. In *Germany. A Winter's Tale* (*Deutschland. Ein Wintermärchen*, 1844) and the essay *Elementary Spirits* (*Elementargeister*, 1837), Heine deconstructs the Barbarossa legend as a political myth of national unification. In a process analogous to the use of irony in the *Harz Journey*, Heine breaks the Barbarossa legend into its component parts and places these back into their historical context. In doing so, Heine exposes the legend, which is shown to be an expression of contemporary political concerns, as empty political rhetoric: Heine's Emperor Barbarossa refuses the demands of the republican nationalist movement that he should seize the moment to bring unity to the German states. He does not want to wake his sleeping troops in the Kyffhäuser, because the first thing he would have to do would be to pay their wages, which are in any case pretty poor: one ducat in one hundred years. For the representatives of outmoded political power, like the imperial throne, the demands for national unity proclaimed with such pathos remain, according to Heine, empty slogans which are quickly sacrificed to class interests. The French Revolution, symbolized by the guillotining of Louis XVI and Marie Antoinette, and the republican overcoming of class hierarchies are denounced by Heine's Barbarossa as attacks on the supposedly natural order. In this way, nothing remains of the political hopes articulated by the legend. By making visible the history evacuated from the

---

[19] See Camilla G. Kaul, *Friedrich Barbarossa im Kyffhäuser. Bilder eines nationalen Mythos im 19. Jahrhundert* (Köln: Böhlau, 2007).

Barbarossa legend, Heine makes clear whose interests it serves as a political myth, in Roland Barthes' sense of the term. He shows how the formulation of hopes for a nation state in terms of the Barbarossa myth divests the national movement of its republican content and its emancipatory dynamic.

Heine's description of the Harz, in which he links the landscape to contemporary political discourses, founded a tradition of portraying the region in terms of a multilayered interpretational model. Writers who came after him repeatedly took up his literary motifs and strategies, and continued to do so after 1945 in the literature of the GDR. It is here above all Irmtraud Morgner and Thomas Rosenlöcher who continue this work on the landscape of the Harz and maintain its prominence as an interpretational model. Both use the literary landscape of the Harz as a model for the deconstruction of the discourses of power and hegemonic interpretations of history.

In episodes of *Amanda. A Witch Novel* (*Amanda. Ein Hexenroman*, 1983), entitled for example, 'Brocken Mythology' ('Brockenmythologie), 'Elbish Brocken Story' ('Elbische Brockengeschichte'), 'Factual Brocken Story' ('Sachkundige Brockengeschichte'), 'Walpurgis Night on the Brocken (Intermezzo in a Major Key)' ('Die Walpurgisnacht auf dem Blocksberg (Intermezzo in Dur)'), Morgner conjures up the various meanings of the Harz above all as discourses: the Harz as a landscape of sublime nature, as the location of figures of folk legend, and the national symbolism of its context in political geography. The specifically discursive character of this description resides in the fact that the landscape of the Harz is not primarily produced as a location in the plot of the novel. Instead the layers of meaning in the landscape are narrated by the protagonists of the novel, Laura, Amanda and Vilma.[20] This means that, in *Amanda*, the Harz as a place is for the most part indirectly present in the Brocken stories that the characters tell. By means of these Brocken stories, social discourses are dialogized and thereby subjected to critique: the discourse of the

---

[20] On the dialogic structure of various meanings of the Harz in *Amanda* and their function, see Ute Wölfel, *Rede-Welten – Zur Erzählung von Geschlecht und Sozialismus in der Prosa Irmtraud Morgners* (Trier: Wissenschaftlicher Verlag Trier, 2007), 173ff.

(natural) sciences and their appropriation of nature, the heterosexual gender order
and its patriarchal power, the historical political geography of the Harz. This
juxtaposition of the different layers of meaning and their respective social
contexts, contained within or placed against the Brocken stories, is the basis of
Morgner's profiling and exploitation of the Harz as an interpretational model.
This can be seen most clearly in the episode 'Factual Brocken Story' (Chapter 59,
'Sachkundige Brockengeschichte'), which combines several layers of meaning of
the Harz. It begins with a description of a hike through the Harz and onto the
Brocken in the tradition and language of the experience of sublime nature:

> High and majestic rises the Brocken above the lower mountains of
> the Harz, a great giant of a mountain, its head. [...] A wonderful
> landscape scene surrounds us. To the right the towering cliffs of
> the Westerberg, to the left the abrupt, vertical cliffs of the
> Ilsenstein with its cross on the top. Around us a gentle valley with
> flowers, blackbirds and siskins.

> Hoch und majestätisch hebt aus der Mitte der niederen Harzberge
> der Brocken, ein gewaltiger Bergriese, sein Haupt. [...] Ein
> herrliches Landschaftsbild umgibt uns. Rechts die aufgetürmten
> Klippen des Westerberges, links die schroffen, senkrechten
> Schichten des Ilsensteins mit dem Kreuz darauf. Um uns ein
> liebliches Tal mit Blumen, Amseln und Zeisigen.[21]

The classical topoi of the Harz as a natural landscape are cited: the wide
view from the Brocken, its dominating visibility, the alternation between
charming and wild nature, hiking as a form of authentic experience of nature and
its liberating character. In what follows, the description of nature, as in Goethe's
Faust, is overlaid with motifs and figures from the world folklore and finally turns
into a re-telling of the legend of Walpurgis Night. The third Brocken story –
'Instructions to Tourists on Correct Behaviour in the Border Area' ('Belehrung
der Urlauber über das Verhalten im Grenzgebiet', A 232) – then places the accent
on the political geography of the Harz after 1945.

---

[21] Irmtraud Morgner, *Amanda. Ein Hexenroman*, (Berlin and Weimar: Aufbau, 1983), 234-35.
Referred to in the following as A.

As might be expected, the folklore of the Harz and its literary reception through Goethe's *Faust* are the key point of reference for Morgner's representation of the Harz. In *Amanda*, the Harz is primarily defined by the witches and devils, that is to say by tales of them. Amanda, Laura and Vilma tell Harz stories with witches and devils as a history of the constitution and perpetuation of patriarchal power and of its deforming effect on society and the individual.[22] The patriarchal order is represented by devils, whereas women who refuse this order with its rationalist division of labour and instrumental reason are represented by the witches. They gather on the Brocken to look for ways of overcoming the patriarchal order. In order to secure their power, the devils drive the witches from the Brocken. When the witches defend themselves, they and the 'following generations of awkward females' ('nachfolgenden Generationen von weiblichen Querköpfen') who 'tried to get a foot-hold on the Brocken' ('versuchten, auch auf dem Brocken Fuß zu fassen', A 118) are locked up in the Höselberg and forced to become prostitutes for the devils. In fact then, it would be more accurate to speak of Höselberg witches than Brocken witches, but this title is rejected by them. With the name of Brocken witch they claim to be holding onto the goal of recapturing the Brocken, in others word of overcoming patriarchal power: 'The title of "Brocken witch" would keep alive the belief in the future of a world without violent confrontation, without the military occupation of mountains' ('Die Bezeichnung "Brockenhexe"' hielte den Zukunftsglauben an eine Welt ohne kriegerische Auseinandersetzungen, ohne militärbesetzte Berge, wach', A 287).

With this reference to the military occupation of the Brocken, the different levels of meaning of the Harz's political geography and their symbolism are called to mind. The devils have also had to leave the Brocken. With the division of Germany, the Brocken has become an important strategic border location for the military where the GDR army allows no interference, including that by 'supernatural forces' such as the devils. The devils are therefore evacuated. The

---

[22] Wölfel, *Rede-Welten*, Chapter 6.4.

return of the witches to the Brocken would, consequently, not only mean the end of the oppression of the witches by the devils, but also the end of German division under the auspices of socialism: for Morgner, the context for the overcoming of the patriarchal order implies the final overcoming of the capitalist social order. Or vice versa: only with the overcoming of patriarchy can socialism become possible:

> Castle Blocksberg on the Brocken, with its outpost in the Hörselberg, makes sure that patriarchal habits do not die out. A socialism, however, which does not abolish male dominance cannot build communism.

> Schloß Blocksberg mit Dependance Hörselberg besorgt nämlich, daß patriarchalische Gewohnheiten nicht aussterben. Ein Sozialismus aber, der die Männervorherrschaft nicht abschafft, kann keinen Kommunismus aufbaun. (A 549)

The various levels of meaning of the Harz and their social context, which Morgner has previously differentiated, are brought together at this point in the utopia of the fulfilling of history through the overcoming of patriarchal power relations. This is the common utopian horizon against which Morgner places the various layers of meaning of the Harz and the discourses of power that govern them. Morgner thereby explicitly links her critique of socialism's failure to overcome patriarchal power relations to the Marxist philosophy of history and reemphasises, despite all doubts, its '[g]rand [...] narrative of the saving of the world through the emancipation of woman'.[23]

For the Harz as literary landscape this social-utopian context means that Morgner configures it as an interpretational model in such a way as to deconstruct the discourse of patriarchal power, a deconstruction which is presented as an intervention in the discourse of socialist power. This deconstruction of the discourse of patriarchal power in the context of this model is based above all on the grotesque and carnivalesque character of the (re-)telling of the layers of meaning of the Harz by Amanda, Laura and Vilma, as well as by the use of

---

[23] Wölfel, *Rede-Welten*, 169. Wölfel demonstrates, however, how fragile this perspective is.

typical figures from folklore (witches, devils, fairies etc.). Even when the utopian model fails at the level of action in Morgner's unfinished trilogy of novels,[24] of which *Amanda* is the second part, the carnevalesque moments potentially overthrow, in Bakhtin's sense,[25] the existing (patriarchal) order, by holding onto the possibility of an order and way of life beyond power as a point of historical orientation.

If Morgner's work is characterized above all by the use of folklore and its literary reception through Goethe's *Faust*, then Thomas Rosenlöcher places his *Harz Journey* (*Harzreise*) in the tradition of literary Harz journeys and their poetic exploitation of the experience of nature as landscape. He wants, he says at the beginning of his text, to go hiking 'in order to at least to be able to begin writing poetry again' ('um wenigstens andeutungsweise wieder Gedichte schreiben zu können');[26] and in 1990, the Harz is the only possible place to go hiking:

> Of course it had to be the Harz, now that Germany was supposed to become one again, and that 'I will climb upon the mountains' had doubtless called to me softly from the bookcase.

> Natürlich mußte es der Harz sein, nun, da Deutschland wieder eins werden sollte, und sicherlich hatte mir jenes 'Auf die Berge will ich steigen' vom Bücherschrank herüber sacht in den Ohren geklungen. (W 9)

Here Rosenlöcher names the two levels on which his use of the Harz as an interpretational model rests: a lyricizing experience of nature and the status of the Harz as a political symbol of German history. The element of folklore does not occur in Rosenlöcher's representation of the Harz.

Rosenlöcher's wanderer cites the Harz journeys of Goethe and Heine again and again as he hikes through the Harz. What Heine only implies has become an irrefutable dictum for Rosenlöcher: it is impossible to hike through the

---

[24] Wölfel, *Rede-Welten*, 271-72.

[25] Mikhail Bakhtin, *Rabelais and his World*, trans. Helene Iswolsky (Bloomington: Indiana UP, 1984).

[26] Thomas Rosenlöcher, *Die Wiederentdeckung des Gehens beim Wandern. Harzreise* (Frankfurt a.M.: Suhrkamp, 1991), 9. Referred to in the following as W. Heine's *Harz Journey* begins with a poem containing the line 'I will climb upon the mountains' ('Auf die Berge will ich steigen').

Harz naively since Goethe's Harz journey, especially if you are a poet. As a 'borrowed experience' (Löwenthal),[27] Goethe's and Heine's landscape experiences have become literary clichés and commonplaces, which have been put in the service of increasing tourist revenue. By consciously performing literary tradition, Rosenlöcher reveals the way in which it has become mediatized and breaks through its logic by attempting to reproduce the typical imagery of Goethe's and Heine's Harz journeys in his own contemplation of nature. The inevitable discrepancy between the inherited literary images and his own experiences (of nature) creates a deliberate irony. A Harz journey in which the contemplation of nature has become a naive idyll of nature – or conversely an accusatory environmental poetry – has become impossible for Rosenlöcher's wanderer:

> For a while I looked down into the river Bode and waited for an experience of nature. But no rippling looked back at me. And the murmuring murmured on past my ears. […] Any stream on TV would have been more real.

> Eine Weile schaute ich in die Bode hinab und wartete auf ein Naturerlebnis. Aber kein Kräuseln schaute mich an. Und das Rauschen rauschte an meinem Ohr vorbei. […] Jeder Bach im Fernsehen wäre wirklicher gewesen. (W 38)

The sublime in the landscape, as invoked by the imagery of Goethe's Harz journey, does not emerge, and appears only to be possible as the mediatized surrogate of the 'stream on TV'. The expected images of sublime nature, formed by tradition, are confronted with the banality of the touristic exploitation of these same images.

The experience of nature is only possible for Rosenlöcher's wanderer in minute observations of the smallest moments:

> He, however, […] had, as an observer of nature, taken every small detail seriously and in his ornithological studies had also once recorded a fly (Musca domestica) as it passed by chance.

---

[27] Leo Löwenthal, 'Humanität und Kommunikation', in *Untergang der Dämonologien* (Leipzig: Reclam, 1990) 235-50 (here 240).

> Er jedenfalls [...] habe als Naturbeobachter jede Kleinigkeit
> wichtig genommen und bei seinen ornithologischen Studien auch
> einmal eine zufällig vorbeikommende Stubenfliege (Musca
> domestica) schriftlich festgehalten. (W 40)

This retreat into the small and the random, into the apparently meaningless and banal, such as the house fly, is characteristic for Rosenlöcher's perspective. He turns his gaze from the great, with its promise of the sublime (in relation to the experience of nature) and the pathetic (with regard to the political geography of the Harz), to the unnoticed and the everyday, to that which is without a voice: 'The fragile bloom [...]. "You", I said so softly that I didn't hear it myself. "You", it says even more softly, so that this time I really couldn't hear it' ('Die hinfällige Blüte [...] 'Du', sagte ich so leise, daß ich es selber nicht hörte. 'Du', sagte sie noch leiser, daß ich es erst recht nicht hörte', W 39). Here Rosenlöcher habitually shows the perspective of what is marginalized in hegemonic discourse. With the figure of the wanderer, the model of experience practised in terms of nature as landscape is transferred to the interpretation of the political meaning of the Harz. The experience of nature beyond the surrogate of media images is said to demand 'the mode of being of the wanderer' ('die Daseinsweise des Wanderers', W 13): conscious slowing down, the insistence on direct observation, the turn to the small and the unnoticed. In the face of the new speed and range of media products,[28] this makes him an untimely and marginalized figure, who – by the very fact of his being – resists the perspective of the (new) hegemonic political and social discourses.

On his journey through the Harz, Rosenlöcher's wanderer registers minutely the changing image of the landscape and the changing modes of behaviour: the new cars, goods, newspapers, signs, social hierarchies and mechanisms of distinction. Just as when he examines patterns of perception on the level of the experience of nature, so Rosenlöcher equally turns his attention to the

---

[28] At what point, the narrator asks himself, for example, did he stop noticing when he was reading a West German newspaper (W 11).

apparently meaningless and untimely when considering society, in other words to
that which is being repressed and marginalized in the process of reunification:

> [...] and [she] sold me a Ruhla wrist watch for almost nothing. Of
> course this unsophisticated timepiece had to be given a good shake
> first; the hands stood motionless for too long, but the watch had
> rightly recognized that its own number was up. Its noisy
> mechanism and its plastic casing had already been superseded by
> the watches without hands, the quietly creeping neon digitalization
> of the Western world [...]. This portent had from the beginning
> been a monument to a downfall, but had now become one in the
> space of a few weeks. The forty frozen years weighed light in my
> hand.

> [...] und verkaufte mir eine fast schon kostenlose Ruhlataschenuhr.
> Freilich mußte das Grobchronometer erst gründlich geschüttelt
> werden; zu lange standen die Zeiger reglos, aber die eigentlich
> herrschende Zeit hatte die Uhr an sich selbst gemessen. An ihrer
> Rasselmechanik und ihrem Plastegehäuse: von vornherein überholt
> von den zeigerlosen, auf leisen Nummernsohlen daherkommenden
> Leuchtschriftuhren der digitalen, westlichen Welt [...] Ein
> Menetekel von Anfang an und nun in wenigen Wochen zu einem
> Untergangsdenkmal geworden. Leicht wogten in meiner Hand die
> vierzig gefrorenen Jahre. (W 36-7)[29]

The clearly banal nature of the everyday moments to which he turns his
gaze creates an effect of the ridiculous, which the deliberate naivety of the
language accentuates further. However, set against the political geography of the
Harz, this ridiculousness attains an enlightening irony.

Rosenlöcher can assume that his German reader knows the meaning of the
Harz as a symbolically charged site of national unity and German division. The
meanings and the context of the political geography of the Harz are so anchored in
the collective memory that the brief observation '[o]f course it had to be the Harz,
now that Germany was supposed to be become one again' is sufficient to invoke
them. This means that, by using the topos of the Harz, Rosenlöcher's description
of a journey on foot through the everyday experience of the German unification
process becomes a commentary on the political and media rhetoric of German

---

[29] A Ruhla was a make of GDR wristwatch.

unification. The pathetic political discourse is countered by Rosenlöcher's everyday lived perspective from below. One image, for instance, invokes the defence of pedestrians against the 'chrome ships' with the Mercedes star:

> Along [...] rocked a chrome ship. To constantly drive around things was its way of experiencing things. [...] My neck tensed. My feet walked as if they were completely automatic. Although the centre of resistance was the rucksack itself. [...] Just like my poor trousers, too. 'Look at them', I thought, 'They alone are the basis for a fairer world'. The motor was already screaming behind me. I could already feel the bumper. In desperation I tried to whistle the International or at least the Marseillaise.

> Da [...] kam schaukelnd ein Chromschiff heran. Beständig herumzufahren, das war ihre Art zu erfahren. [...] Mein Nacken versteifte sich. Meine Füße gingen, als wären sie vollautomatisch. Wobei das Widerstandszentrum der Rucksack selber war. [...] Wie auch meine dürftigen Hosen. 'Schau sie dir nur an', dachte ich. 'Sie allein sind die Basis für eine gerechtere Welt.' Schon heulte der Motor dicht hinter mir. Schon konnte ich die Stoßstange spüren. Verzweifelt versuchte ich noch, die Internationale zu pfeifen oder doch wenigstens die Marseillaise. (W 24)

Here Rosenlöcher uses his wanderer as a figure of resistance who does not just stand up to the occupation of the landscape by the car, but who also, in his citation of the International and the Marseillaise, brings together the historical discourses of emancipation and the socialist movement to provide a context for his actions. Against the hierarchies and stigmatizations of the social order represented by the driver of the Mercedes, which he is constantly confronted with as a walker, he calls upon the memory the utopia of a more just society.

As a reader, one is tempted to accuse Rosenlöcher's wanderer of ideological overinterpretation. The strong politicization creates an effect of the ridiculous. Together with Rosenlöcher's equally strong and continuous irony, it makes Rosenlöcher's wanderer appear as a picaresque figure. Yet the naivety is only the performance of naivety. Rosenlöcher's emphasizing of the Harz as an interpretational model is based on the collapse of the function of observation and the meaning it is supposed to produce, a collapse which is performed in the naive language. It seems ridiculous to represent the demise of a social order by means of a simple plastic watch. Signifier and signified do not fit together. The banality of the everyday world and the world of experience work against the pathos of the meaning ascribed to the 'big history' of German unification. This is precisely Rosenlöcher's target in his use of the Harz as an interpretational model: enlightening irony towards the political spirit of the times and its hegemonic view of history. Unlike Morgner, Rosenlöcher does not seek to counter this hegemony with another utopian grand narrative. Instead, he undermines the political narrative of German unification, and history itself, with critical observations on its everyday consequences, in other words on the Westernisation of everyday life.

Translated by David Clarke

CHAPTER 7

Paradise Regained:
Topographies of the Self in the Prose Fiction of Angela Krauß

Ute Wölfel

> This is how the place looks that I have been imagining for a long time: to move among people who get what they wish for. From the very beginning we are constructing the scenery of fulfilment, strange cities occupy hidden worlds, through which expectant inhabitants wander.

> So sieht der Ort aus, von dem ich lange Vorstellungen gehegt hatte: unter Menschen einherzugehen, die bekommen, was sie sich wünschen. Von Anfang an bauen wir an der großen Erfüllungsszenerie, seltsame Städte besiedeln unsere verborgene Welt, durch die erwartungsvolle Bewohner streifen.[1]

In her prose fiction Angela Krauß drafts places of the imagination. Driven by longing and expectation, Krauß's protagonists search the inner and outer world for 'sceneries of fulfilment', that is for places to stage or perform their feelings, wishes, ideals, virtues etc. and thus reinforce their identity. As the term 'scenery' implies these places are linked to the arts and as such form places outside the daily routine. In the words of Foucault they are heterotopias, i.e. 'real places [...] which are something like counter-sites, a kind of effectively enacted utopia in which real sites, all the other sites that can be found within the culture are simultaneously represented, contested, and inverted'.[2]

'Sceneries of fulfilment' have been central to Krauß's texts from the beginning, though the (textual) conditions and circumstances of fulfilment have changed considerably with the fall of the Wall and German unification. The

---

[1] Angela Krauß, *Milliarden neuer Sterne* (Frankfurt a.M. Suhrkamp 1999), 20-1.
[2] Michel Foucault, 'Of Other Spaces', *Diacritics*, 16.1 (1986), 22-27 (here 24).

scenery of fulfilment emerges as a topos in Krauß's debut *The Celebration* (*Das Vergnügen*, 1986); it may even be said that the creation of such a scenery is the text's objective. This first scenery of fulfilment is generated by the narrative destruction of the literary conventions and expectations that had shaped the industrial topos in the literature of the German Democratic Republic. The result of that literary dismantling is the discovery of the aesthetic dimension of the old briquette factory in the industrial region of Bitterfeld which is at the centre of the novel. Krauß's approach turns the industrial space into a lustrous stage on which the workers open a scene of mistaken and found identity along the lines of Shakespeare's *Midsummer Night's Dream*.[3] The spectacle inverts and contests the daily practices and roles and allows the workers existential insights.

The destruction of literary conventions and expectations and the aesthetic reassessment of the industrial topos in *The Celebration* rely on an identity that is based on the 'industrial collective' not (anymore) in a political or economic sense but in the social sense of a milieu. The industrial milieu is seen as a nurturing undercurrent or soil of life in which the individual is rooted. With the fall of the Wall and German unification this home milieu disappears and the need to re-locate identity ensues. In texts like *The Woman Flying Across* (*Die Überfliegerin*, 1995), *Millions of New Stars* (*Milliarden neuer Sterne*, 1999) or *How Do We Go On* (*Wie Weiter*, 2006), Krauß's protagonists appear uprooted and homeless; they travel the world from Moscow to New York and San Francisco, they roam their home town (Leipzig and its surrounding industrial areas), they leave their flats and factories and frequent the 'other places' such as the zoo, cafés, planes and the cemetery; they travel into their past, memories and fantasies. They find themselves drifting and in need of stabilizing their threatened identities.

This chapter looks at *Summer on the Ice* (*Sommer auf dem Eis*), a seminal text of Krauß's published in 1998, seven years after German unification, in order

---

[3] For the ambivalent, problematic depiction of the industrial milieu in *The Celebration* see Ute Wölfel, 'Die autonome Produktion: Arbeitswelt in der DDR-Prosa am Beispiel Angela Krauß' *Das Vergnügen*, in: Wölfel (ed.), *Literarisches Feld DDR. Bedingungen und Formen literarischer Produktion in der DDR* (Würzburg: Königshausen & Neumann 2005), 31-51.

to discuss the changing function of the sceneries of fulfilment, these crucial places of identity. *Summer on the Ice* revisits the industrial landscape of the debut and looks at the difficulties and distress the individual faces due to the completely changed circumstances. With the disappearance of the home milieu, identity is no longer supported by the industrial collective. Instead, the individual is thrown back upon itself and forced to embark on a highly subjective journey of self-discovery. The sceneries of fulfilment which before 1989 provided the opportunity to stage or perform identity within the objective framework of the home milieu are now the sole source for the individual in its attempt to cope with crisis; they replace an objective framework and its meaning, cohesion and coherence. With the end of the industrial milieu, the daily routine and its 'common places' seem to lose relevance for the individual in favour of sceneries of fulfilment with heterotopic qualities.

In order to address the issues highlighted, the chapter is divided into three sections. The first section looks at the function of industrial space as home in Krauß's early texts, while the other two sections examine the re-appropriation of that space by the threatened individual.

All of Krauß's post-unification protagonists experience some form of being uprooted. This is mostly due to changes in the world of work, which in Krauß's texts before 1990 functioned as a component of life that was as absolute as a natural phenomenon. On the maps of Krauß's texts, work and more precisely industry provided an existential space that one could fall back upon. The following passage from 'Streams' ('Ströme', 1988) describes the industrial quarter of a town as the home from which the narrator sets off into the 'unknown':

> The house I had been invited to is not really on my way, I first had to check a map of the town and find it in a distant suburb. On account of the good weather I went on foot, which took over an hour, straight through the old, reddish industrial area I live in, where in some streets those narrow, hundred-year-old factories stand one beside the other, over whose courtyards women walk in flowery aprons on weekdays; looking as if they have interrupted their domestic spring cleaning to fetch raspberry soda from the

shop across the way, whilst here and there an older man is out and about in those black shoes with the acid-proof soles, carrying something away on a cart or letting it fall onto a heap. On such days, the whole area stews in the stolid, familial warmth of pre-industrial manufacturing. [...] I walked through my neighbourhood and had the impression that it was sleeping. Exhausted like an old man asleep in a railway hut next to his thermos flask, from whose long ears wiry hairs are growing that look like iron filings. And who knows nothing of himself.

Das Haus, in das ich eingeladen war, steht nicht an meinem täglichen Weg, ich habe mich erst auf dem Stadtplan vergewissern müssen und es dabei in einem entfernten Viertel gefunden. Wegen des schönen Wetters bin ich über eine Stunde zu Fuß dorthin gegangen, quer durch das alte, rötliche Industriegebiet, in dem ich wohne, wo in manchen Straßen eine dieser engen hundertjährigen Fabriken an der anderen steht, über deren Höfe werktags Frauen mit geblümten Kittelschürzen laufen, die so aussehen, als unterbrächen sie kurz ihr häusliches Großreinemachen, um im Konsum gegenüber eine Brause mit Himbeergeschmack zu holen, während hier und dort ein älterer Mann in diesen schwarzen Schuhen mit den säurefesten Sohlen unterwegs ist, etwas wegkarrt oder etwas auf einen Haufen fallen läßt. Die ganze Gegend brütet an solchen Tagen unter der dumpfen Familienwärme vorindustriellen Manufakturwesens. [...] Ich ging durch meine Gegend und hatte den Eindruck, sie schliefe. Erschöpft wie ein alter Mann im Wartehäuschen der Bahn neben seiner Thermosflasche schläft, aus dessen Ohren lange drahtige Haare wachsen, die aussehen wie Eisenspäne. Und der nichts von sich weiß.[4]

The industrial quarter is depicted as deeply familiar; like its inhabitants it seems natural, i.e. unaware of itself. As a place it emerges through a number of architectural features and social practices referred to in details such as the domestic spring cleaning, the apron, the thermos flask, the shoes or the raspberry soda. The gaze that registers these details is careful and caring, and scans the place gently as if looking at an interior. This depiction of an industrial environment must not be misunderstood as reverence for the GDR, the self-

---

[4] Angela Krauß, 'Ströme', in *Kleine Landschaft. Erzählungen* (Frankfurt a. M.: Suhrkamp, 1989), 7-31 (here 9-10).

proclaimed state of workers and peasants. Krauß depicts a working class milieu originating in the nineteenth century and disappearing for good with German unification and globalization.[5] The identity that such places supposedly gave the individual dissolved when East Germany was being restructured after 1990. With the fundamental change undergone by work and life, the old places vanish and the individuals that were rooted there appear threatened with dissolution. One of the most striking examples of change in this respect is unemployment, a fate that Krauß's first-person narrator in *Summer on the Ice* shares with many East Germans. Unemployment here means not only the end of earning money but the end of a routine, of a set of social practices, which established relationships to other people, institutions and places, and thus created the place where the narrator was at home. Consequently, unemployment results in the dissolution of place and identity:

> Last Monday I had decided again to change my life, I walked around and looked at the same things again and again: the houses, the walls, the off-licence. For some time I had already been catching myself always looking at the same things. [...] I forget myself contemplating a kerb [...] I was even still staring at it with an absent expression at night, until the contours began to move and became larger or smaller of their own accord, constantly back and forth, larger or smaller, narrower and wider. It is, for example, a difficult exercise not to make any judgement. [...] Last Monday I had decided to learn how to do that again. That is how it happened that everything began to become so large and to change its shape, because it could not be stopped by means of an instant judgement. You lose power over your impressions of the things around you.

> Letzten Montag hatte ich wieder beschlossen, mein Leben zu ändern, ich ging herum und sah mir immer dasselbe an: die Häuser, die Mauern, den Getränkeshop. Ich ertappte mich schon seit einer Weile dabei, wie ich immer wieder auf dasselbe schaute. [...] [I]ch vergesse mich selbst in Betrachtung einer Rinnsteinkante [...]. Ich starrte es mit einem abwesenden Gesicht sogar noch nachts an, bis die Umrisse anfingen sich zu bewegen und von selbst größer und kleiner wurden, immer hin und her, größer und kleiner, enger und

---

[5] In an interview with Ingrid Jarmatz, Krauß herself stressed that what she depicted was a milieu. See 'Biste für immer hier? Auskünfte von Angela Krauß', *Sonntag*, 15 July 1984, 4.

weiter. Es ist zum Beispiel eine sehr schwierige Übung, kein Urteil zu fällen. [...] Letzten Montag hatte ich beschlossen, das wieder zu erlernen. So kam es, dass alles anfing, so groß zu werden und in den Formen zu schwanken, weil nicht durch sofortige Beurteilung Einhalt geboten wurde. Man verliert die Gewalt über das, was außer einem selbst noch vorkommt ringsum.[6]

The narrator, who finds herself without purpose and aim, tries to restore identity by 'reading' the environment of her old life. This attempt fails as the place itself loses its coherence and meaning. Despite the narrator's efforts to understand the disintegration as liberation from limiting routine, the threat of that disintegration to her self is palpable. In contrast to the collapse of (situated) identity, the narrator remembers her past working life as a place, in which all parts were clearly defined and related to each other and herself:

> I began to think of my earlier life as something wonderfully clear, I was visited by images of wide fields, over which a quiet and at the same time lively peacefulness lay: my life as a worker. [...] The past formed itself into a great overpowering landscape, in which nothing seemed left to chance, and everything seemed large, simple and meaningful.

> Ich begann, an mein früheres Leben als etwas wunderbar Klares zu denken, Bilder mit weiten Feldern, über denen eine friedliche und zugleich lebendige Ruhe lag, suchten mich heim: mein Leben als Arbeitskraft. [...] Die Vergangenheit formierte sich zu einer überwältigenden Landschaft, in der nichts zufällig, alles groß, schlicht und sinnvoll gewesen zu sein schien. (SE 56)

The impact that the loss of the familiar place has is also stressed by the story of the boiler-attendant, which frames the narrator's story. Unlike the narrator, the boiler attendant is still employed and has thus not yet lost her roots and identity. Again, her rootedness shows in her relationship to her surroundings:

> The place is dream-like to her, she does not have to see the landscape in order to know it as an extension of her body. The landscape is the extension of her physical form. As is the factory. She reaches out with the factory and the landscape into the

---

[6] Angela Krauß, *Sommer auf dem Eis* (Frankfurt a.M.: Suhrkamp, 1998), 38. Referred to in the following as SE.

surrounding world. There is absolutely nothing mysterious about it, it is a completely concrete self-perception, like when you pull on very large wellingtons.

Die Gegend ist ihr vertraut, sie muss die Landschaft nicht sehen, um sie um sich zu wissen als Fortsetzung ihres Körpers. Die Landschaft ist ihre erweiterte Körperform. Ebenso die Fabrik. Sie reicht mit der Fabrik und der Landschaft in die sich anschließende Welt hinaus. Daran ist überhaupt nichts Geheimnisvolles, es handelt sich um eine ganz konkrete Selbstwahrnehmung, wie wenn man sehr große Gummistiefel anzieht. (SE 13)

Continuation and stability experienced as a deep sense of belonging are depicted against the background of the anticipated explosion of one of the boilers. The detonation is going to destroy not only the factory but also the attendant. The violence and finality of the explosion reflect the end of the old way of living. Though the end is anticipated, the narrative stops 'three seconds' before the catastrophe actually happens, which freezes the ultimate destruction in mid air, always pending but never taking place; the old way of living is given a memorial in the shadow of termination.

The end of the industrial milieu forces the narrator in *Summer on the Ice* to re-locate herself. This is done by remembering her childhood and testing her individual biography as endowing meaning and coherence. The reason for engaging with the past is not any supposedly undisturbed happiness of the early years, but the experience of existential crisis, which the child was able to resolve; this ability is to be remembered.

Krauß describes growing up in terms of a loss of unity and harmony and at the same time in terms of finding or founding an ideal, which the narrator still pursues for her identity. The re-enforcement of that identity is bound to sceneries of fulfilment. Both the remembered childhood and the process of remembering result in a subjective remapping of the industrial landscape along these sceneries producing a 'bio-map' of heterotopias.

In the beginning there was paradise, namely the unity of child, mother and world:

work is an enthusiastic exertion, nothing but wonderful being, in
which you construct the world, and enjoyment and effort are the
same, and horror and delight are hardly distinguishable. The scent
of my mother's skirt that I buried myself in, roses as big as
washing-up bowls on the black background, while she read a
telegram. I could wrap my head in a rose and sniff at the base of it.
And turn the base upwards, diagonally between my mother's
exposed legs, so that the light from the rose petals showered my
head, while she read the telegram about the death of her mother
and the messenger flew off like a bee on his yellow motorbike
outside.

die Arbeit ist eine begeisterte Anstrengung, nichts anderes als das
herrliche Dasein, in dem man sich die Welt zusammensetzt und
Lust und Mühe dasselbe sind und Schrecken und Entzücken noch
kaum unterscheidbar. Der Duft des Rockes meiner Mutter, in den
ich mich grub, Rosen groß wie Waschschüsseln auf schwarzem
Grund, während sie ein Telegramm las. Ich konnte meinen Kopf in
eine Rose wickeln und auf dem Grund der Rose schnüffeln. Und
den Rosengrund aufwärts wenden, schräg zwischen die entblößten
Beine meiner Mutter gelehnt, so dass das Licht von Rosenblättern
auf meinen Kopf sickerte, während sie das Telegramm vom Tod
ihrer Mutter las und draußen der Telegrammbote auf dem gelben
Motorrad wie eine Biene wegflog. (SE 49)

This is an image of beginning. First and last things are still mingled: life is not yet
differentiated and all essential elements form a unity. In the succession of mothers
and daughters, life and death are fused: the mother-daughter group with the
daughter standing between her mother's legs and 'digging' herself into her
mother's black skirt is an image both of birth and of the grave. The girl's
exploration of the rose pattern and the bee simile link the gravity of death to joy
and playfulness. Both bee and rose image are objects of the child's innocent
pleasure as well as complex symbols: the bee represents abundance but also the
message of death while the rose, the symbol of transience and eternity, life and
death, fertility and virginity, passion and purity, anticipates mystery and paradox
as the condition of the individual. The girl still lives in a blissful, ignorant
familiarity with phenomena. It is important to note that this paradise-like state is
essentially 'placeless'; except for the space between her mother's legs the girl

does not occupy any place in the world and has no notion of it. This changes when the child grows older:

> Earlier there had still been days with back lighting. For some reason I have not known any for a long while now. The first had a vaulted horizon, quite deep, almost at the uppermost point of the path I stood on. The horizon was the colour of clay and as gently vaulted as the globe that at that time I would often contemplate in the atlas, which, when opened up, would cover my outstretched legs, and on the northernmost end of which my shoes would poke up, turned slightly inward. Over the clay-coloured arc of the earth stood the sun, only a metre above. We had lost my mother in the wood. The sun was dark red like the heart of a fire. Next to me was my little companion, who had circular nostrils and an irascible way of riding his scooter, as if he were trying to leave petrifying impressions in the soft tar of our street. He recognized the human form in the solar disk better than I, which extended like a tiny figure in the distance on a plateau over sea. For him there were not yet any distances. He plunged towards it, throwing the scooter against me, and in fact the figure was standing only thirty metres away from us, and it also really was our mother, as I could see from his small, desperate, hard neck, as he threw himself against her.

> Früher gab es noch Tage mit Gegenlicht. Aus irgendeinem Grund sind mir seit langem keine mehr bekannt. Der erste hatte einen gewölbten Horizont, ziemlich tief, fast auf der Höhe des Weges, auf dem ich stand. Der Horizont war tonfarben und so zart gewölbt wie die Erdkugel, die ich damals oft lange im Atlas betrachtete, der aufgeklappt meine ausgestreckten Beine bedeckte und an dessen nördlichem Ende meine Schuhe hervorsahen, ein wenig einwärtsgekehrt. Über der tonfarbenen Wölbung der Erde stand die Sonne, nur einen Meter darüber. Meine Mutter hatten wir im Wald verloren. Die Sonne war ein dunkelroter Brandherd. Neben mir mein kleinerer Gefährte hatte kreisrunde Nasenlöcher und eine jähzornige Art, Trittbrettroller zu fahren, so als wollte er versteinernde Abdrücke im weichen Teer der Straße hinterlassen. Er erkannte die Gestalt in der Sonnenscheibe, die sich wie eine kilometerweit entfernte winzige Figur auf einem Plateau über dem Meer ausnahm, eher als ich. Für ihn gab es noch keinerlei Entfernung. Er stürzte, den Roller gegen mich schleudernd, auf sie zu, und tatsächlich stand sie nur dreißig Meter von uns weg, und sie war auch wirklich unsere Mutter, was ich an seinem kleinen,

verzweifelten harten Nacken sah, als er sich ihr entgegenwarf. (SE
44)

The vignette depicts a still early state of life, albeit in the story of first separation.
Though the separation ends in reunion and the terror in bliss, the episode denotes
the beginning of differentiation and self-awareness. Most importantly, this stage is
linked to the mapping of the world, the emergence of space and topography.
Though the perceived landscape is still primary, the girl compares the sight of the
earth with the globe she used to look at in the atlas. The girl knows and operates
with images and develops a notion of her own scale, the space she occupies
physically and mentally. This is accompanied by the loss of immediacy, a fact the
narrator underlines when comparing her former self with her brother, who unlike
her had not yet developed a sense of distance. Growing up is thus defined by the
acquisition of skills and self-awareness, and the detachment or alienation this
generates.

　　One of the central childhood memories is the first time the girl is in love.
The boy she is attracted to is a visiting pioneer of the Communist Party of Italy;
she takes him to the cemetery for a first 'taste' of love:

> It was high summer, I knew every corner of the cemetery and the
> marble faces that peeped through the juniper bushes. I knew the
> turns where you could suddenly be confronted with a group of
> mourners when you wanted to shoot around the corner with the
> handcart, over the edges of which stuck out the slimy stalks of the
> wilted wreaths. I spent some days with the women gardeners. [...]
> I [...] loved [...] the cemetery with the dead and their barely
> clothed guardian angels, and with the women who kneeled in the
> rose beds in their aprons with flower patterns: the little boys went
> and stood in front of them when they were weeding and let them
> look at the ladybirds they had caught in matchboxes.

> Es war Hochsommer; ich kannte jeden Winkel auf dem Friedhof
> und die marmornen Gesichter, die durch die Wacholderbüsche
> guckten. Ich wusste die Biegungen, wo einem plötzlich ein Zug
> Trauernder gegenüberstehen konnte, wenn man mit der
> Schubkarre, über deren Rand die glitschigen Stengel der
> verwelkten Gebinde stießen, in die Kurve schießen wollte, ich
> verbrachte manche Tage bei den Gärtnerinnen. [...] Ich [...] liebte

> [...] den Friedhof mit den Toten und ihren kaum bekleideten
> Schutzengeln und den Frauen, die in den Rosenbeeten knieten in
> ihren Kleiderschürzen mit Blumenmustern: die kleinen Jungen
> stellten sich vor sie hin, wenn sie beim Jäten waren und ließen sie
> in ihre Zündholzschachteln mit den gefangenen Marienkäfern
> sehen. (SE 28-9)

Unlike the early childhood vignette, which depicted the unity of the elements of life, the cemetery scene enfolds their fundamental cultural concepts. This indicates the girl's socialization; transience and eternity, fleetingness and permanency, love and death, spirit and matter are now differentiated into small details, singular scenes and gestures, such as the roses, the wheelbarrow with dead flowers, the marble sculptures, the little boys with ladybirds in matchboxes, the housewives with aprons tending graves etc. The depiction of the cemetery scene denotes complex cultural relations between the girl and her surroundings laid out on an ever more concrete map with specific places. The detailed description of the cemetery underlines a heightened sense both of reality and symbolic meaning.

Love becomes the girl's ideal. It is first performed in the cemetery. It promises a paradise-like (re)union and wholeness, albeit taking the form of a mystery, as from the beginning it is present only as an illusion, something virtual. Love can be staged, yet does not solidify and cannot be located. In that sense it does not seem accomplishable. Love remains the kind of fantasy art produces and which contests the material world and its utilisation. According to Foucault the cemetery is a heterotopia, 'a space of illusion that exposes every real space, all the sites inside of which human life is partitioned, as still more illusory'.[7] The cemetery as a stage for the love ideal in Krauß's text calls into question the structure of everyday, i.e. its organisation along the lines of production and consumption and the exploitation of the material world as depicted in the industrial plant.

This stage in the girl's development is characterized by skills. The letters and the diary entry she writes *in her best handwriting* about the cemetery episode

---

[7] Foucault, 'Of Other Spaces', 27.

underline her skilfulness. Her best handwriting (*Schönschrift*) signifies effort and years of learning and practice; it stresses the link between identity and toil. The letters and diary entry can be seen as an attempt to materialize and locate love in *Schönschrift*. However, this only results in the (re)production of its illusive presence:

> Towards the end, I could not fail to notice how something developed within me from all the letter-writing, which, the more passionately I wrote, became ever more buzzing, airy, transparent, until it was finally truly ungraspable, an enchanted spirit, as transient as a figure described in the air by the centre of gravity of a dancing body.
>
> Gegen Ende entging mir nicht, wie vom vielen Briefeschreiben in mir etwas entstand, das, je inbrünstiger ich schrieb, immer schwirrender, luftiger, durchsichtiger wurde, schließlich wirklich ungreifbar, ein bezauberter Geist, flüchtig wie die Figur, die der Schwerpunkt des tanzenden Körpers in der Luft beschreibt. (SE 27-8)

The passage compares love to an enchanted spirit and to the figure described by the body when dancing. Here the central metaphor of the text for the narrator's re-founded identity is introduced: the girl's obsession with figure skating. Figure skating provides a model of the performance of the love ideal; it is at the core of the individual's development and life-map:

> I never believed that matter was the most important thing in the world. I believed in the art of the great Oleg and his figure-skating partner, who could stretch up her leg as perpendicular as a candle, so that it touched the bun in her hair whilst Oleg let his knee drag across the ice in a pose of adoration. I believed in her devotion as she stretched on her back across his thigh, when he laid his arms like eagle's wings over her body and his small head, that always seemed slightly bald, sank between his shoulders. With my own eyes, I saw that love creates the figure. I believed in life as an ideal, in life as longing, as desiring, and that everyone is born in order to work on this art.
>
> Ich glaubte nie an die Materie als Schwerpunkt der Welt. Ich glaubte an die Kunst des großen Oleg und seiner Kunstläuferin, die das Bein steil wie eine Kerze nach hinten heraufstrecken konnte,

> bis es ihren Dutt berührte und Oleg sein in Anbetungspose
> gebeugtes Knie vor ihr auf dem Eis schleifen ließ. Ich glaubte ihrer
> Hingabe rücklings auf seinem Schenkel, wenn er die Arme
> adlerschwingengleich über ihren Leib breitete und sein kleiner,
> immer etwas kahl wirkender Kopf tief zwischen die Schultern
> rutschte. Mit eigenen Augen sah ich, dass die Liebe die Figur
> schafft. Ich glaubte an das Leben als Ideal, an das Leben als
> Sehnsucht, als Begehren, und dass jeder dazu geboren ist, an
> diesem Kunststück zu arbeiten. (SE 47-8)

Figure skating, more precisely the figure skating of Oleg Protopopov and Ludmila Belousova, is here described as a staging of love, that is: the staging of an ideal of beauty, desire and devotion. The staging of this illusive ideal appears as the objective of life contesting all other claims of use, usefulness and profit. This is stressed by the skill needed for figure skating which itself contests the weight, gravity and limits of the material world.

For the narrator in *Summer on the Ice*, remembering her childhood and its ideal first of all means remembering how in winter she practiced figure skating on Slurry Pond 4. The pond is a place of the everyday. With its highly polluted water, and as outlet of the waste water system of a cooling tower, it belongs to the industrial topography. In winter the children play ice hockey or do figure skating there after school. Despite the commonness and bleakness of the place, for the narrator it was and is the site where existential crisis and alienation are resolved and the self is (re)affirmed. This makes Slurry Pond 4 another scenery of fulfilment.

The existential crisis of the child is not only a result of separation and differentiation, but also of the girl's physical development. Becoming aware of herself as a sexual being, she experiences her own body as well as others' bodies as alienated. Physical estrangement is caused by the sight of a school friend's mature breasts, which to the girl seem uncontrollable and cause confusion and fear:

> The breasts were long and pale like Annelore's face, with the same
> tendency to greyish brown freckles, they had something evasive
> about them, something that was in flight from the rest of the body.

My school friend had no power over these breasts that she had grown over night. From then on there was clearly something about her body that she was no longer in charge of.

Die Brust war lang und blaß wie Annelores Gesicht, auch mit dieser Neigung zu graubraunen Sommersprossen, sie hatte etwas Entweichendes, dem übrigen Körper Entfliehendes, meine Schulkameradin hatte nicht Gewalt über diese Brust, die ihr über Nacht gewachsen war. Seitdem gab es offensichtlich etwas an ihrem Körper, über das sie nicht gebieten konnte. (SE 22)

The incident illustrates adolescence as the loss of physical harmony. This is reminiscent of Kleist's *On the Puppet Theatre* (1810), which in its famous Spinario episode also links the loss of grace to self-consciousness caused by sexuality. The comparison with Kleist's conversation between a first-person narrator and a dancer highlights key aspects in Krauß's text. In both Kleist and Krauß the loss and retrieval of human harmony are at stake. The dancer in Kleist's essay focuses on the human loss (fall) through self-consciousness. He supports his case by showing how the unconscious marionette and beast on the one hand and the infinitely conscious god on the other hand are exempt from the fall. For self-conscious man, he speculates, a back door to paradise might be open once man has completed his ungraceful journey 'around the world'[8] and eaten 'of the tree of knowledge a second time'.[9] Krauß's narrator faces the same problem as Kleist's protagonists but instead of focusing on the loss, she looks for the back door. This necessarily releases the potential of paradox inherent in Kleist's text and has Krauß's novel participate in the concept of romantic irony.[10]

In an attempt to solve her crisis, the girl begins to practice figure skating on Slurry Pond 4, trying to regain the body's centre of gravity; this reads like a further elaboration of the dancer's statement in Kleist's text. Krauß's narrator

---

[8] Heinrich von Kleist, 'On the Puppet Theatre', in Kleist, *An Abyss Deep Enough: Letters of Heinrich von Kleist with a Selection of Essays and Anecdotes*, ed. by Philip B. Miller (New York: Dutton, 1982), 211-16 (here 214).

[9] Kleist, 'On the Puppet Theatre', 216.

[10] Paul de Man, 'Allegory and Irony in Baudelaire', in *Romanticism and Contemporary Criticism*, ed. by E.S. Burt, Kevin Newmark, Andzej Warminski (Baltimore and London: John Hopkins 1993), 101-19.

avoids the negative statement and instead explains the complexity of the body's centre of gravity:

> In movement, the centre of gravity has a certain correct position: it should not be regarded as a simple point, but rather as the result of all the centres of gravity of the individual limbs and extremities of the body. [...]
>
> At first sight, one assumes that it is not difficult to calculate the resultant of the centres of gravity of the head, the shoulders, the arms, the hips, the legs in any given position. These partial centres of gravity are not, however, constant, for if they were, ice skating would lose one of its greatest attractions.

> In der Bewegung hat der Schwerpunkt seine bestimmte korrekte Lage: er ist nicht als einfacher Punkt, sondern vielmehr als die Resultierende aller Schwerpunkte der einzelnen Gliederteile und Extremitäten des Körpers anzusehen. [...]
>
> Auf den ersten Blick sollte man glauben, dass es nicht schwer ist, die Resultierende der Schwerpunkte des Kopfes, der Schultern, der Arme, der Hüfte, der Beine in jeder beliebigen Lage zu berechnen. Diese Teilschwerpunkte sind jedoch wieder keine konstanten Größen, sonst würde der Eislauf seinen größten Reiz einbüßen. (SE 26)

The complexity is 'mastered' by a simple but effective insight, which essentially reverses the problem:

> The centre of gravity of the body is not a constant point, that is to say that it is not always a constant point. Because we possess bodies equipped with self-determining movement, the centre of gravity is only constant in one particular case, namely in a state of absolute rest.

> Der Schwerpunkt des Körpers ist aber kein konstanter Punkt, das heißt, er ist nicht immer ein konstanter Punkt. Da wir über einen mit freier selbsttätiger Bewegung ausgestatteten Körper verfügen, ist der Schwerpunkt dieses Körpers nur in einem einzigen Fall ein konstanter Punkt. Nämlich im Zustand der absoluten Ruhe. (SE 23-4)

Clearly, this solution is ironic in its antipodal logic; it outlines the narrator's route to identity taking paradox as a modus operandi. It could be claimed that the inversion of the problem is an attempt to find the 'other end of the world'. This is best illustrated by the pond as scenery of fulfilment. Figure skating does not serve any outside objective. It could be called *l'art pour l'ideal*. That the girl/ narrator chooses a place like the pond is consistent, as it too serves no outside purpose and cannot be utilized or exploited. Indeed, the freedom from utility forms an essential part of the pond's stage features. Again, this follows the inverted logic of heterotopia, as the pond's suitability for use is ironically due to its status as a waste product.

The central skating figure that the girl invents is a 'ship', a symbol of the vast dimension of her longing and expectations. She creates it in a reaction to the discovery of her friend's mature breasts during an x-ray check-up at school:

> I remained there for a while in love and cowardice, then jumped into the air and invented a figure in which my leg appeared backwards above my forehead like a ship's mast on the horizon. In this way it slowly pushed upwards. It was connected with sudden, throbbing pain, then I threw my head back in such a way that my mouth brushed down along my leg, which seemed as foreign to me as if it were inorganic, or rather: my mouth brushed up along my leg from the steel blade of the skate, and over the heel along the Achilles tendon with little pinching kisses.

> Ich verharrte noch eine Weile in Liebe und Feigheit, dann sprang ich in die Höhe und erfand eine Figur, bei der mein Bein rückwärtig über meiner Stirn auftauchte wie ein Segelmast am Horizont. So schob es sich langsam herauf. Es war mit einem jähen ziehenden Schmerz verbunden, dann bog ich meinen Kopf so zurück, dass mein Mund an dem Bein, das mir bis zum Anorganischen fremd erschien, hinabglitt, was eigentlich hieß: hinauf, von der Stahlkufe über die Ferse die Achillessehne hinauf mit kleinen zwickenden Küssen. (SE 24)

The girl reacts in an emotional and direct, very skilful but naive way. Self-consciousness is still limited to skill and not yet to knowledge. This next stage is only achieved by the grown-up narrator when she chooses a highly reflexive approach to overcome her crisis thus marking the transformation from skill to knowledge. Unlike her former childhood self, the narrator does not actually skate on the frozen pond but lies on a blanket during a hot summer and practices figure skating in thought. The physical movement has thus translated into the movement of the soul as the real centre of the individual's gravity. This transformation is linked to knowledge which here is self-knowledge. Full knowledge is gained when the narrator suddenly realises that she is free and dispensable, herself effectively a waste product:

> So I was free. Nothing and nobody held me back. I was relieved of all obligations, nobody expected anything from me. Basically, it was not necessary for me to exist.

> Ich war also frei. Nichts und niemand hielt mich. Ich war aller Verpflichtungen ledig, niemand erwartete etwas von mir. Es war im Grunde nicht notwendig, dass es mich gab. (SE 59)

That self-knowledge is the realisation of one's dispensability or uselessness is ironic again. Self-knowledge causes despair and drives the woman to attempt suicide by drowning herself in the old Slurry Pond 4. However, when at the edge of the pond the narrator, caught in the antipodal logic, does not drown, but enters her own vision of paradise, the absolute scene of fulfilment, a big white ship slowly appears behind the brushwood there:

> The highest branches dragged against its rump, the motors ran almost noiselessly, only a rectangular shadow fell across the woman on the bank, who could once have become a great ice skater. [...] The ship appeared like the low sun when it sometimes emerges unnaturally large from behind a wood: with that expression of complete independence with which it governs our lives.

> Die höchsten Äste schrammten am Rumpf entlang, die Motoren liefen nahezu lautlos, nur ein kastenförmiger Schatten fiel über die Frau am Ufer, die einst eine große Eisläuferin hätte werden können. [...] Das Schiff erschien, wie die tiefstehende Sonne manchmal übergroß hinter einem Waldstück hervortritt: mit dem Ausdruck jener vollkommenen Unabhängigkeit, mit der sie über unser Leben entscheidet. (SE 60)

The ship that the woman sees is the overwhelming appearance of her own ice skating figure, which she seems to have conjured up. Ironically, self-knowledge generates the wish to die and only the wish to die re-enforces the identity longed for. The ship is the ideal-come-true and as such has on board the new lover of the narrator/woman;[11] thus only in its most illusive form as dream or vision does love actually materialize.

The 'ship' belongs to the virtual space of dreams and visions. Art has a constitutive part in that space, not only because of its origin in figure skating but also because of the 'envisioning' of the pond by the beholder. The woman's gaze transforms the scene of fulfilment into an old painting:

> At the same time her gaze lay on the ship as if she were looking at an old panel in a museum that had previously hung for four hundred years in the Santo Spirito Church, from where it had disappeared in the confusion of wartime, been taken to heart by an illegitimate owner and then ended up in a museum [...].
> The picture showed a great white ship in a landscape, which stretched over hills and snow-covered peaks all the way to the cypresses of Lebanon, without the details losing their sharpness as they got smaller.

> Dabei ruhte ihr Blick auf dem Schiff, als würde sie im Museum lange ein altes Tafelbild betrachten, das vorher vierhundert Jahre lang in der Kirche Santo Spirito gehangen hatte, von wo es durch Kriegswirren verschwunden, einem unrechtmäßigen Besitzer ans Herz gegangen und daraufhin in dieses Museum gelangt war [...].
> Das Bild zeigte ein großes weißes Schiff in einer Landschaft, die über Hügel und Schneegipfel bis zu den Zedern des Libanon sich hinzog, ohne dass die Einzelheiten im Kleinerwerden an Schärfe verloren. (SE 65)

The reference to art has a twofold function. Firstly, it underlines the reflective nature of the process of remembering (and indeed writing). Secondly, the topoi such as the biblical cedars of Lebanon and the historical context are significant in that the (virtual) pond with the ship is not a simulation of Nature, but a cultural construct fully displaying its elements of construction. This de-naturalization applies to the narrator herself. In the moment of fulfilment she splits in two when looking at the ship in the picture, where she sees a woman looking at a ship. The

---

[11] As this last episode of the text is told by a third-person narrator, the double denotation is necessary.

narrator's splitting seems a sign of complete detachment, which becomes palpable also in the shifting of the narrative voice from a first-person to a third-person narrative:

> The woman on land looked at the picture with the great white ship. It seemed to her now as if there was a woman standing there looking at a ship, which gave the whole even greater depth. Suddenly she was herself part of the picture. It was as if the picture was flowing around her on either side and closing behind her. And now she saw her own figure from behind standing in front of the ship and the landscape stretching out into the distance. Suddenly she was more sure than she had ever been before in her life that she physically existed. The picture was the proof.

> Die Frau an Land betrachtete das Bild mit dem großen weißen Schiff. Es schien ihr jetzt, als stünde da eine Frau in Betrachtung eines Schiffes, was dem Ganzen noch größere Tiefe verlieh. Sie war auf einmal selbst Teil des Bildes. Es war, als flösse das Bild beiderseits um sie herum und schloß sich hinter ihr. Und sie sah nun ihre Gestalt in Rückenansicht vor dem Schiff und der in die Tiefe führenden Landschaft. Auf einmal war sie sich so sicher wie niemals vorher in ihrem Leben, dass sie leibhaftig existierte. Das Bild war der Beweis.' (SE 68-9)

Yet in the logic of paradox, complete detachment and fulfilment, paradise lost and paradise regained, dream and reality coincide and 'both ends of the ring-shaped world interlock'.[12] Here, Kleist's text offers further explanation. Kleist's dancer ends the conversation about the loss and retrieval of grace with a mirror simile, stating that

> just as our image, as we approach a concave mirror, vanishes to infinity only to reappear before our eyes, so will grace, having likewise traversed the infinite, return to us once more [...].[13]

This is a philosophical as well as a spatial metaphor describing scenery of fulfilment. When the narrator/woman looks at the painting of a ship in which she sees a woman looking at a ship, she gains not only the greatest distance from herself in order to come closest to her self, but her self returns as an image. This

---

[12] Kleist, 'On the Puppet Theatre', 214.
[13] Kleist, 'On the Puppet Theatre', 216.

reflection makes her 'more sure than she had ever been before in her life that she physically existed'.

The spatial explanation for the travel through infinity and back can be found in Foucault:

> I believe that between utopias and these quite other sites, these heterotopias, there might be a sort of mixed, joint experience, which would be the mirror. The mirror is, after all, a utopia, since it is a placeless place. In the mirror, I see myself there where I am not, in the unreal, virtual space that opens up behind the surface; I am over there, there where I am not, a sort of shadow that gives my own visibility to myself, that enables me to see myself there where I am absent: such is the utopia of the mirror. But it is also a heterotopia in so far as the mirror does exist in reality, where it exerts a sort of counteraction on the position that I occupy. From the standpoint of the mirror, I discover my absence from the place where I am since I see myself over there. Starting from this gaze that is, as it were, directed toward me, from the ground of this virtual space that is on the other side of the glass, I come back towards myself; I begin again to direct my eyes toward myself and to reconstitute myself there where I am.[14]

The ship acts as a (concave) mirror; it reflects the woman's wishes and longing and enforces her identity. Like a mirror, it is at the same time a heterotopia and a utopia. It is a utopia in that it is just a dream or vision of the woman's ideal; yet it is also a heterotopia, a real 'other place' that counters the disintegrating industrial space. Dissolution is countered not only by the appearance of the ship and the man onboard with whom the woman/narrator falls in love and who seems the materialization of the ideal; more generally the ship brings passengers with whom the narrator/woman begins an exchange again which indicates the possibility of a new community.

The passengers have come to the Bitterfeld region, one of the most desolate, polluted and ruined landscapes of eastern Germany, in order to find paradise there, an Eden, pure and untouched, which is said to have emerged precisely because of the desolation and neglect of the industrial wasteland:

---

[14] Foucault, 'Of Other Spaces', 24.

The passengers had booked a trip after they had heard and read ever more frequently of a miracle, which had, however, never been shown on television. This region was named repeatedly in terms of a miracle: the miracle of the chemical triangle. The natural miracle of central Germany. And even: The wonder of the world of the third millennium after Christ.

Die Passagiere hatten die Fahrt gebucht, nachdem sie immer häufiger von einem Wunder gehört und gelesen, niemals aber Bilder davon im Fernsehen gesehen hatten. Diese Region wurde immer wieder im Zusammenhang mit dem Begriff des Wunders genannt: das Wunder im Chemiedreieck. Das mitteldeutsche Naturwunder. Sogar: das Weltwunder im 3. Jahrtausend nach Christus. (SE 70)

For the passengers the industrial space which the narrator/woman tries to escape from figures as utopia. This inversion indicates an asynchronism between individuals that stresses the loss of the collectivity of the old milieu. At the same time the inversion restores a positive potential to the ruined place rooted in the passengers' wishes and longings which repeats the subjectivity of space and place. Most importantly, the passengers look also into a 'mirror' when they enter into an exchange with the narrator/woman from the 'u-topos' on board of the 'hetero-topos', in order to reconstitute their identities by telling the narrator/woman the 'stories of their lives'.

The lonely and subjective journey through her past in order to re-locate and enforce uprooted and threatened identity thus ends with fulfilment in a new community. Unlike the old milieu this community seems temporary, instable but also based on active communication and mutual recognition. It seems to rely on openness and transformation. This community depends on heterotopias, the 'other places' and their potential for inversion and paradox. However, the irony inherent to the constitution of this communal fulfilment indicates its fragility if not illusiveness.

CHAPTER 8

Steam Bath and Eloquent Library:
Budapest as a Topography of Modernism in Franz Fühmann's
Twenty-two Days or Half a Life

Stephan Krause

In 1973 the GDR author Franz Fühmann published *Twenty-two Days or Half a Life* (*Zweiundzwanzig Tage oder Die Hälfte des Lebens*), which was originally planned as a simple travel book based on a three-week visit to Budapest between 14 October and 4 November 1971, just before his fiftieth birthday. The aphoristic and, in places, lyrical heterogeneity of the text is nevertheless evidence that it represents a distinctive change of style for an author whose early work had been politically and structurally conformist. Given this central importance for his career development, it has often been read as a public confession. Such mainly biographical readings concentrate, for example, on the social differences between the reality of the German Democratic Republic, as the literary-historical context of the book's reception, and the People's Republic of Hungary, which forms the background to the text.

Taking into account the fact that this text also marks a poetic and poetological turning-point in Fühmann's career, however, it is more important to privilege the aesthetic originality of the text. This can be achieved, for example, by means of an analysis of a number of its intertextual and linguistic practices, which ultimately demonstrate its high *literary* quality. *Twenty-two Days* is analysed here as a strongly fictional text and not as a travel journal with a (partially) documentary intent. In *Twenty-two Days*, Fühmann creates an almost unprecedentedly rich and varied topography of modernism in Budapest. In this process, the urban landscape becomes simultaneously a modernist interior and an exotic, yet familiar space full of colourful impressions, including those from Fühmann's own journeys to Budapest; a place extensively inscribed and described by others, a place in which to read, translate and create poetry.

The journey through the changing topographies of Fühmann's work after these inauspicious beginnings takes us by way of his involvement in the collaborative process of *Nachdichtung* – helping to translate the poetry of major Hungarian authors such as Attila József – to this independent writing of what lies within the significant exterior of Budapest.[1] This diary-like text performs a search for points of reference where biographically none are to be found, and imagines an urban literary space whose deictic marking identifies it as a τόπος τρίτον (third place), which is signalled in the title of the text as a temporal one. The explicitly open-ended text defines its focus in relation to Hölderlin's question in his poem 'The Middle of Life' ('Hälfte des Lebens'): 'Alas, where shall I find, when winter comes, the flowers, and where the sunshine and shadows of the earth?' ('Weh mir, wo nehm' ich, wenn / Es Winter ist, die Blumen, und / Den Sonnenschein, / Und Schatten der Erde?').[2] In doing so it thematizes the heterochronic and announces a quest through the internal spaces of Budapest, a heterotopia presented as a place in which time 'never stops building up'.[3] Fühmann's journey to Hungary, and the change of location it indicates , sets in motion a movement into the Other. As a text, *Twenty-two Days* represents Fühmann's 'real entry into literature' ('eigentlichen Eintritt in die Literatur'), as he described the book in an interview ten years later.[4]

To walk a path and to open up that path as one walks it means, after Dante, to accept that it will be impossible to walk in a straight line and to accept the

---

[1] The term *Nachdichtung* refers to a form of translation widely practice in the GDR, which was characterized by a division of labour between the translator and a poet. The translator did not produce poetry, but simply the raw material that the poet transformed into a version in the target language, which, given its quality, could easily have been published as a poem in its own right. See 'Über die Kunst des Nachdichtens' [Protokoll der Sitzung des Übersetzeraktivs des Schriftstellerverbands], *Weimarer Beiträge*, 19.8 (1973), 34-74, and my 'Der aufgespannte Widerspruch: Franz Fühmanns nachdichterische Spurensuche bei Attila József', *Jahrbuch der ungarischen Germanistik* (2004), 133-49.

[2] Friedrich Hölderlin, 'The Middle of Life' ('Hälfte des Lebens'), in Hölderlin, *Selected Verse*, ed. by Michael Hamburger (Harmondsworth: Penguin, 1961), 242. [The English prose translation cited here is Hamburger's. Tr.]

[3] Michel Foucault, 'Of Other Spaces', *Diacritics* 16.1 (1986), 22-7 (here 26).

[4] Franz Fühmann, 'Im Gespräch mit Wilfried F. Schoeller', in Fühmann, *Den Katzenartigen wollten wir verbrennen. Ein Lesebuch*, ed. by Hans-Jürgen Schmitt (Hamburg: Hoffmann und Campe, 1983), 363.

consequent twists and turns of the way: in this sense Fühmann's text is both open-ended and incapable of being completed. By emphasizing both thematically and formally the presence in the city of the 'prose of the world' ('Prosa der Welt'),[5] Fühmann is able to capture the contemporary distinctiveness of Budapest. The entrance into the 'acoustic cave'[6] of this city-text anticipates the subterranean descent into the mine in Fühmann's unfinished novel *Inside the Mountain* (*Im Berg*).[7] The entrance into the artificial world of the text simultaneously marks the point of exit from the easily decipherable prose of the real world.

The penetration of the city of Budapest occurs in the form of a text, yet above all metonymically *through* texts and *with* texts. One such trope is the immediate impression of the almost babylonian variety of languages present in the city, which Fühmann at one point lists.[8] The graphical juxtaposition of the enumeration of the languages at the same time expresses the almost simultaneous rushing past of their users . Each language listed stands for the fleeting moment it can be identified. This is a kind of *flaneurism* in reverse, represented as a stream of languages rushing past, which also indicates, like the 'noise of many languages', the polyglossia of the city.[9] Budapest appears as one of the modern 'polyglot cities, the cities which [...] had acquired high activity and great reputation as centres of intellectual and cultural exchange',[10] an exchange that Fühmann sees as particularly strong because it crosses linguistic boundaries and

---

[5] Georg Wilhelm Friedrich Hegel, *Vorlesungen über die Ästhetik I* (Frankfurt a.M.: Suhrkamp, 1999), 199.

[6] Hans Blumenberg, *Höhlenausgänge* (Frankfurt a.M.: Suhrkamp, 1996), 80.

[7] This unfinished mine novel appeared posthumously in 1992. Franz Fühmann, *Im Berg*, ed. by Ingrid Prignitz (Rostock: Hinstorff, 1992).

[8] Franz Fühmann, *Twenty-two Days or Half a Lifetime*, trans. Leila Vennewitz (London: Jonathan Cape, 1992), 55. Franz Fühmann, *Zweiundzwanzig Tage oder Die Hälfte des Lebens*, in Fühmann, *Werkausgabe*, 9 vols. (Rostock: Hinstorff, 1993), III, 281-506 (here 324). In the following, references to texts by Fühmann are taken where possible from the *Werkausgabe* and are indicated by the abbreviation WA followed by the relevant volume and page numbers. References to Vennewitz's translation of *Zweiundzwanzig Tage* are indicated by the abbreviation TD.

[9] Malcolm Bradbury, 'The Cities of Modernism', in Bradbury and James McFarlane (eds.), *Modernism: A Guide to European Literature 1890-1930* (London: Penguin, 1991), 96-104 (here 97).

[10] Bradbury, 'The Cities of Modernism', 96.

barriers.[11] Budapest functions multilingually as the 'intersection of every imaginable historical and spiritual line' (TD 13; 'Kreuzpunkt aller nur denkbaren historischen und geistigen Linien', WA III, 287). As a topography of such lines, *Twenty-two Days* inscribes these places within the city, and in so doing turns them into literature.

The wide-ranging reception of literary texts in *Twenty-two Days* is an integral element of an aphoristic narration of Budapest, in which the city simultaneously narrates itself and makes itself present as a city of modernism: 'What is modern, it seems, is the idea that the narration about the city is superseded by the city's narration of itself'.[12] For Fühmann, Budapest is 'inherently the most poetic of all material',[13] with a wealth of intertextual associations which can be incorporated in exemplary fashion into his own text.

On at least seven occasions the text refers to the view of a window that the narrator can see from his hotel room. Fühmann mostly incorporates these episodic details into his narration of the end of a day. The shutters on this window are 'just like last year [...] half raised and aslant' (TD 32; 'noch immer wie voriges Jahr halbaufgezogen und schräg', WA III, 304). This defect means that the narrator can see only 'human torsos in sweaters and pants [...] against subdued light' (TD 32; 'vor mattem Licht menschliche Mittelstücke in Pullover und Hose', WA III, 304). The act of looking is here not the optical penetration of an interior, but actually the realization that the interior is shielded from the outside world and the narrator's gaze. This can also be seen in the way Fühmann describes this separation and the way it changes. The shutters stand as a division between

---

[11] In an interview with Hans-Georg Soldat, Fühmann explains: 'I believe that what I am doing goes beyond this limit, goes beyond borders, is considered to be of value beyond these borders' ('Ich glaube, daß das, was ich mache, über diese Grenzen hinausgeht, als über diese Grenzen hinaus von Bedeutung empfunden wird [...].') Hans-Georg Soldat, 'Gespräch mit Franz Fühmann 1979', *Sinn und Form*, 50.6 (1998), 844-54 (here 853). Fühmann is referring here to the borders of his country, which may also be the meaning of this little scene in *Twenty-two Days*.

[12] Klaus R. Scherpe, 'Nonstop nach Nowhere City? Wandlungen der Symbolisierung, Wahrnehmung und Semiotik der Stadt in der Literatur der Moderne', in Scherpe (ed.), *Die Unwirklichkeit der Städte* (Reinbek bei Hamburg: Rowohlt, 1988), 129-52 (here 131).

[13] George M. Hyde, 'The Poetry of the City', in Bradbury and McFarlane (eds.), *Modernism*, 337-48 (here 338).

outside and inside, but the extent to which they move determines the perception of what may lie beyond them. Clearly, the theme here is the possibility of penetrating the barrier, if only optically to begin with, as the end of the entry for 21 October demonstrates: 'In the building across the lane, the shutters otherwise always half open and aslant are suddenly closed' (TD 83; 'Im Nachbarhaus sind die sonst immer halboffenen schrägen Rolläden plötzlich geschlossen', WA III, 348). The third time that the shutters are mentioned, they are hanging down across the window 'like a fan' (TD, 84; 'wie ein Fächer, WA III, 349). This fan then becomes, in the sixth such episode, 'Mallarmé's fan' (TD 227; 'Mallarmés Fächer', WA III, 479). This reference to Mallarmé's poem 'Madame Mallarmé's Fan' is an example of how Fühmann inscribes modernist poetry into the cityscape of Budapest. Like the fan of the poem, the shutters shield a 'very precious abode' from the eyes of the observer, but are also a medium that simultaneously hides and reveals something.[14] The poem is at one and the same time the fan itself and the language through which the 'verse of the future' becomes visible. The fan's movement, a 'fluttering towards the skies',[15] places its inscribed paper surfaces between the face of the woman spoken to and the speaking subject. That is, however, only one of its functions since, wing-like, the fan also acts as a means of communication in a quite literal sense as the carrier of a message, since Mallarmé wrote this and his other fan poems on actual paper fans.[16] Now Fühmann projects Mallarmé's text onto the shutters, also imitating the fluttering of the fan, which is manifested in the variations in the raising and lowering of the shutter. Drawn out over a number of days, it is possible to see in Fühmann's intertextual use of the fan image a slowing down of the movement described in Mallarmé's poem, whilst the individual changes in the position of the shutters have the character of sudden

---

[14] The relationship between the shutters and what lies behind them comes very close to 'appearing in a non-appearance and not appearing in what appears'. Dieter Mersch, *Ereignis und Aura* (Frankfurt a.M.: Suhrkamp, 2002), 145.

[15] Stéphane Mallarmé, 'Éventail de Madame Mallarmé', in Mallarmé, *Oeuvres complètes*, ed. by Henri Mondor (Paris: Gallimard, 1992), 57-8 (here 57).

[16] This is also the case for the two other fan poems. See Mallarmé, *Oeuvres*, 1474 and Mallarmé, *Poésies*, ed. by Bertrand Marchal (Paris: Gallimard poésie, 1992), 227-29.

events. For example, on the fourth occasion the shutters are completely raised, opening up a view into the room. This happens only 'for a moment' (TD 117; 'für einen Augenblick', WA III, 378), yet the person who opens the shutters here is Franz Molnár's classic figure of the Budapest 'N'er-do-well', Liliom.[17] This moment reveals a rich interior, which could have fulfilled the dreams of this dramatic hero, who Molnár portrays as a real good-for-nothing and womanizer. Fühmann has thus also skilfully inserted the protagonist of Molnár's play of 1909 on to the stage of the room opposite his hotel window. The viewer then expresses his disappointment when the shutters are closed: 'black box; where is the input' (TD 212; 'black box; wo ist der input', WA III, 466). The building opposite clearly remains unreachable and the site of an illusory world of the Other. The narrow alley still divides these two worlds as fully, as they are kept apart by Mallarmé's fan and its binding permeability, in the most dramatic of the seven episodes: the sixth scene (TD 226-27; WA III, 478-79) unites the figure of the ruffian Liliom with two women, who resemble siren-like witches. The sparkling eyes of these two enticing blond ladies might well be taken from the world of Mikhail Bulgakow's *The Master and Margarita* (1966), behind whom Fühmann's Liliom appears like Casanova. The end of the scene has all the hallmarks of the end of a theatrical performance:

> Past the yellow moon flies Margarita, and the curtains begin to close on the laughter; the faces disappear, the lights go out; Líliom lets down the shutters, and one of them catches and remains at an angle to the windowsill, Mallarmé's fan, subdued light behind it, and silence, and Blue flits past , and then nothing more (TD 227)

> am gelben Mond fliegt Margarita vorbei, und da gehen im Lachen noch die Vorhänge zu; die Gesichter verschwinden, die Lichter verlöschen; Líliom [*sic*] läßt die Rolläden nieder und einer hakt und bleibt schräg zum Fensterbrett stehen, Mallarmés Fächer, gedämpftes Licht dahinter, und Stille, und einmal huscht Blau vorbei und dann ist nichts mehr (WA III, 478-79)

---

[17] Otto F. Beer, 'Nachwort', in Franz Molnár, *Liliom*, trans. Alfred Polgár (Stuttgart: Reclam, 1979), 114. In *Twenty-two Days*, Fühmann uses the incorrect spelling 'Líliom' throughout.

The end of the scene is contextualised through the intertexts. Besides *Liliom*, the explicit intertext here is Mallarmé's poem. Added to this are the aspects of the diabolical, whose origins in Bulgakow's novel can be demonstrated with reference to the introduction of the flying figure of Margarita.[18] As becomes apparent from the last reference to the building opposite the hotel room, in which 'all [the] shutters [are] closed' (TD 241; 'alle Rolläden geschlossen', WA III,492), this is also the finale of this series of episodes. The observer, who had earlier stood on Mount Gellért carving out a metaphor for Budapest's bridges over the Danube, now adopts the position of a reader, who uses the text as a means of creating a montage of references. The complex linking of intertexts into this topography of modernism reveals a mode of observing that expresses itself through the insertion of appropriate texts[19] that inscribe the places observed . The diary-like account records meetings, incidents and events alongside one another in a way that is informed by the same consideration that occupies Homer's Odysseus as he begins to tell his tale to Alcinous: 'what shall I tell you first, what shall I leave for last?'[20]

A similar sense of the impossibility of achieving completion emerges from Führmann's reception of James Joyce, which can also be traced through *Twenty-two Days*.[21] Joyce's hero Leopold Bloom appears in the Lukács Baths, which Führmann also depicts as a Cretan labyrinth. There several men sit in the warm and hot baths, where the 'waterlover' Bloom is also in his element:[22] 'Thirteen Leopold Blooms: what a metamorphosis' (TD 74; 'Dreizehn Leopold Blooms:

---

[18] In Bulgakow's novel, Margarita turns into a witch, who flies on a broom (chapter 20). The motif of the moon is mentioned in a number of instances during her first flight, but plays a greater role in her final flight in chapter 32. Here the moonlight, which appears in a number of colours, a transformative power for Voland and his followers. Mikhail Bulgakow, *The Master and Margarita*, trans. Diana Burgin and Katherine Tiernan O'Toole (London: Picador, 1997).
[19] See Philip Fisher, 'City Matters: City Minds. Die Poetik der Großstadt in der modernen Literatur', Scherpe (ed.), *Die Unwirklichkeit*, 106-28 (here 121): 'the imposed way of seeing can reach the same complexity as the mode of representation'.
[20] Homer, *The Odyssey*, trans. Walter Shewring (Oxford: OUP, 1980), 99.
[21] For an account of Fümann's Joyce reception, see Dennis Tate, 'Undercover Odyssey: The Reception of James Joyce in the Work of Franz Fühmann', *German Life and Letters* 47.6 (1994), 302-12.
[22] James Joyce, *Ulysses* (London: Penguin, 2000), 783. Referred to in the following by the abbrevation U and the relevant page numbers in parantheses.

welche Metamorphose', WA III, 340).[23] Fühmann inserts this line, as if it has just occurred to him, into the otherwise continuously narrated Lukács Baths episode. The intertextual reference is set apart from the more narrative segments of the episode by its verbless structure. In the relevant episode in Joyce's novel, Bloom is at Paddy Dignam's funeral:

> Bloom stood far back, his hat in his hand, counting the bared heads. Twelve. I'm thirteen No. The chap in the macintosh is thirteen. Death's number. Where the deuce did he pop out of? He wasn't in the chapel, that I'll swear. Silly superstition that about thirteen. (U 139)

In the Lukács Baths too, only the heads of the bathers can be seen above the water.

In the funeral scene of the so-called Hades chapter, Bloom wonders what it would be like if 'we were all suddenly somebody else' (U 139), which Fühmann takes as a cue to make reference to the notion of metamorphosis, thereby thematizing the motif of sudden change that can be found in both *Twenty-two Days* and *Ulysses*. In the Lukács Baths episode this motif appears as an intensification of the idea of transformation[24] central to his earlier work, now

---

[23] See Ursula Heukenkamp's analysis of this line with regard to Fühmann's number games. Heukenkamp, 'Die große Erzählung von der befreiten Arbeit. Ein Richtungswechsel des Erzählers Franz Fühmann', in Brigitte Krüger (ed.) *Dichter sein heißt aufs Ganze aus sein. Zugänge zu Poetologie und Werk Franz Fühmanns* (Frankfurt a.M.: Lang, 2003), 15-35 (here 29-30).

[24] This classic Fühmann theme is discussed extensively in studies of his work. For example: Irmgard Wagner, *Nachdenken über Literatur* (Heidelberg: Carl Winter, 1989), especially chapters 1-3, 4, and 8; Ihmku Kim, *Franz Fühmann – Dichter des „Lebens"* (Frankfurt a.M.: Peter Lang, 1996); Hans Richter, *Franz Fühmann – Ein deutsches Dichterleben* (Berlin: Aufbau, 1992); Wilfried F. Schoeller, 'Wandlung als Konzept', in Brigitte Krüger, Margrid Bircken, and Helmut John (eds.), *'Jeder hat seinen Fühmann': Herkunft – Prägung – Habitus: Zugänge zu Poetologie und Werk Franz Fühmanns* (Frankfurt a.M.: Peter Lang, 1998), 25-40; Horst Lohr, 'Vom Märchen zum Mythos. Zum Werk von Franz Fühmann', *Weimarer Beiträge* 28.1 (1982), 62-81; Klaus-Dieter Schönewerk, 'Sein Werk spiegelt historische Wandlung. Zum Gedenken an Franz Fühmann', *Neues Deutschland*, 9 July 1984; Ulrich von Bülow, 'Von der Geschichtsphilosophie zur Anthropologie. Fühmanns ästhetische Wende in seinem Essay "Das mythische Element"', in Krüger, Bircken and John (eds.), *'Jeder hat seinen Fühmann'*, 59-78; and von Bülow, *Die Poetik Franz Fühmanns. Vom geschichtsphilosophischen Märchen zum anthropologischen Mythos* (Neuried: ars una, 2001).

linked with the element of water, which pleases Bloom because of its streaming movement and its transmutability.[25]

In the preceding lotus-eaters chapter, Bloom collects exotic impressions on his way to the cemetery. The no less exotic appearance of lotus blossoms in Budapest's Lukács Baths could represent a reference to this. In Joyce there is no explicit mention of the lotus, yet the intoxicating perfumes and flowers call to mind the lotus-eaters' island from the *Odyssey*:

> The far east. Lovely spot it must be: the garden of the world. Big lazy leaves to float about on, cactuses, flowery meads snaky lianas they call them. Wonder is it like that. Those Cinghalese lobbing around in the sun, in *dolce far niente*. Not doing a hand's turn all day. Sleep six months out of twelve. Too hot to quarrel. Influence of the climate. Lethargy. Flowers of idleness. The air feeds most. Azotes. Hothouse in Botanic gardens. Sensitive plants. Waterlilies. Petals too tired to. Sleeping sickness in the air. Walk on roseleaves. (U 87)[26]

In Fühmann, the exotic lotus blossom is perhaps not only an intertextual reference to Joyce's novel, but equally shows a peculiarity of the thermal spas of Budapest. The *Lexicon of Antiquity*'s entry on 'Lotus' points to 'the curious position of the white lotus in the warm springs of the Bishop's Baths of Großwardein (Oradea) and the Emperor's Baths at Ofen (Buda) in Hungary',[27] the latter of which, the *Császárfürdő*, are particularly recommended by a taxi-driver in *Twenty-two Days* (TD 66; WA III, 333).

Shortly afterwards, in *Ulysses*, Bloom thinks about taking a bath: 'Time to get a bath round the corner. Hammam. Turkish. Massage' (U 105). At the end of

---

[25] Bloom's admiration for the transmutability of water is discussed in Winfried Eckel, 'Odysseus im Labyrinth. Zum Konzept der unendlichen Irrfahrt in James Joyce' *Ulysses*', in Kurt Röttgers and Monika Schmitz-Emans (eds.) *Labyrinthe. Philosophische und literarische Modelle* (Essen: Die blaue Eule, 2000), 74-91 (here 84).

[26] Up until the end of the chapter the element of water, which Bloom so admires, appears on a number of occasions: to begin with as an intertextual reference to the suicide of Ophelia (U 97), and then as a drink ('lovely cool water out of the well stonecold', U 97); further on there is talk of holy water, the 'waters of oblivion' at Lourdes (U 99), and the question is raised in parentheses whether communion wafers are kept in water (U 99).

[27] *Lexikon der Antike* (Stuttgart: Metzler, 1927), XIII.

the chapter, he expands upon this idea when he moves from thinking about the 'stream of life' to the more intense desire for a bath:

> Heatwave. Won't last. Always passing, the stream of life, which in the stream of life we trace is dearer than them all.
>   Enjoy a bath now: clean trough of water, cool enamel, the gentle tepid stream. This is my body.
>   He foresaw his pale body reclined in it at all, naked, in a womb of warmth, oiled by scented melting soap, softly laved. He saw his trunk and limbs riprippled over and sustained, buoyed lightly upward, lemonyellow: his navel bud of flesh: and saw the dark tangled curls of his bush floating, floating hair of the stream around the limp father of thousands, a languid floating flower. (U 107)

The emphasis on the corporeal in this passage finds an echo in Fühmann's observations on the 'Hungarians' [entirely naïve] relationship to water' (TD 68; '[ganz naives] Verhältnis der Ungarn zum Wasser', WA III, 335) and in the memory of the orgiastic wallowing 'in body-temperature mud' (TD 68; 'im blutwarmen Modder', WA III, 335) at Hévíz.[28] Bloom's attachment to water and its meaning in *Twenty-two Days* demonstrate clear similiarities. Fühmann also describes a sixty-year-old man slowly entering the water and experiencing a moment of pleasure that is very similar to the hydrophilia of Leopold Bloom, which is in turn shared by that driver whom Fühmann describes as having lovingly collected and brought home waters from the springs of the Balaton region.

The connection between metamorphosis, Bloom and water allows us to demonstrate a further relationship between *Ulysses* and *Twenty-two Days*, which helps to explain why Fühmann makes Joyce's hero appear at this moment. Amongst the wide range of advantages that Bloom attributes to water are 'its healing virtues' (U 784), which can be experienced in the *Gyógyfürdő* (therapeutic bath) of the Lukács Baths. In *Twenty-two Days*, this issue has already come up when the narrator falls ill and is recommended a cure for an illness, involving

---

[28] Hévíz is a town on the southwest tip of Lake Balaton. It has a lake in a volcanic crater with warm, sulphurous, black water and, attached to this, a therapeutic spa.

bathing in a series of pools of increasing temperature. In Joyce, water has a further metamorphic quality ('its metamorphoses as vapour, mist, cloud, rain, sleet, snow, hail', U 784), which provides a further intertextual basis for reading Fühmann's own discussion of it here in these terms. Bloom's wave-like 'stream of life'[29] can be read in this context as a topos which draws parallels between the idea of transformation and the flow of water. In the explicit reflection on the notion of transformation and the thoughts about its representability in *Twenty-two Days* (TD 108-11; WA III, 370-73), the following line is inserted: 'Metamorphosis – Queen of the Mythologems' (TD 109; 'Metamorphose – Königin der Mythologeme', WA III, 371). In this way, this term is placed in the appropriate context and is, furthermore, identified as a formal category to be developed in Fühmann's later mythopoetics.

The appearance of Bloom in Budapest also refers to an important aspect of the heritage of Joyce's protagonist. Bloom is the descendant of the Jewish-Hungarian exile Virag Lipoti, his grandfather, and Rudolph Virag, his father, who both hail from Szombathely (U 628).[30] The name of the grandfather is the Hungarian equivalent of Leopold Bloom (*virág* means flower or bloom).[31] The hydrophilia that Fühmann notes in Hungarians creates a further analogy to Bloom that, from this perspective, reveals his Hungarian roots. In this way, the ancient Hungarians, those 'heroes of the land seizure, the seven vassals of Álmos' (TD 72; 'Helden der Landnahme, die sieben Getreuen des Álmos', WA III, 338), who meet in the steam bath in the 'maw of Hell' (TD 72; 'Rachen der Hölle', WA III,

---

[29] See the references to water in *Ulysses*: '[…] which in the stream of life we trace is dearer than them all. […] clean trough of water […] the gentle tepid stream […]' (U 107); 'How can you own water really? It's always flowing in a stream, never the same, which in a stream of life we trace. Because life is a stream.' (U 193); 'Its universality: its democratic equality and its constancy to its nature in seeking its own level' (U 783); 'its variety of forms in loughs and bays and gulfs and bights and guts and lagoons and atolls and archipelagos and sounds and fjords and minches and tidal estuaries and arms of sea' (U 785).

[30] The correct Hungarian spelling of the name should almost certainly be Virág Lipot. See Tate's reference to this connection: 'Leopold Bloom emerges unexpectedly – or perhaps not so unexpectedly, as the fictional son of an Hungarian father – in the text of Fühmann's Budapest Diary'. Tate, 'Undercover Odyssey', 310.

[31] Bloom's father's change of name, as mentioned in the Cyclops chapter, is therefore a straightforward translation of the Hungarian into English (U 438). See also Bloom's examination of the documents that refer to the change of name and Virág as 'formerly of Szombathely' (U 852)

338), can also be seen as the forebears of the Dubliner: Their appearance is followed by that of Bloom. In the labyrinthine passages of the text that deal with the Lukács Baths, the 'brown-skinned Magyar warriors' (TD 72; 'braunhäutige[n] magyarische[n] Recken') make their appearance in the everyday space of the Baths just as Joyce's hero does in the Dublin of 16 June 1904. The much-discussed relationship between the mythical setting invoked by the title and its presence in the narration of *Ulysses* seems to exist in a similar fashion in these sections of *Twenty-two Days*: 'The heroic seems [...] to be reduced everywhere to the everyday; the everyday, on the other hand, is stylized more into the archetypical'.[32] This tendency can also be observed elsewhere in *Twenty-two Days*, for example in the scene describing the author's departure by train from Berlin's Ostbahnhof, in which Poseidon, Prometheus and Epimetheus are considered as potential station masters (TD 10; WA III, 284). Fühmann now shows the water testers from the era of the *honfoglalás* (land seizure) in the steam bath. A sixty-year-old in the swimming pool outside swims 'out into the Sea of Azov toward the wilds of Maeonia' (TD 68; 'durchs Asowsche Meer zum mäotischen Urland', WA III, 335), as if the migration of the Hungarians was still taking place in the middle of Budapest.

Fühmann's Joyce reception in the context of *Twenty-two Days* can be seen as a constitutive aspect of the modernist topography of Budapest. The presence of Bloom in the Lukács Bath becomes the presence of Joyce's novel in Fühmann's writing of Budapest. The kind of openness that characterizes *Twenty-two Days* can therefore be made to correspond to the twisting paths of Joyce's hero in Dublin. Fühmann's *Twenty-two Days* creates out of its expedition from Berlin to Budapest and back to Berlin a landscape of modernism, the writing of which is far from being exhausted by the return to Berlin at the end of the book. That 'restlessness' (U 785) that Bloom discovers in the water as in the 'stream of life', and which fascinates him, creates the continuity that is contained in Fühmann's

---

[32] Eckel, 'Odysseus im Labyrinth', 78.

deliberations about ending at the beginning and beginning at the end of his text .[33] It is precisely the erratic nature of this path through Budapest that allows the labyrinth to be understood as a space of transit between the transposed exit and entrance signs that mark the passage through the steam bath (TD 70, 75; WA III, 336, 341).

'Myths are movements in space' (TD 236; 'Mythen [sind] Bewegungen im Raum', WA III, 487), writes Fühmann in the entry for 2 November. There are further statements in *Twenty-two Days* that describe the difference between fairy-tale and myth in spatial terms. To begin with, the mythical is seen as three-dimensional, finally even as 'multidimensional' (TD 236; 'vieldimensional', WA III, 487). At another point, myth is described as 'abysmal', whereas the fairy-tale only points towards abysses (TD 235; WA III, 486).

In this context, the movement in the urban space of Budapest could be described as a movement *to* and *in* a mythical place, which initially achieves this quality, however, as a literary place , in which the interpretation and writing of texts occurs , and which shows itself to be a process of dissemination in which the writing of existing texts is continued. The textual traces incorporated into *Twenty-two Days* thereby create a place whose aphoristic multiplicity and thematic limitlessness at first lacks a climax or tangible centre. Or at least, the text does not obviously reveal them.

To return to the beginning of *Twenty-two Days*, this can be described not only as a entrance to the text, but also as a journey out of it that marks a 'moving out into the open'.[34] The fifteen minutes before midnight on 14 October that frame the diary's opening entry would therefore be the entrance into the text as an exit from the first day of travel following his departure from Berlin. This ambivalence is repeated in reverse in the final sequence, which contains the (re)entry into Berlin as an exit from the text.

---

[33] Compare the final sentence in *Twenty-two Days*: 'To begin? Or: to end?' (TD 258; 'Anfangen? Oder: Aufhören?', WA III, 506).
[34] Wagner, *Nachdenken über Literatur*, 27.

The visit to the steam bath in Budapest's Lukács Baths demonstrates an analogous phenomenon. There the way *into* the steam bath is 'through a door marked EXIT' (TD 70; 'durch eine Tür mit der Aufschrift AUSGANG', WA III, 336 – capitalization in original). The crossing of the threshold into an extraordinary interior space happens furthermore in the form of entering into a building from outside in the open air.[35] In this way, reaching the interior is shown as a stepping out of the exterior, which is reached again at the end of the episode by using the ostensible entrance as an exit. The points of transition are marked in the text in each case by placing the words 'ENTRANCE' and 'EXIT' in capitals. These capitals separate the steam bath episode from the rest of the text. The confusion of the entrance and exit to the steam bath shows a reversal of inside and outside. The exit into the steam bath remains the entrance into another space, which as an interior nevertheless represents an outside, just as the departure from Berlin to Budapest is simultaneously a stepping outside one place and an entrance into another.

The same dialectic of entry and exit links Fühmann's later topos of the mine in *Inside the Mountain* to the steam bath . This is the case not just for the descent into the depths as an entering and, conversely, for the ascent to the surface as an exit. Fühmann shows the perpendicular mine shaft at the same time as both the entrance to and the exit from the mine, which not only represents its labyrinthine qualities, but also clearly makes it – in terms of the process of entering it and moving away from it – a (much) bigger sibling of the steam bath.

Moving through by means of being permitted entry as well as exit means passing through a space in between. The existence of this space can only be identified by passing through it, a process that, for the steam bath as well as for the mine, is also a linguistic point of transition, whether represented in terms of the stylistic peculiarities of the steam bath episode or by Fühmann's inclusion of

---

[35] Fühmann's description reads as follows: 'Sunshine and silence, I shiver in the air' (TD 67; 'Sonne und Stille, mich friert an der Luft', WA III, 334). In the interior of the building are found the therapeutic baths with their thermal water pools and steam bath. See the description in *Meskó Csaba: Heilbäder*, trans. Veronika Stöckigt and Dagmar Fischer (Budapest: Mayor's Office Budapest), 2001, 42-7.

miners' terminology in the other text. In the Lukács Baths the exit leads equally to a place whose present is clearly differentiated from that of the text that surrounds it, so that the steam bath episode also particularly represents a linguistic exit from the interior of the text of *Twenty-two Days*.

One attendant checks the tickets before letting customers in, whilst another one distributes the towels. The entrance to the place of the steam bath is in this way doubly marked by a ritual of gaining access, and is therefore made distinct from the rest of the spa.[36] Entry to the mine is marked by an even broader range of rituals. As with the attendants in the Lukács Baths in Budapest, there is an exchange or offering of various tokens in the pit-head baths, although in the mine this is primarily for reasons of safety. The ritual in the steam bath involves a series of exchanges. Despite the differences in these processes, what is key is that they are both obligatory in order to gain access to a particular place.

The entrance into the bath is the entrance into the 'Minos palace' (TD 70; 'Minospalast', WA III, 336) and an entering into the Cretan myth that this name evokes. Therefore this is at the same time a stepping out of the realm of reality. As Fühmann writes in his almost contemporaneous essay 'The Mythical Element in Literature' ('Das mythische Element in der Literatur'): 'Myth is clearly that which reality is not, and the world we can experience and its laws begin where myth ends' ('Der Mythos ist offensichtlich das, was die Wirklichkeit nicht ist, und erfahrbares Dasein mit seinen Gesetzen fängt dort an, wo der Mythos aufhört', WA VI, 91). The dual entrance and exit to the steam bath marks a border, whose clearly dialectical character is shown in this passage through it, in which every exit contains an entrance and every movement inside contains a movement outside. Within the text of *Twenty-two Days*, the possibility of stepping outside the text is suggested, and is indeed played out in the language it deploys. The textual form of the following pages shows not only thematically, but also in terms of language, the presence of a place that represents an outside due to its mythic

---

[36] It should be noted that the entrance to the Lukács Baths is '[t]here where there is nothing' (TD 66; '[d]ort, wo nichts mehr ist', WA III, 333). There is, however, no description of the entrance to the spa. In this respect also the entrance to the steam bath is emphasised.

connotations. The link between this place and the context of Budapest remains nevertheless just as present. With his labyrinthine text on the steam bath, Fühmann creates a literal equivalent to this place and its form. In the passage in question, the text reproduces the spatial organisation of the steam bath, so that the movement of reading through and with the text follows the contours of a place, which does not appear *in* the text, but whose presence the text reproduces as an aesthetic experience.[37] Part of this is a preparatory and ritualized moment of entry into the labyrinth of the steam bath, which can be described in Foucault's terms as a heterotopia.

> Heterotopias always presuppose a system of opening and closing that both isolates them and makes them penetrable. In general, the heterotopic site is not freely accessible like a public place. Either the entry is compulsory […] or else the individual has to submit to rites and purifications. To get in one must have a certain permission and make certain gestures. Moreover, there are even heterotopias that are entirely consecrated to these activities of purification that is partly religious and partly hygienic, such as the hamman of the Moslems, or else purification that appears to be purely hygienic, as in Scandinavian saunas.[38]

The way into the steam bath in Fühmann's text demands two rituals of admission, in each case from a 'goateed' (TD 70; 'knebelbärtigen', WA III, 336) attendant. Passage through the door marked 'exit' has all the trappings of an entrance, down to the changing of clothes. The exactness of the checks made in order to establish that the right of entry and the double ritual of exchange stand in almost grotesque contrast to the subsequent 'odyssey' (TD 75; 'Irrfahrt', WA III, 341) through the labyrinth of the changing room. Hypotactic fragments of sentences, lists, repetitions and interjections follow one another relentlessly. The entrance to the labyrinth of the steam bath and the twisting path through it are reproduced as an aesthetic experience through the mediality of this section of the

---

[37] As Pascal Quignard observes, 'to read is to follow the invisible presence with one's eyes'. Pascal Quignard, *Le sexe et l'effroi* (Paris: Gallimard, 1994), 271. In this way, the labyrinthine experience of the bath can be understood as a moving through the text with one's eyes.
[38] Foucault, 'Of Other Spaces', 26.

text. The text does not only describe the labyrinth, but rather writes the labyrinth itself.

Typologically, Fühmann has incorporated two different forms of labyrinth.[39] The motif of the wandering quest belongs to the modern type, in which the world is understood as a labyrinth with no clearly prescribed and walkable path and the movement through it reflects the labyrinthine nature of the pursuit of understanding. The archetypal journey home of the Homeric wanderer turns out to be a detour that both takes him backwards and leads him towards understanding. . In this sense, 'experience is an extensive spatial process which must be completed and which will not tolerate short cuts'.[40] Opposed to this is a reading that is directed towards the lower rooms of the real steam bath, which appear to be a goal that will be reached at the end of the odyssey . There, 'at the heart of the turning screw' and 'in the sacrificial pit' (TD 74; 'im Herzen der Schraube, in der Opfergrube', WA III, 340), the Minotaur is to be found. The path does not lead just anywhere, but rather, like the route taken by Theseus, to the mythical labyrinth-dweller. This second variant of the labyrinth begins in Fühmann's text with a narrowing, as 'the labyrinth narrows down to a passage, and the passage winds its way, ever more crooked and narrow into the maw of Hell' (TD 72; 'das Labyrinth verengt sich zum Gang, und der Gang schraubt sich, in unendlicher Krümmung sich verengend, hinunter in den Rachen der Hölle', WA III, 338). This part conforms more to the classical or ancient model of the labyrinth, which leads on a winding, confusing, but nevertheless directed path to a particular goal. Before reaching the heart of the turning screw there is time for a passing glance into one of the saunas. Fühmann lets the seven princes of the Hungarian tribes ('Hetumogens' from the Hungarian *Hétmagyar*, TD 72; WA III, 338) appear. They are shown gathered around Álmos, their elder. Here Fühmann makes a connection to Imre Madách by quoting from the phalanstery scene from

---

[39] On the typology and categorization of labyrinths, see Monika Schmitz-Emans, 'Labyrinthe. Zur Einführung', in Röttgers and Schmitz-Emans (eds.), *Labyrinthe*, 14ff. and 25; Hermann Kern, *Labyrinthe. Erscheinungsformen und Deutungen. 5000 Jahre Gegenwart eines Urbilds* (Munich: Prestel, 1999), 13-42.
[40] Hans Blumenberg, *Die Lesbarkeit der Welt* (Frankfurt a.M.: Suhrkamp, 2000), 108.

The Tragedy of Man (1861) that he examines in detail elsewhere: "'"Valóban nagy tudós vagy, idegen..."'" (TD, 72; WA III, 338 – 'You are a scholar, foreigner...'). This line is the answer of a scientist to the curiosity of the visitor Adam, who constantly demands in the course of their dialogue to see and learn more. In *Twenty-two Days* the eye of the narrator falls on the phalanstery-like setting of the meeting of the tribal princes in the sauna. The scene is also closely related in terms of circumstances and setting to that later story in which Fühmann focuses on a trio of naked men. In both cases, these are groups cut off from the outside world, which openly practice the exclusion of the *idegen* (foreigner). Fühmann's story 'Three Naked Men' ('Drei nackte Männer', WA I, 509-22) similarly presents a clique of three men (representative of the political elite) during a semi-ritualized visit to a sauna. The cold hermeticism of the group in this story stands in direct contrast to the heat of the sauna and the detailed and very intimate representation of the behaviour of the three occurs from an unbridgeable narrative distance: any verbal contact between the first-person narrator and the men is entirely precluded by the behaviour of the latter .

This episode in *Twenty-two Days* again takes up the story of the Hungarian land seizure in a kind of dramatization. The way Fühmann does this demonstrates the nature of his mythopoetics. The exit from the space of 'the world we can experience' ('erfahrbaren Daseins',WA VI, 91) leads into another space, as the heroes of legend appear and enter into the subjective experience of the first-person narrator. Fühmann lets the 'Magyar warriors' (TD 72; 'magyarische[n] Recken', WA III, 338) appear themselves and lists their names and genealogies. In this place of myth, Fühmann presents *his* telling of the legend he has referred to earlier. Its presence remains that of a process of reception, in which the double quality of the mythic material reveals itself, making it possible here to work on the land-seizure legends by working them into his mythic conception. In Fühmann's linking of the Minotaur myth with the appearance of the Hetumogens, he discovers the fixity of form that allows him to inscribe both of them into his representation of Budapest:

> The fact that reception is not simply an addition to myth [...], but
> that myth can only be passed down and known in the form [...] of
> something which finds itself in a process of reception, is based,
> despite its iconic constancy, on the malleability of its elements;
> that is to say, on the fact that it is not – as Bernay [...] has it –
> made up of *granite figures*, for which any appropriation must be a
> misappropriation.[41]

Fühmann's appropriation is a movement through a space. His labyrinth of
the baths, with its external dimension clearly marked, has its place in the text
itself. The effect of his reading is equally inscribed into the text. The 'ghetto-like
thicket' (TD 71; 'Ghettowirrsal', WA III, 337) of the bath can be wandered
through in the form of its own text. The reader has to follow the 'twisted and
tangled' (TD 71; 'verfitzt- und verfilzten', WA III, 337) turns of the path in
unending hypotaxis without the prospect of ever finding the exit. The forward
flow of the text and the sense of being caught up in it that, echoing again Joyce's
'stream of life', 'takes hold of you and washes you into the unknown' (TD 72;
'[dich] erfaßt und spült dich ins Unbekannte', WA III, 338), only relents in that
moment, marked with a colon, when the narrator freezes at the entrance to the
sauna. The narrowing of the path of the labyrinth is accompanied by a tendency to
make the linguistic material increasingly dense. If the text is characterized by
series of attributes and lists of nouns at the beginning of the visit to the labyrinth,
its textual coherence is increased by the ever more frequent use of alliteration. At
the beginning, for example, we read that the narrator is in 'a tiled passageway
traversed by sheeted figures and leading nighmarishly from the darkness of a
screw's turn up to an iron ladder' (TD 70; 'in einem von Laken durchwandelten,
alptraumhaft aus der Nacht einer Schraubendrehung zu einer Eisenleiter
hochführenden Kachelgang', WA III, 336). Yet, after passing the two attendants
he wanders through

> cage upon cage formed by lathes, lattices, staves, grilles, slats, slits,
> joists, holes, air, numbered with unholy abandon and finding

---

[41] Hans Blumenberg, *Arbeit am Mythos* (Frankfurt a.M.: Suhrkamp, 1996), 240-41. Emphasis in original.

[himself] is the one cage that is perspicuous from all sides and hence unfathomable (TD 70)

der aus Latten, Leisten, Stäben, Rosten, Lamellen, Ritzen, Fugen, Löchern und Luft gebildeten, heillos durcheinandernumerierten, käfighaft zwischen Käfigen über Käfige in den einen, rundum offen nach allen Seiten durchschau- und eben darum unergründbaren Käfig dieses Labyrinths (WA III, 337)

The cabin that the narrator is looking for is found, but this does not mean that the end of the labyrinth has been found. The climax of the journey through the labyrinth is reached by way of a series of alliterations, first of all moving from the shortest possible sentence to a series of nouns alliterating on the letter L.

And with a sigh or relief you enter, undress, stand naked, look around, peer out and descry beyond lathes and slats and slits and slats and lathes nothing but sheeted and loinclothed figures (TD 71)[42]

und aufatmend trittst du ein, ziehst dich aus, stehst nackt, schaust dich um, lugst hinaus und schaust hinter Latten und Leisten und Luken zwischen Leisten und Luken und Latten nur Lakenumhüllte und Lendenbeschürzte (WA III, 337)

Fühmann intensifies this process by amalgamating the individual words into alliterative compounds. This is followed by a list characterized not only by its omission of the commas that have hitherto been included, but also above all by its phonological microstructure, which borrows a phenomenon from tongue-twisters. Here the occlusives [k] and [g], which are differentiated phonetically from one another only in terms of their being voiced or unvoiced, appear as the initial sounds of alternate words:

for the sake of a lousy loincloth and re-enter the twisted and tangled lathedstavedgrilledslattedslittedjoistedjointedlabyrinth of cage-like cubbyholes grottoes cabins gratings canals gangways crannies grooves corners grilles cubicles (TD 71)

um eines lumpigen Leistenschurzes willen zurück ins verfitzt- und verfilzte Leistenlattenlamellenlöcherlukenluftlabyrinth käfighafter

---

[42] [Unfortunately, the full extent of the alliteration in this passage is not conveyed by the English translation. Trans.]

Kauen Gaupen Kojen Gaden Koben Gänge Kanäle Gatter Kabinen
(WA III, 338)

The centre of the labyrinth lies further below. Movement in the mythical
place is not only a wandering that seems endless in its twists and turns, but also a
'descent into hell' ('Höllenfahrt')[43] and 'into the unknown' (TD 72; 'ins
Unbekannte', WA III, 338). The visit to the labyrinth remains a passing through
and moving past, the goal of which is this movement itself. The visit is an
excursion from the exit back to the entrance, which stands as an exit from the
labyrinth at the end of the twisted path of the text and text of the path. Below in
the Hadean place, where the shades of Homeric heroes do not weep, but where
instead the ancient Magyars gather to confer , the Joycean labyrinth-walker
emerges. Thirteen Blooms appear.

At the centre of the labyrinthine path is a point of transition marked by a
ritual. It constitutes not only the centre of the labyrinth, but is at the same time the
place where a striking moment of corporeality can be observed in the form of
complete exposure, followed by an immediate covering of nakedness. At first the
mythical occupant of the labyrinth, the Minotaur, stands there, who Fühmann does
not make appear as an ugly chimera, but rather as a handsome young man. His
animal half in this case is the half that is clothed: 'a youth, handsome and black as
only a Pasiphaïde can be, he stands there bare to the waist in the middle of the pit'
(TD 74; 'Ein Jüngling, schön und schwarz wie nur ein Pasiphaïde steht er bis zum
Gürtel nackt in der Mitte der Grube', WA III, 340). Each bather must give the
Minotaur his loin cloth and uncover himself completely for a moment before
moving on covered with a sheet. In the following room 'forty shrouded bodies'
('vierzig vermummte Leiber') lie 'motionless and pale and hideously groaning'
(TD 75; 'reglos und bleich und schauerlich ächzend', WA III, 341).

The way back 'by way of the tiled passage as it unwinds from the night'
(TD 75; 'durch den der Nacht sich entschraubenden Kachelgang', WA III, 341) to

---

[43] Thomas Mann, *Joseph and His Brothers*. trans. H. T. Lowe-Porter (Harmondsworth: Penguin,
1978), 32. Mann, *Joseph und seine Brüder* (Frankfurt a.M.: Fischer, 1964), 7.

the changing booth and to the entrance that leads outwards is no easier, but its narration is shorter. The movement along the way to the 'heart of the turning screw' (TD 74; 'Herzen der Schraube', WA III, 340) made the time of narration and the narrated time, as demonstrated above, almost identical. Now the stations of the way down appear again in reverse order and in the briefest possible form. Gyula, one of the seven princes, intervenes to help the narrator avoid a wrong turn through the 'landscape of lathes and lattices' (TD 75; 'Landschaft der Latten und Leisten', WA III, 341). The labyrinthine complexity now only shimmers through in the short alliteration of the three words. Even before the threshold has been reached the same man's question announces immediately that we are back in world of experience. When he asks after the GDR author Günter Kunert, his mythical mask as the land seizure hero Gyula disappears.

The journey through the labyrinth has been an 'odyssey' (TD 75; 'Irrfahrt', WA III, 342), the reader is told, from which the visitor returns visibly aged. After stepping out over the threshold of the entrance, the return to the sphere of experience is accompanied by a feeling of unease. Furthermore, and almost as a consequence, the problem of whether experience can be written about emerges. In answer to the question, posed with 'cutting sceptical irony' (TD 77; 'schneidend skeptischer Ironie', WA III, 342), if a book about Budapest is planned, the text demonstrates its poetological self-referentiality:

> Don't worry, Ferenc, don't worry, I don't feel competent to write so much as an essay about one of the bridges, I'm keeping a diary, [...] and if particles of Budapest are reflected in it, it's not Budapest (TD 76)

> Keine Sorge, Ference, keine Sorge, ich fühle mich ja nicht befugt, auch nur einen Aufsatz über eine der Brücken zu schreiben, ich führe mein Tagebuch weiter, [...] und spiegeln sich auch Splitter von Budapest drin, so nicht Budapest (WA III, 342).

Following on from the linguistic complexity of the previously highlighted labyrinth episode, this statement is puzzling. It only makes sense, coming as it does in the middle of a highly allusive book on Budapest, in the context of the reflection that continues later. Fühmann seems to be referring to the link between place and individuality, rather than negating what he has just created with his apparently obscure intertextualities. This has nothing to do with a 'topographical image' (TD 100; 'topographisches Abbild, WA III, 363), but has to do instead with the spirit of a place, and is also nothing to do with an attempt to reproduce the real in its completeness, which would founder on the impossibility of achieving such totality. The idea of having a clear goal for the text has now also become less important than its effect, as can be seen in the literary praxis of the labyrinth episode. This praxis would at least provide a practical answer to the poetological questions raised later in the text:

> Could one describe a street, a quarter, a city, a country by means of the thoughts dreams memories feelings that come to one under their spell? Could someone else see those places from such jottings, would he recognize them, or could he visualize them? (TD 100)

> Könnte man eine Straße, ein Viertel, eine Stadt, ein Land durch die Gedanken, Träume, Erinnerungen, Gefühle beschreiben, die einem in ihrem Bannkreis kommen? Sähe ein Zweiter aus solchen Aufzeichnungen jene Stätten, erkennte er sie wieder, oder könnte er sich ein Bild von ihnen machen? (WA III, 363)

This question touches precisely not upon the idea of a arriving at a place, which the text would necessarily overstretch itself trying to reproduce. It has to do instead with offering an intellectual topography, which can be distinguished as a textual landscape from a descriptive one. In this way, the labyrinthine reading experience of the Lukács Baths episode is not the labyrinth itself and the reader's path through the twists and turns of the text is at best that 'following of the invisible presence'.[44] This presence is of course expanded when shrouded in the textual object, yet it remains, in Fühmann's 'movements in space' (TD 236; 'Bewegungen im Raum', WA III, 487), the appearance of a 'a non-appearance in that which appears'.[45]

---

[44] Quignard, *Le sexe et l'effroi*, 271.
[45] Mersch, *Ereignis und Aura*, 145.

That place 'by the Danube', which Attila József had already occupied, hardly hearing 'the surface chatter. From the depths: not a word' ('hogy fecseg a felszin, hallgat a mély'), would be for Fühmann 'a good place to take stock' (TD 93; 'ein guter Ort Bilanz zu ziehen', WA III, 356).[46] This place becomes readable not as the chattering surface of a descriptive piece of travel writing, but rather in the co- and contextual boundlessness of a 'uncompleted change' (TD 185; 'unvollendete[n] Wandlung', WA III, 442). The intertextually defined locus of this encounter with Budapest is the experience of literature. It is above all texts that inscribe and describe this place of metamorphosis and that are shown to be written into the landscape. This quality of an eloquent library is part of the present of Budapest and of being present in its reality. The urban *flaneur* is able to penetrate the reality of Budapest as a repeated deep submergence in the city. Even as the text writes the city into itself, it is also speaking of itself and demonstrating *its own* performance as a presence. Fühmann creates this presence in the present tense of reading, which does not simply proceed as a parallel reception of place and text or of texts in places. Rather, the readability of Budapest is achieved in terms of its presence.

This opens up a perspective that, by approaching what it means to arrive in a place, creates what Fühmann calls 'another point of view' ('anderen Augenwinkel' [*sic*]).[47] The text demonstrates that Budapest's urban landscape of modernism possesses that 'atmosphere of intellectual creativity' ('Atmosphäre schöpferischen Geistes'),[48] and precisely because in it 'the broad impact of modernism' can be seen.[49] In this openended τόπος 'amongst the art nouveau houses' ('unter den Jugendstil-Häusern')[50] the writer can find not only a location of poetic metamorphoses that is open to the whole world. At least as importantly,

---

[46] Attila József, 'By the Danube', *Winter Night. Selected Poems*, trans. John Bátki (Budapest: Corvina, 1997), 102-4 (here 102). Attila József, 'A Dunánál', *Összes versei II. köt., kritikai kiadás*, ed. by Stoll Béla (Budapest: Balassi kiadó, 2005), 334-38.

[47] Endre Kiss, 'Ich versuche Petőfi zu übersetzen: Ein Gespräch mit Franz Fühmann', *Budapester Rundschau*, 11 December 1972, 6.

[48] Kiss, 'Ich versuche Petőfi zu übersetzen'.

[49] Tate, 'Undercover Odyssey', 303.

[50] Kiss, 'Ich versuche Petőfi zu übersetzen'.

he can also find, in the cave of the city[51] – in that 'inherently most poetic of all material'[52] – that entry into incompletability, which finds its poetic and literary medium in myth – for example in the 'the allegory of digging a pit' (TD 252; 'Gleichnis vom Grubenausheben', WA III, 502) –, and which Fühmann will later locate definitively amidst the underground passages of the mines.

Translated by David Clarke with Dennis Tate

---

[51] On the city as cave, see Blumenberg, *Höhlenausgänge*, 76: 'The city is a repetition of the cave with other means. [...] it [is] the essence of artificiality'.
[52] Hyde, 'The Poetry of the City', 338.

CHAPTER 9

Brandenburg as a 'Spiritual Way of Life'?: Günter de Bruyn and the Appeal of Living 'off the Beaten Track'

Dennis Tate

At first glance Günter de Bruyn's literary work appears to be based on an exceptionally stable sense of place, arising from a lifetime spent in one part of Germany, involving regular movements between the complementary environments of the city of Berlin and the Brandenburg countryside. Since the beginning of a career stretching back to the late 1950s he has written a succession of topographically precise novels and autobiographical narratives that provide a strong visual impression of the places he has lived, within a world constricted first by the circumstances of a Third Reich childhood, then by his forty years as an adult in the German Democratic Republic. (It is also a world, it has to be stressed, whose horizons he has never sought to extend whenever the opportunity to do so has arisen.) Partly for this reason, partly also for the intimately informed way he has promoted the work of his literary forebear most associated with the same area, he is often seen as the Theodor Fontane of contemporary German literature. When he was awarded an honorary doctorate by the Humboldt University in Berlin in 1998, the centenary of Fontane's death, it was no surprise that he chose to speak about Fontane in his acceptance speech.[1] In the oration that celebrated de Bruyn's own achievements, Roland Berbig further underlined this idea of a shared sense of place:

> Günter de Bruyn's literary development is as unthinkable without Berlin as it is without the countryside that surrounds the city: the Brandenburg Marches [...]. Like his literary model Fontane, [de Bruyn] is torn between the city and its surrounding area, and like

---

[1] Günter de Bruyn, *Altersbetrachtungen über den alten Fontane: Festvortrag anläßlich der Verleihung der Doktorwürde* (Berlin: Humboldt-Universität, 1999), 25-36. Republished in de Bruyn, *Deutsche Zustände: Über Erinnerungen und Tatsachen, Heimat und Literatur* (Frankfurt a.M.: Fischer, 1999), 206-23. *Deutsche Zustände* is referred to in the following as DZ.

Fontane he draws his literary energies from this tension – with an
awareness of history, without false pathos, in friendship, but also
with that sense of critical irony which makes the story-teller de
Bruyn so irreplaceable to us.[2]

This biographical continuity makes de Bruyn's life appear very different to
those of many other contemporaries associated with the GDR, since their shared
generational turning-point of 1945 was not marked in his case by the enforced
upheaval from an Eastern European homeland and the psychological dislocation
that accompanied it. In contrast to authors such as Christa Wolf, Franz Fühmann
and Johannes Bobrowski, who ended up to a greater or lesser degree by chance on
the previously unknown territory of what was to become the GDR, de Bruyn was
able to return from military service to his childhood surroundings in the summer
of 1945.

From the perspective de Bruyn adopts in *Taking Stock: Growing Up in
Berlin* (*Zwischenbilanz. Eine Jugend in Berlin*, 1992) the autobiography he
published after German unification, his decision to remain in the Berlin area after
the GDR was established in 1949 was based on a mixture of emotional and
cultural rather than ideological reasons: to be with his widowed mother, living
initially with her in a summerhouse amidst the pine forests of the Brandenburg
countryside, to experience the cultural richness of the still open city of Berlin, and
not because of any deeper commitment to the GDR itself.[3] Returning in 1945 to a
'settlement of weekend houses off the beaten track' ('abseits gelegene
Wochenendsiedlung', Z 302) had evidently been an unproblematic 'homecoming'
('Heimkehr', Z 299) for him, while a 'double life' ('Doppelleben', Z 363) doubly
divided between the country and the city and between the eastern and western
sectors of Berlin was an unique opportunity to be seized. This image of
untroubled post-war continuity (albeit amidst the material deprivations of postwar
life in and around the former capital) seems poles apart from the self-imposed

---

[2] Roland Berbig, 'Laudatio', in de Bruyn, *Altersbetrachtungen*, 15-23 (here 21).
[3] Günter de Bruyn, *Zwischenbilanz. Eine Jugend in Berlin* (Frankfurt a.M.: Fischer, 1992), 297-
303 and 371-8. Referred to in the following as Z.

suffering experienced by an author like Franz Fühmann, who spent two decades desperately trying to suppress his longing for a childhood spent in a German-speaking area of Czechoslovakia that had become indelibly tainted because of its association with 'Sudeten German' fascism and to generate an alternative identity within the GDR, before acknowledging the impossibility of implementing an enforced *Heimatverbot* ('denial of his origins') of this kind.[4]

De Bruyn was born in 1926 on the southern edge of Berlin in Britz, just to the west of the dividing-line later created by the erection of the Berlin Wall. He experienced this rapidly growing suburb (part of the borough of Neukölln) as a self-contained urban village, a place that had managed to retain its 'village character' ('dörflichen Charakter') and was best known to outsiders for its wayside inn, the "Buschkrug", off the beaten track amongst the fields and meadows' ('abseits zwischen Feldern und Wiesen gelegene[n] Buschkrug', Z 24). His description of this sheltered environment blends neatly with his account of the determination of his self-sufficient Catholic family to protect him from the perils of fascist indoctrination at school and in youth organisations.[5] Although he was 'growing up in Berlin', as the subtitle of his first volume of autobiography indicates, his relationship with the cultural and social heart of the city in these years was that of an occasional visitor rather than a young man shaped by regular exposure to metropolitan life. His gradual separation from his roots resulting from the demands of paramilitary training and conscription to anti-aircraft duties only become an unmitigated reality when the family home was destroyed in an Allied bombing raid late in 1943. When he returned from the trauma of war service as a reluctant conscript he found his mother – as already indicated – living in the family's summerhouse near Königs Wusterhausen, an enforced move to an area

---

[4] See my article '*Böhme[n] am Meer*, "Bohemien mit Heimweh": Franz Fühmann's Competing Identities and his Tribute to *Tonio Kröger*', in Nigel Harris and Joanne Sayner (eds), *Festschrift for Ronald Speirs* (Oxford: Lang, 2008, forthcoming).

[5] This is at any rate the way de Bruyn constructs his childhood in *Taking Stock*. For a discussion of his changing self-presentation see my monograph *Shifting Perspectives: East German Autobiographical Narratives Before and After the End of the GDR* (Rochester NY: Camden House, 2007) esp. 178-83.

where she was to remain for the rest of her life, thus heightening the significance of the Brandenburg countryside for de Bruyn himself from this time onwards. He then found his first job as a temporary teacher at a village primary school to the west of Berlin, in the Havelland, before the cultural counter-attractions of the divided city became irresistible, starting his training as a librarian in the East as the GDR was created and embarking on his career as a writer just before the Berlin Wall went up.

The move from the southern suburbs of East Berlin to a flat in the proletarian heart of the old city as he became a professional author created the impression, which was to last for at least two decades, that he had now integrated fully there, thriving amidst the streets and buildings associated with Berlin's rise to cultural prominence in the late eighteenth century as he found his distinctive ironic voice as a writer of prose fiction. In an interview published in 1981 he responded forcefully to the question of whether he could imagine living away from the city:

> No, I am really bound to Berlin. It is a lively city. And I also always need a lot of local knowledge, a lot of historical background in order to feel at home in a city.

> Nein, mit Berlin bin ich wirklich verbunden. Es ist eine lebendige Stadt. Und ich brauche auch immer viel Kenntnisse, geschichtlichen Hintergrund, um in einer Stadt heimisch zu sein.[6]

Some of his readers might have had their doubts, even then, whether de Bruyn's attachment to his native city had remained as strong as he claimed in this interview. In his previous work of fiction, *Researches in the Brandenburg Marches* (*Märkische Forschungen*), published in 1979, his perspective on East Berlin had markedly changed. A notably distanced, if not alienated, narrator, was now depicting the city as the sphere of a complacent and corrupt GDR elite, a place that appealed superficially to his country-based protagonist Ernst Pötsch

---

[6] Karin Hirdina, 'Interview mit Günter de Bruyn', *Günter de Bruyn: Leben und Werk* (Berlin: Volk und Wissen, 1981), 7-26 (here 8).

until he realised that he would have to compromise himself intellectually to live there. The author offered no explanation of this apparent discrepancy until 2005, when his volume *Off the Beaten Track: A Declaration of Love to a Landscape* (*Abseits: Liebeserklärung an eine Landschaft*), was published, and even then there were important issues left unresolved.

In *Off the Beaten Track*, de Bruyn highlights the year 1968, just seven years after his move to the centre of East Berlin and more than two decades before the collapse of the GDR, as the turning-point in his post-war life. It was then, he tells us, that he discovered the dilapidated cottage in the hamlet of Blabber/Görsdorf in the Brandenburg countryside which he was able to purchase cheaply and then painstakingly renovate over many years. Once it was habitable, at some point in the 1980s, he began to spend more of his time there, gradually coming to see it, rather than his flat in Berlin, as his home. His accidental discovery of the cottage during a country walk is described here as an epiphany, the moment when he realized it would be possible to establish a safe haven, protecting his integrity within an increasingly alienating GDR without the emotional upheaval that the alternative of emigration to the Federal Republic would involve:

> The certainty I suddenly felt was one of knowing we belonged together. Here was the place that was meant for me. I had found it without having looked for it. And [...] it [provided] everything it seemed to promise in that first moment.

> Die Gewißheit, die ich da plötzlich spürte, war die des Zusammengehörens. Hier war der Ort, der für mich bestimmt war. Ich hatte ihn gefunden, ohne nach ihm gesucht zu haben. Und [...] er [hielt] alles, was er auf den ersten Blick zu versprechen schien.[7]

Almost four decades later, however, he was still finding it difficult to decide what this actually meant for his relationship with his native Berlin. In the account of his discovery of the cottage, what he welcomes is the prospect of

---

[7] Günter de Bruyn, *Abseits: Liebeserklärung an eine Landschaft* (Frankfurt a.M.: Fischer, 2005), 45. Referred to in the following as A.

deepening his links with Brandenburg without moving too far away from the familiar surroundings of the city, thereby keeping alive his longer-term hopes of achieving the bipolar sense of *Heimat* he had inherited from Fontane:

> This wilderness, not far from familiar Berlin, but still hard to reach, in a landscape that was no less familiar, became a refuge for me, an exile without any difficult changes, an escape without having to leave home.

> Diese nicht weit vom vertrauten Berlin entfernte, aber schwer erreichbare Einöde in einer nicht weniger vertrauten Landschaft konnte ein Asyl für mich werden, ein Exil ohne schwierigen Wechsel, eine Flucht ohne Heimatverlust. (A 47-8)

In his introduction to *Off the Beaten Track*, however, de Bruyn talks in terms of his 'choice of a new home' ('Wahl einer neuen Heimat'), of having broken his emotional and physical links with his 'original home' ('angestammte Heimat') in Berlin in favour of this new 'second home' ('zweite Heimat', A 8-9) in Brandenburg, indicating that this has become a more radical break than he originally imagined, but without shedding light on the intervening process of reorientation, which would be of obvious interest in relation to the notion of an evolving topography of identity. There are obvious conceptual echoes here of the earlier aspirations of adoptive GDR citizens like Fühmann to establish a new *Heimat*, whether on the Baltic coast, as depicted in his story 'Bohemia by the See' ('Böhmen am Meer'), or in the part of Brandenburg he was exploring in the footsteps of Fontane around the same time that de Bruyn was discovering his future home slightly further to the south.[8] In view of Fühmann's painful failure to make an emotional leap that GDR propaganda viewed as unproblematic it would be illuminating to gain some insight into the manner in which de Bruyn believes he has achieved his less dramatic shift of allegiance, and at what personal cost. De

---

[8] Franz Fühmann, 'Böhmen am Meer', in *Erzählungen 1955-1975* (Rostock: Hinstorff, 1977), 283-318 and *Das Ruppiner Tagebuch: Auf den Spuren Theodor Fontanes* (Rostock: Hinstorff, 2005). See also note 4 above.

Bruyn has, however, shown a marked reluctance to confront this issue, whether in *Off the Beaten Track* or his other post-unification writing.

Readers of the second volume of de Bruyn's autobiography, *Forty Years* (*Vierzig Jahre*, 1996), which, as its title indicates, covers his life during the GDR era, would have been aware of the author's discovery of his country retreat (described in detail in a chapter called 'Walden' in acknowledgement of Thoreau's idyll)[9] but would probably have assumed that this was a short-lived fantasy, in view of the self-mocking account that follows of his failure to turn himself into a self-sufficient smallholder. Apart from a passing reference to time spent in the 1970s 'in the woods' ('im Wald', V 202), the predominantly political emphasis of this part of his autobiography gives the impression that he remained essentially a city-dweller as he struggled against censorship and the State Security Police, at least until we are told about his 'ever shorter stays in Berlin' ('immer kürzer werdenden Berlin-Aufenthalte', V 258) during the GDR's final years. Although this is partly understandable in terms of the agreement he tells us he has reached with his partner to avoid any discussion of the private sphere of their relationship in his autobiography (V 115 and 129), it leaves the reader with no insight into the process of transition that is said to be complete by the time *Off the Beaten Track* is written.

The final chapter of *Forty Years*, describing the author's return to the streets and places of his childhood in West Berlin on the day after the opening of the Wall in November 1989, still suggests a link between past and present places, in the sense that Britz is still described – as it was at the beginning of *Taking Stock* – as being ' off the beaten track' ('abseits') away from the centre of the city, where the eyes of the world are focused (V 260), but this short journey is recalled as if it were an act of leave-taking rather than a belated opportunity to reconnect. As an author well-known for his encyclopedic understanding of the history of Berlin and his commitment to keeping alive the notion of the 'cultural nation'

---

[9] Gunter de Bruyn, *Vierzig Jahre. Ein Lebensbericht* (Frankfurt a.M.: Fischer, 1996), 148-59. Referred to in the following as V.

('Kulturnation') – now represented symbolically by the reunification of its old capital – de Bruyn might have been expected to be vigorously reasserting his identity as a Berliner. Why he remained reluctant to do so as the physical barriers dividing the city disappeared is another aspect of this problematic transition.

The speech that de Bruyn made some six months later, in the city of Lübeck, acknowledging the award of its prestigious Thomas Mann prize, exemplifies this unexpected ambivalence. The year of the fall of the GDR regime was in many respects an *annus mirabilis* for de Bruyn: his literary status was finally being recognized in the (old) Federal Republic as the GDR collapsed, and the Thomas Mann prize was only the first of three major awards he received in 1990, a process that was to continue through the 1990s, when he was widely regarded as an author with whom Germans right across the old divide could identify.[10] The title he chose for his acceptance speech in Lübeck was '*Germany* as a Spiritual Way of Life' ('*Deutschland* als geistige Lebensform', my emphasis).[11] In doing so he was evidently seeking to pay tribute to Thomas Mann's famous speech of 1926 marking his return to his home city for its seven-hundredth anniversary – 'Lübeck as a Spiritual Way of Life' ('Lübeck als geistige Lebensform') – while expressing his joy at the end of the era of German division. What is striking when his speech is reread outside the context of rapidly approaching unification is the fact that de Bruyn avoids drawing any comparison between Mann's homage to Lübeck and the importance of Berlin for his own identity as an author. He could have made a good deal of the parallel between the restoration of his links to Berlin as a whole, almost thirty years after the building of the Wall, and Mann's acknowledgement of the enduring impact of his upbringing in Lübeck in providing the moral and spiritual core of his creative

---

[10] The others included elevation to the Deutsche Akademie für Sprache und Dichtung (October 1990) and the Heinrich Böll prize (November 1990). For the wider process of public recognition see my article 'Günter de Bruyn: The "gesamtdeutsche Konsensfigur" of post-unification literature?', *German Life and Letters*, 50.2 (1997), 201-13.
[11] De Bruyn, 'Deutschland als geistige Lebensform', in *Jubelschreie, Trauergesänge: Deutsche Befindlichkeiten* (Frankfurt a.M.: Fischer, 1994), 143-57.

work over the similar period of his (self-imposed) exile. For Mann this festive occasion was an appropriate moment to emphasize an unexpectedly deep dimension of continuity:

> The day and the hour came when it became clear to me that the apple never falls far from the tree; that as an artist I was much more 'genuine', much more of an apple from Lübeck's tree, than I had supposed; [...] that my whole identity as an artist was [...] not some bohemian and rootless virtuosity, but rather a way of life, *Lübeck as a spiritual way of life*.

> Es kam der Tag und die Stunde, wo mir klar wurde, daß niemals der Apfel weit vom Stamme fällt; daß ich als Künstler viel 'echter', viel mehr ein Apfel vom Baume Lübecks war, als ich geahnt hatte; [...] daß es sich [...] bei meinem ganzen Künstlertum [...] nicht um irgendwelches bohemisierte und entwurzelte Virtuosentum, sondern um eine Lebensform, um *Lübeck als geistige Lebensform* handelte.[12]

This was the first opportunity he had been given since the local scandal caused by his all-too-revealing depiction of his native city in his novel *Buddenbrooks*, published in 1901, to comment in public there on its enduring importance. He admitted how surprised he had been that such a topographically precise novel as *Buddenbrooks* had struck such a powerful chord, not just across Germany but in contemporary Europe as a whole, making it 'at the same time a pan-German and a European book' ('zugleich ein überdeutsch-europäisches Buch'):

> One expresses the most personal of feelings and is surprised to discover one has struck a national chord. One expresses the most national of feelings – only to find one has struck a general and the most human of chords – and struck them much more surely than if one had programmatically set out to achieve an international impact.

> Man gibt das Persönlichste und ist überrascht, das Nationale getroffen zu haben. Man gibt das Nationalste – und siehe, man hat das Allgemeine und Menschlichste getroffen – mit viel mehr

---

[12] Thomas Mann, 'Lübeck als geistige Lebensform', in *Das essayistische Werk*, ed. by Hans Bürgin, 8 vols. (Frankfurt a.M.: Fischer, 1968), VIII: *Autobiographisches*, 177-94 (here 184).

Sicherheit getroffen, als wenn man sich den Internationalismus programmatisch vorgesetzt hätte.[13]

Readers of de Bruyn's work would not have been surprised that he used this quotation as he approached the climax of his speech.[14] He had previously defended the 'concreteness of place' ('Ortskonkretheit') in his own work against GDR critics who viewed it as too parochial, by aligning himself with Thomas Mann and other internationally respected authors: 'The great literature of our century – whether Thomas Mann, Kafka or the South Americans – is always very regionally concrete' ('Die große Literatur unseres Jahrhunderts – ob Thomas Mann, Kafka oder die Südamerikaner – ist immer regional sehr konkret').[15] On this occasion, however, he avoids any specification of what is ' most personal' ('das Persönlichste') in his own work or any consideration of whether the reuniting of the two halves of Berlin had confirmed its importance to him as a 'spiritual way of life'. For the purposes of his speech he seems intent on omitting the local dimension of his identity in order to place his emphasis on the continuing vitality of the idea of the 'cultural nation' and on the European context in which the humanistic values associated with Thomas Mann can now be realized. The reasons for his avoidance of any topographical self-definition are not clarified here. Perhaps the very thought of comparing his own career with that of his illustrious predecessor under these circumstances would have seemed inappropriate to a genuinely modest author. From the new perspective opened up by *Off the Beaten Track*, however, it appears more likely that the obvious comparison no longer applied.

When we go a step further and reread de Bruyn's earlier works in the light of the decisive shift of allegiance described in *Off the Beaten Track*, the impression that he had maintained a Fontane-like balance between the spheres of Berlin and Brandenburg in his earlier GDR years also proves ill-founded. There

---

[13] Mann, 'Lübeck als geistige Lebensform', 183.
[14] Cf. de Bruyn, 'Deutschland als geistige Lebensform', 155.
[15] Hirdina, 'Interview mit Günter de Bruyn', 17.

too we find a tendency to fluctuate uncertainly between these two environments as his fictional protagonists seek to stabilise their identity in the exceptionally unstable surroundings of divided Germany. This process can be exemplified with reference to three prose works that span his career up to the 1980s, *The Ravine* (*Der Hohlweg*, 1963), *Buridan's Ass* (*Buridans Esel*, 1968) and *Researches in the Brandenburg Marches* (1979).

In the first of these texts, *The Ravine*, the semi-autobiographical novel of education, which the author has long viewed as fatally flawed by the concessions he made to ideological expectations of a conciliatory ending, his postwar feeling of being torn between the disorientating diversity of city life and the promise of integration into a protective rural community provides the tension around which the novel is structured. His protagonist Weichmantel is increasingly drawn to the village where some of his closest friends of the war years have settled and where he immediately feels 'as if he had returned home a second time' ('als wäre er selbst noch einmal heimgekehrt').[16] For his oldest friend Eckart, however, who has himself rapidly reintegrated into metropolitan life, the idea of a 'retreat into this puffed-up provinciality' ('Rückzug in diese aufgeblasene Abseitigkeit', H 499) is incomprehensible, yet the appeal of a small community that offers him a new beginning as a teacher in the village school is ultimately stronger. The revised account of the same period in his life provided thirty years later in *Taking Stock* depicts the Havel community as a backwater to which he is consigned by a bureaucrat as punishment for displaying intellectual independence, a cosmopolitan trait which, he is told, in a telling reversal of his original image, 'will only get you stuck out here off the beaten track' ('nur ins Abseits führ[t]' (Z 325). The fact that the original construction of life in a country community was produced in support of state propaganda raises concerns that the later celebration of a successful retreat into another rural backwater might again derive from an

---

[16] Günter de Bruyn, *Der Hohlweg* (Halle: Mitteldeutscher Verlag, 1963), 356. Referred to in the following as H.

unacknowledged need to resolve a complex city-country tension in an over-simplified way in one direction or the other.

De Bruyn's second work, *Buridan's Ass*, is in contrast to *The Ravine* not just his best piece of fiction but also one of the few successful 'Berlin novels' of the GDR era. Here we find a protagonist, the ironically depicted Karl Erp, moving in the other direction, from a childhood in the Brandenburg countryside to a post-war career as librarian in East Berlin that broadly reflects the same period in de Bruyn's own life. The alternative life-styles open to Erp in the 1960s when his midlife crisis strikes him are now conditioned by this move to the city: an affluent existence as a member of the GDR's new social elite, living with his wife and family in a suburban villa, or a radical switch to a shabby tenement in the old city-centre in pursuit of a fulfilling new relationship with his young library colleague Fräulein Broder. Erp fails miserably to rise to a challenge similar to the one that was to transform de Bruyn's life in the same decade, even though he initially seems just as fully committed to the city-centre as his creator in terms of his precise topographical awareness and sense of its political and cultural history. De Bruyn's loving depiction of this new world opening up for Erp suggests that it is an island of human vitality cut off from the changes that are threatening the rest of East Berlin in the GDR era, a place where 'the new order' ('die neue Ordnung') has so far been kept at bay: 'there the chaos and the lawlessness of the officially long-gone postwar era still reigned' ('dort herrschten noch immer das Chaos und die Gesetzlosigkeit der offiziell längst erledigten Nachkriegszeit').[17] And although de Bruyn guards against portraying this potential 'spiritual way of life' as a long-term solution – reminding his readers regularly of the physical grimness of Fräulein Broder's environment ('the stink, the crumbling plaster, the din of the pigeons, the sound of the television next door, Frau Wolff's chit-chat, the desert of stones'; 'den Gestank, den bröckelnden Putz, das Gurren der Tauben, die Fernsehunterhaltung von nebenan, die schwatzende Frau Wolff, die Steinwüste',

---

[17] De Bruyn, *Buridans Esel* (Munich: dtv, 1971), 37. Referred to in the following as B.

B 188) – the lovers' discussions about escaping from the city to the outer darkness of a provincial library in Angermünde on the Polish border are recounted so satirically that they are never intended to represent a serious alternative. The dream of 'finding happiness in a quiet little corner of the world' ('Glück [...] im stillen Winkel', B 150) is seen as having died out with Erp's father, while Erp's regular Sunday trips to remote corners of Brandenburg serve purely to extend his cultural knowledge of Berlin's hinterland.

A decade later, with the publication of *Researches in the Brandenburg Marches*, de Bruyn's depiction of the place in which a fulfilled life might be achievable has decisively changed, for reasons that are never explained in the text. In the present-day of the 1970s, the centre of Berlin has ceased to exist as an environment offering the prospect of self-fulfilment to a much younger protagonist, Ernst Pötsch, who is tempted to follow in Erp's footsteps by abandoning his native Brandenburg countryside in pursuit of a professional career. No attempt is ever made to describe the 'two-room apartment in the city centre' ('Zweizimmerwohnung in der Innenstadt') on offer to Pötsch and his wife in exchange for giving up the struggle to maintain the large country house with 'two acres of garden, two pigsties in the process of falling down, a barn that had already fallen down, a dog, two cats and 13 hens' ('zwei Morgen Garten, zwei im Verfall begriffene Ställe, eine bereits verfallene Scheune, ein Hund, zwei Katzen und 13 Hühner),[18] which he has inherited from his father and in which his entire extended family currently lives. One of the pleasures of rereading *Researches in the Brandenburg Marches,* in the light of de Bruyn's account in *Off the Beaten Track* of his discovery of his current home, is to savour the self-mocking exaggerations in his earlier fictionalization of what is essentially the same property. It is no surprise that the featureless urban alternative to this distinctively shambolic home environment never develops into a serious proposition.

---

[18] Günter de Bruyn, *Märkische Forschungen* (Frankfurt a.M.: Fischer, 1981), 43-4. Referred to in the following as M.

The city centre of Berlin continues to exist as the location of the workplace of the other main characters in the story, the satirically conceived *Central Institute for Historiography and Historiomathy* (*Zentralinstitut für Historiographie und Historiomathie*, or *ZiHiHi* for short), which offers Pötsch his only chance of an academic career. Yet it is no longer, in any sense of the phrase, a living environment. The competing 'spiritual ways of life' now consist of his run-down country house and the exclusive estate of well-appointed villas (again in the southern suburbs of Berlin where Erp's villa was located), where his antagonist, the career historian Professor Winfried Menzel, lives. In the former, as embodied by Pötsch, the cultural heritage of the area is honestly explored with old-fashioned thoroughness, while in Menzel's environment historical facts are cynically manipulated and distorted to serve the interests of state propaganda. The contrast has now taken on a polemical directness in response to what can now be seen as de Bruyn's final alienation from the GDR, although still with the implication that the counter-attractions of the city have only been tainted temporarily by the corrupt presence of the SED hierarchy.

Even though Pötsch's prospects of achieving self-fulfilment may appear brighter than those of Weichmantel und Erp in the earlier novels, since he has always been in the right enviroment and has not suffered any prolonged agonies of choice between the available alternatives, he is prevented in other ways from flourishing 'in the woods' ('im Walde', M 8) – the term used in the title of the first chapter – or what Menzel later refers to dismissively as his 'village' ('Dorf', M 140). Not only has he been conceived on one level as a comic figure; his GDR environment of the 1970s is also a more threatening one than those depicted in the earlier works. As shown by the bleak closing image of Pötsch searching obsessively on a rubbish tip for the engraved brick that will confirm his version of the historical facts, there is no chance, as long as the GDR continues to exist, of him overturning one of the revolutionary myths on which the legitimacy of the state (and Menzel's academic reputation) is based.

The question of whether de Bruyn's alienation from Berlin would be overcome after the reunification of the city was not to be resolved until well after his ambivalent Lübeck speech of May 1990. In the course of the following decade it gradually became clear that this alienation was not just politically determined. In de Bruyn's many speeches and essays about the unification process there are frequent references to his native city, yet the comments tend to relate to its symbolic status as the focal point of national change rather than to his concerns as a Berliner seriously re-engaging with his home environment. A representative example of this unchangingly distanced relationship is his essay of 1999, 'Berlin as an Example' ('Berlin als Beispiel', DZ 86-99). Here he makes the point that Berlin is 'representative of the nation' ('stellvertretend für die Nation') in its tradition of welcoming immigrants fleeing persecution, in the 'east-west diversity' ('ost-westliche Vielfalt') of its population and in the speed of its post-unification transformation. He does now use the term 'way of life' in connection with the city, but in the plural, as part of a disappointingly generalized statement that it has always been easy to acquire an identity as one of its citizens:

> Here people have always been used to living with new arrivals, and because they always quickly felt at home in this ever growing and changing city, it was always easy to become a Berliner. Not having been born in Berlin never meant that you would not be seen as a Berliner.

> Man war hier also immer gewohnt, mit Zugereisten zu leben, und da diese in der stets wachsenden und sich wandelnden Stadt mit ihrer Vielfalt von Lebensformen schnell heimisch wurden, war es immer leicht, zum Berliner zu werden. Nicht in Berlin geboren zu werden, bedeutete nie, nicht als Berliner angesehen zu werden. (DZ 86-8)

Moreover, the mood of the essay changes markedly when the focus switches from praise for Berlin's historical openness to change and diversity to an assessment of how the city has changed since 1945. The relationship between 'new beginnings' ('Aufbruch') and 'demolition' ('Abbruch'), as encapsulated by processes of architectural change, is viewed increasingly negatively. His examples are taken predominantly from the East of the city during the GDR era: the ideologically enforced demolition of the ruins of the royal palace of the Hohenzollerns and the creation of the Stalinallee (referred to by its original, historically tainted name) in the early years; the 'greyness' ('Trostlosigkeit') of the Alexanderplatz and the insensitive building of the television tower alongside the Marienkirche as legacies of the 1960s; the 'concrete pseudo-cosiness of the Nikolai Quarter' ('betonierte Pseudogemütlichkeit des Nikolaiviertels') as a typical product of the Honecker era, and so on. He suggests that West Berlin fared little better, but refrains from giving examples of 'town planning concepts that left a lot to be desired' ('städtebauliche Gesamtkonzepte [, die] viel zu wünschen übrig ließen') on that side of the post-war divide (DZ 94-6). More revealing is his view that the reconstruction of Berlin as the capital of united Germany has so far done little to regenerate an historically based sense of metropolitan identity. The new Potsdamer Platz is a missed opportunity, 'more showy than beautiful' ('mehr protzig als schön', DZ 96), and people still tend to think locally, in terms of their 'love of their neighbourhood' ('Liebe zum Kiez'), rather than acknowledging their 'responsibility for the whole' ('Verantwortlichkeit für das Ganze', DZ 99). Only in the final sentence does he identify himself as a native Berliner and mention his pleasure (although speaking of himself in the third person) at seeing the city reunited, but only in the strangely impersonal terms of being able to travel freely again:

> the joy [...] that Zehlendorf and Kleinmachnow are now close to each other again and that he can use the underground station under the Friedrichstrasse, which for 28 years he could only hear and feel under the soles of his shoes.

> die Freude [...,] daß Zehlendorf und Kleinmachnow nun wieder dicht beieinander liegen und er die U-Bahn unter der Friedrichstraße, die er 28 Jahre lang nur hören und unter den Sohlen spüren konnte, wieder benutzen kann. (DZ 99)

Although de Bruyn was still prepared in this essay to express a degree of optimism that a sense of responsibility for the city as a whole would gradually re-emerge, his mood had become noticeably darker just two years later, in the long essay he wrote to mark his seventy-fifth birthday, with the unexpectedly Nietzschean title 'Untimely Observations' ('Unzeitgemäßes'). He now talks about his 'growing alienation' ('wachsende Fremdheit') in relation to contemporary German society in general and the capital in particular.[19] The endless debates about Berlin's monuments around the millennium have culminated in the banality of the Hans Haake's 'bucket of flowers' ('Pflanzenkübel') in front of the Reichstag with its politically correct neon-lit dedication 'to the population' ('der Bevölkerung') and in the anticipated 'concrete wilderness' ('Betonödnis') of the Holocaust Memorial.[20] He is no longer willing to conceal his anger at the failure of successive post-unification governments and the citizens of Berlin to build on its classical traditions as they shape its future. While continuing to pay his own intimately informed tributes to the city's history and culture in volumes such as *Unter den Linden* (2002) and *Good Enough for Poetry: Lives of Berlin Artists 1786 to 1807* (*Als Poesie gut: Schicksale aus Berlins Kunstepoche 1786 bis 1807*, 2006) he now evidently finds little to satisfy his conservative expectations of continuity in the increasingly globalized Berlin of the early twenty-first century.

Only with the publication of *Off the Beaten Track* in 2005 does it become clear that he has definitively abandoned his 'original home' in favour of his new adoptive home in Brandenburg. Although he initially seems to suggest that he has paid a high price for this switch of allegiance, in terms of losing his connection with the 'paradise of my childhood' ('Paradies der Kindheit') in Berlin, he immediately sees the possibility of compensating for this through 'living my way into the collective memory of my new surroundings' ('ein Einleben in das kollektive Erinnern der neuen Umgebung', A 8-9). The key to this act of creative

---

[19] Günter de Bruyn, *Unzeitgemäßes: Betrachtungen über Vergangenheit und Gegenwart* (Frankfurt a.M.: Fischer, 2001), 7.
[20] *Unzeitgemäßes*, 14-15 and 23. The artwork by Hans Haake that de Bruyn refers to here is a flower bed in which members of parliament were invited to tip earth from their constituencies: the seeds contained in the earth were then allowed to grow. The dedication is a play on the motto 'To the German people' ('Dem deutschen Volke'), which adorns the Reichstag building.

empathy is his reconstruction of the history of the family who owned his new
home between the 1920s and the 1960s, the Bahrs, with the help of a collection of
letters, photos and other documents he discovered in the attic after moving in (A
167-77). He identifies particularly with their son, Rudi Bahr, a near-contemporary
who suffered the fate that de Bruyn himself narrowly avoided, of being killed on
military service during the war. Despite the fundamental differences between their
social backgrounds and intellectual sensitivities they have enough shared
experience as children growing up in the Third Reich for de Bruyn to turn Rudi
Bahr into an *alter ego* with a past capable of replacing the one in Berlin that he
has now abandoned. This reconstructed biography stands at the heart of the
community history pieced together by de Bruyn with the help of surviving school
and church chronicles from the 1930s and 1940s. It allows him to 'individualize'
it[21] and thus merge it with those parts of his own post-1945 life he has spent in the
area in order to lay claim to the unipolar sense of place that is now so important to
him.

Two particular conclusions emerge from this examination of the work of
an author whose life-pattern initially suggested that a complementary and
fulfilling city-country relationship was achievable. Firstly, the idea of thriving on
the productive tensions of a life divided between Berlin and the Brandenburg
countryside has proved unsustainable in practice. For de Bruyn there has always
been a choice to be made between these two competing environments, a dilemma
around which he has structured his major works of fiction and autobiography and
which he has resolved in different ways at different periods in his life. The issue
he has avoided confronting is that of his relationship with Berlin since the late
1970s: the impression that he was alienated by the GDR's cultural and
architectural disfigurement of East Berlin and would thus be able to reassert his
urban identity after the fall of the Wall has proved to be misleading. The
combination of factors that have hindered his reintegration other than at the level

---

[21] 'In [Rudi Bahr] recent local history becomes individualized' ('In [Rudi Bahr] individualisiert
sich jüngere Heimatgeschichte', A 80).

of celebrating the cultural achievements of earlier eras includes a conservative distaste for the post-modernist innovations that have, for many other Berliners, signalled the city's recent breakthrough to international distinctiveness.

Secondly, it would be just as much of an over-simplification to take the recurrence in his work of the motif of living 'off the beaten track' as an indicator of a long-term preference for rural tranquillity and small country communities. As we have seen, de Bruyn has at different times in his life associated the idea of a fulfilling existence with the contrasting city settings of suburban Britz and proletarian Berlin-Mitte as well as with the dilapidated cottage hidden away amidst the pine forests of Brandenburg that he celebrates in his 'declaration of love to a landscape' of 2005. This is, on closer inspection, not a sense of community based on a particular place, adopted or otherwise, but rather the indicator of an environment in which he feels able to develop his individuality at a distance from otherwise ubiquitous social pressures to conform and compromise. Apart from his evident closeness to the small circle of family and friends whose privacy he is always intent on protecting, the strongest sense of community that de Bruyn acknowledges is in relation to the authors of previous generations whose work is integral to his creative identity. Locating himself 'off the beaten track' evidently satisfies a general emotional need in de Bruyn to assert his continuing status as an outsider while the different environments in which he has lived undergo one fundamental change after another. This makes the relationship between identity and place in his work as a whole just as complex as that found in contemporaries whose biographies have been more obviously fractured by external circumstances. By giving his new volume the title *Off the Beaten Track* and attempting there to link together the independence of the outsider and integration into a rural environment in an artificially restricted way – even though this is only one aspect of an absorbing piece of local history – he has ended up replacing one biographical myth with another.

CHAPTER 10

In Dialogue with the City:
Gert Neumann's Leipzig

David Clarke

Nearly two decades after German unification, the east German author Gert Neumann remains something of an insider tip: a figure who, despite being championed by the likes of Martin Walser and the well-known Berlin Professor of German literature Frank Hörnigk, has remained marginalized in the contemporary literary scene.[1] Whilst his implacable opposition both to official literary aesthetics in the GDR and what he calls the 'critical' writing of many of his contemporaries left him unpublishable in East Germany outside the literary underground, the inherent difficulty of his texts has proved unpalatable to the post-unification public. Whilst his status as a dissident perhaps assisted him in being taken up by the West German Fischer publishing house in the 1980s, alongside fellow Leipzig writers Wolfgang Hilbig and Wolfgang Hegewald, his output was confined to small presses and bibliophile editions during the 1990s, the only exception to this being his most recent novel *Attack* (*Anschlag*), published by Dumont in 1999.[2] Neumann's career has been characterized by a single-minded pursuit of his own aesthetic in the face of state oppression and, following unification, public indifference.[3] Even before unification, however, he was more than aware that the

---

[1] See Martin Walser, 'Geist und Sinnlichkeit: Gert Neumanns deutsch-deutsches Gespräch', in Gert Neumann, *Verhaftet: Dresdner Poetikvorlesung 1998* (Dresden: Thelem, 1999), 93-5; Frank Hörnigk, 'My Friend Gert Neumann', trans. Sarah B. Young, in Jost Hermand and Marc Silberman (eds.), *Contentious Memories: Looking Back at the GDR* (New York: Peter Lang, 1998), 1-3.

[2] For a full bibliography of Neumann's works until the turn of the millennium, see Walter Schmitz, 'Gert Neumann: Bibliographie', in Neumann, *Verhaftet*, 133-46.

[3] As Hörnigk reports, Neumann has continued to work at a number of jobs, for example as a metal-worker and bookseller, in order to be able to continue writing. Neumann details some of these experiences in his Dresden lectures of 1998. Hörnigk, 'My Friend Gert Neumann'. Neumann, *Verhaftet*.

challenge of his texts was unlikely to be taken up by a society in which literary discourse itself is increasingly sidelined by mass media.[4]

The focus of this chapter, in keeping with the theme of this volume, will be an exploration of Neumann's aesthetics that takes particular account of the role of place, and in particular of the role of the city of Leipzig, where Neumann lived from 1967 until 1988. Having originally come to the city to study at the 'Johannes R. Becher Institute for Literature', the officially sponsored writers academy of the GDR founded in 1954, Neumann remained in Leipzig following his politically-motivated exmatriculation from the Institute along with his wife Heidemarie Härtl and several of his friends in 1969.[5] He became a significant figure in the local underground literary scene, taking part in the now near-legendary 'motorboat reading' on the Muggelsee in 1969 and becoming closely involved in the publication of the underground literary magazines *Attack* (*Anschlag*) and *Second Person* (*Zweite Person*) in the 1980s.[6] The texts that Neumann wrote about everyday life in Leipzig, however, reflect relatively little of this existence in countercultural literary and artistic circles. Instead, alongside numerous shorter texts published in various periodicals, the novels *11 O'Clock* (*Elf Uhr*, 1981) and *The Clandestinity of the Boiler Cleaners* (*Die Klandestinität der Kesselreiniger*, 1989), which could both originally only be published in West Germany, detail Neumann's experience of working in the city as a manual labourer, whilst at the same time trying to find spare moments to write. This dual theme of working in the city and writing in the city is most central to the former text, which will be my main focus here.

Eleven O'Clock is, despite announcing itself as a novel, generically uncategorizable, being partly a diary, and therefore autobiographical, partly a

---

[4] Egmont Hesse, 'Gespräch mit Gert Neumann', *Frankfurter Rundschau*, 98.2 (1987), 5-20 (here 13).

[5] For further details see David Clarke, 'Parteischule oder Dichterschmiede? The Institut für Literatur "Johannes R. Becher" from Its Founding to Its *Abwicklung*', *German Studies Review*, 29.1 (2006), 87-106.

[6] On the Muggelsee reading, see Uta Grundmann, Klaus Michael and Susanna Seufert, *Revolution im geschlossenen Raum: Die andere Kultur in Leipzig 1970-1990* (Leipzig: Faber & Faber, 2002), 107

treatise on poetics, partly a putting into practice of that poetics, and partly also a commentary on the day-to-day realities of work and social life in Leipzig in the late 1970s. The diary element, which structures the text into individual dated entries between 24 February 1977 and 27 February 1978, also contains many references to and quotations from sources as diverse as the philosophers Martin Buber, Ludwig Wittgenstein and Jakob Böhme, and writers such as Boris Pasternak, Stephane Mallarmé and Novalis, very often motivated by the author's current reading on the day in question. In this way, *Eleven O'Clock* does not just explore the relationship between working in the city and writing about it, but also considers the further dimension of the city as an environment in which literature is consumed, for example on park benches and in trams. The particular significance of the time given in the title is the narrator's search for a few moments' peace and quiet in a place where he can write during his break at eleven o'clock each day. The text that he is working on is the novel *Eleven O'Clock* itself, so that the work furthermore functions as a commentary on its own genesis, which is often impeded by unwanted interruptions from the city going about its business around the writer. This does not imply, however, that the writer is primarily seeking a refuge from the city around him. Instead, the encounter with the city becomes, as I will argue here, a central element of the poetics that the novel develops. Nevertheless, as I will also demonstrate, the clear and specific locatedness of the writing process and the events described in the text does not imply in Neumann's case an attempt to discover or define the identity of place. Rather, the city provides the raw material for a poetics which refuses any such fixed meaning, whether of place or the text produced in and about it.

This poetics is, in the context of the GDR, highly politicized, in that it sets itself against the particular forms taken by state ideology and critiques the relationship between that ideology and the reality it claims to describe. That claim to describe reality is, in Neumann's view, the means by which the regime seeks to dominate society, so that the issue of language and its adequacy or otherwise to lived experience becomes a central concern. For the author, state socialism has become a 'textual fossil' ('Textfossil')[7] that seeks a total occupation of the world of experience, or the 'landscape' ('Landschaft') as Neumann sometimes terms it (e.g. K 14). In this respect, Neumann's critique of ideology is a critique of language: he accuses ideology of seeking to create an all-encompassing description of the world, or a *Realität* in Neumann's terms, that suppresses what the author describes as *Wirklichkeit*.

This distinction, which is already not automatically clear in German, is difficult to express in English, due to the fact that the two terms are both normally translated as 'reality'. In German, *Realität* is a word borrowed from the French (*réalité*) and relates to the adjective *real*, meaning real or actual. One can speculate that Neumann chose this word for his negative term on account of a number of its associations and connotations. In the political sphere, one thinks of Bismarck's *Realpolitik*, the politics of power, but perhaps more pertinently of the phrase 'real existierender Sozialismus' (really existing socialism), the official term used by the ruling SED (Sozialistische Einheitspartei Deutschland or Socialist Unity Party) to describe the social formation allegedly achieved by the GDR on its way to full communism. This ideological manoeuvre, which also provides an example of the replacement of reality with rhetoric that Neumann is attacking, was in part an explanation for failure of the GDR and the rest of the socialist world to make more rapid progress towards a genuine state of communism, in which the state would necessarily wither away, but also implied that the population was required to accept this situation indefinitely. Whatever is *real* implicitly has to be recognized as the given and unavoidable state of affairs, as in the similar English usage of 'having to face reality' (in German: *die Realität erkennen müssen*). *Wirklichkeit*, however, is not just what really exists, that is what is *wirklich*, but also that which has an effect (*wirken*), a distinction that will be important in terms of Neumann's usage of the term.

---

[7] Gert Neumann, *Die Klandestinität der Kesselreiniger: Ein Versuch des Sprechens* (Frankfurt a.M.: Fischer, 1989), 14. Referred to in the following as K.

This distinction between the *Realität* that Neumann rejects and the *Wirklichkeit* that is at the centre of his literary project can be perhaps best understood in the context of his critique of other GDR authors. *Realität*, as I have already shown, is synonymous for Neumann with the ideology of the East German regime as a static 'interpretation of the world' ('Interpretation der Welt', E 29), but is equally regarded as the product of any 'realism' that produces a 'static text of static signs' ('statischen Text aus statischen Zeichen', E 354). Yet it is not just the regime that is guilty in this respect: Neumann is critical of other GDR authors such as Rainer Kunze and Erich Loest, since their work, with its claims to authenticity, produces a realism that lacks that quality of literariness or 'poetry' ('Poesie') that he claims for his own writing. The function of literature, Neumann states, is not to represent the real, but rather 'to order the material of life according to poetic laws' ('das Material des Lebens nach poetischen Gesetzen zu ordnen', E 117). Rejecting the notion of literature as 'a documentation' ('eine Dokumentation', E 145), Neumann argues that the GDR regime and its 'oppositional' literature in fact complement each other, in that they rely on a notion of a coherent *Realität* that, whilst it is the object of a struggle for power in terms of its definition, binds them together: 'the well known oppositional writers and the dictatorship require a consensus about reality. Art is precluded' ('renommierte Opposition und Diktatur benötigen eine Übereinkunft auf die Realität. Kunst is ausgeschlossen', E 289).[8] For Neumann, the conflict between regime and certain oppositional writers is basically a matter of who controls this static description of the world, which is in itself 'a crime against the dignity of humanity' ('ein Verbrechen an der Würde des Menschen', E 354). Unsurprisingly, perhaps, Neumann cites the French philosopher Michel Foucault in this context, whose theory of discourse is founded on the notion that the act of describing society is also to a large extent an attempt to impose control upon it (E 30). Literary language nevertheless holds the key to a liberating *Wirklichkeit*. Instead of offering a closed and coherent world-view through language, which

---

[8] See also his similar comments in *Die Klandestinität der Kesselreiniger* (K 80).

demands of the subject that she accept this world-view as a framework for her own experience, Neumann proposes *Wirklichkeit* as 'a form of resistance' ('eine Form des Widerstands', E 64) that exploits rather than forecloses the true possibilities of 'poetry'.

It is worth stressing here that Neumann is not, like the oppositional authors he criticizes, attempting to pit his version of *Realität* against that imposed by state ideology; he is not offering a coherent alternative world-view that differs only in its content from that of the SED. This claim is initially relativized in the novel *Eleven O'Clock* by the quite extensive descriptions of everyday life under state socialism that are even more radical in their criticism than the observations of more conventionally critical writers. The cynicism of the workers when faced with official ideology and their forced attendance at official events such as the 'School of Socialist Work' ('Schule der sozialistischen Arbeit') or the 1 May parade, the inhumanity of the prison GDR system, the failings of educational institutions, the suspicions raised by the generally acknowledged presence of state security police informants in the workplace and in social life, the censorship of texts such as Rudolf Bahro's *The Alternative* (*Die Alternative*, 1977), the dehumanizing effects of an economy of shortage, the laziness and apathy of Neumann's colleagues: all of these 'realities' are presented in the plainest fashion, thereby of course guaranteeing that *Eleven O'clock* would not find a publisher in the GDR. However, these observations are for the most part by-products of Neumann's description of his struggle to move beyond a literature of 'opposition' which relies on the documenting of such social problems and towards a literature which produces a 'positive resistance to the ruling consensus about reality' ('positiven Widerstand gegen den herrschenden Realitätspakt', E 302). His observations of GDR life reflect the social conditions under which he struggles to work both as a manual labourer and as a writer, but he does not believe that their representation alone is enough to produce a true literature of resistance. Neumann's *Wirklichkeit* is that which is excluded from state ideology, but not simply on the level of content: it is what lies beyond the static language of the state and the 'oppositional' realism of other critical GDR authors; it is what Neumann enigmatically refers to as 'Absence' ('Abwesenheit', e.g. E 53).

As the narrator of Neumann's short story 'Necessary' ('Notwendig') recognizes, the relationship between language and the world is a fraught one, in that words become detached from the objects they supposedly describe. Not only this, but the order created by language supplants the world it is supposed to represent until 'words are really taken for things' ('die Wörter wirklich für die Dinge gehalten werden').[9] According to Neumann, the 'language of things' ('Sprache der Dinge') itself cannot be brought into the *Realität* of static realist language without being destroyed (S 114). For this reason, Neumann very often refers to this 'language of things' in terms of a 'silence' ('Schweigen') or as 'the voice of silence' ('die Stimme des Schweigens'), but this emphasis on that which lies outside of the limits of expression in the conventional sense does not mean, as Colin B. Grant has claimed, that 'a logical adherence to [Neumann's] poetics would condemn him to silence'.[10] Rather, this rejection of the static language of ideology and of critical realist literature leads to the search for a form of writing which makes this silence speak whilst avoiding the trap of formulating a new non-dynamic description of the world.

As Michael Thulin observes, this concern for the difference between language and the world it claims to describe, informed by an awareness of the relationship between language and power, was a significant feature of underground literature in the GDR in the 1980s, particularly in relation to the

---

[9] Gert Neumann, *Die Schuld der Wörter* (Rostock: Hinstorff, 1989), 114. Referred to in the following as S.

[10] Colin B. Grant, 'Beyond the Guilt of Words? On Gert Neumann's Poetics and the *Wende*', in Stuart Parkes and Arthur Williams (eds.), *The Individual, Identity and Innovation* (Frankfurt a.M.: Peter Lang, 1994), 221-31 (here 229). Grant may be referring to Neumann's observation, in his interview with Hesse, that the censorship of his literature in the GDR means that his work cannot reach 'the people of praxis' ('die Menschen der Praxis') for whom it is conceived. This does not, however, amount to a loss of faith in the power of literary language *per se*. See Hesse, 'Gespräch mit Gert Neumann', 13.

younger poets of the Prenzlauer Berg,[11] for whom, as Peter Böthig argues, the 'totalitarian centralism in the GDR manifested itself [...] in language. Much more than in pluralistic societies, power was a discursive structure, which consisted to a great extent of mere rhetoric'.[12] Indeed, Neumann and his associate Wolfgang Hilbig have been credited as the forerunners of this later movement.[13] However, one should be careful not to equate Neumann's poetics with that of this (actually itself quite diverse) group of younger writers. Despite their shared scepticism in relation to language as an instrument of oppressive ideology, Neumann does not, like many of his younger colleagues, retreat into an entirely self-referential language. Instead, Neumann's work remains committed to an engagement with everyday reality in search of the traces of that mysteriously absent *Wirklichkeit* that would break the bounds of ideological *Realität*. There are certainly congruencies between Neumann's formulation of this theme, at least in terms of terminology, and that proposed by Hilbig. For Hilbig, too, the GDR state creates a 'superficial speech' ('oberflächliche Rede') that spreads itself 'like a viscous film over the real silence' ('wie ein dickflüssiger Film über das eigentliche Schweigen') and serves to impose the 'ideas of the administration' ('Ideen der Verwaltung') on the world.[14] According to Hilbig the text created by ideology can only be opposed by the creation of a new 'identity in writing' ('Identität in der Schrift'), as the writing subject slips into 'invented roles' ('erdachte Rollen'),[15] which are ultimately as much linguistic constructs as the identity offered to him by ideology.

---

[11] Michael Thulin, 'Sprache und Sprachkritik: Die Literatur des Prenzlauer Bergs in Berlin/DDR', in Heinz Ludwig Arnold (ed.), *Text+Kritik: Sonderband: Die andere Sprache: Neue DDR-Literatur der 80er Jahre* (Munich: Text + Kritik, 1990), 234-42 (here 235).

[12] Peter Böthig, *Grammatik einer Landschaft: Literatur aus der DDR in den 80er Jahren* (Berlin: Lukas, 1997), 143.

[13] See, for example, Ekkehard Mann, *Untergrund, autonome Kunst und das Ende der DDR* (Frankfurt a.M.: Peter Lang, 1996), 141. David Bathrick has described Neumann as a 'paradigm for the Prenzlauer Berg'. Bathrick, *The Powers of Speech: The Politics of Culture in the GDR* (Lincoln: U of Nebraska P, 1995), 238.

[14] Wolfgang Hilbig, *Zwischen den Paradiesen: Prosa und Lyrik* (Leipzig: Reclam, 1992), 171.

[15] Hilbig, *Zwischen den Paradiesen*, 178.

Neumann's approach to this problematic is more optimistic than Hilbig's in terms of moving beyond the false language of *Realität* in order, paradoxically, to make 'absent' the realm of 'silence' speak. Nevertheless, his optimism and commitment to the power of literary language is frequently tempered by the frustrated recognition that, more often than not, the writer is forced to participate in that struggle for the right to describe *Realitäten* which he sees as incommensurable with true 'poetry'. In order to defend himself against the interference of the regime, the author is often forced to respond to SED bureaucrats in their own terms, playing them at their own language game in order to further his immediate interests, whether protesting at the confiscation of a manuscript at the GDR border or the refusal of an East German publishing house to print his manuscripts. Sometimes, the author speaks to officials of the regime on behalf of others or helps them to formulate a tactical response to the language of the state, for example when he recounts helping colleagues who are being harassed by officials. In this latter case, the results of Neumann's assistance may be satisfactory for the individuals concerned, in that the state backs down. Yet the author recognizes that this is a hollow victory, a mere manoeuvring around the obstacles of everyday life in a dictatorship which substitutes for a true creation of *Wirklichkeit*.[16]

In *Eleven O'Clock*, the setting for Neumann's pursuit of *Wirklichkeit* is the city streets of Leipzig and its source the observation of moments of everyday life in and around the department store where the author was employed whilst he worked on the manuscript. A certain arbitrariness is at work in the selection of these moments, even though we know that the individually dated texts are reworked by the author and that not every day in the year of writing the book is represented with its own entry. Although some shaping and selecting is clearly part of the writing process, the author's decision to set aside his break from 11 a.m. until midday every working day to write his texts in public spaces either

---

[16] Gert Neumann, 'Die Wörter des reinen Denkens', in Klaus Michael and Thomas Wohlfahrt (eds.), *Vogel oder Käfig sein* (Berlin: Galrev, 1992), 185-91.

within or in the environs of the department store where he works means that he is
repeatedly presented with a slice of GDR life that finds its way, sometimes against
the intention of the author, into the text. These encounters with people and places
are often without clear meaning, in that they do not seem to demonstrate or
illustrate any particular point and are also clearly not comic anecdotes. Instead,
the reader is presented with a coming-into-relation of heterogeneous and
incommensurable elements, whether people or objects, from the point of the view
of the writer, who does not attempt to impose meaning upon this interaction. For
example, in the text for 4 May 1977, Neumann observes a Leipzig street scene:

> Several times I saw the feet of the passengers, by looking
> underneath the bus, choosing different places to alight, until, in
> ever new variations, one of the pairs of parallel feet lifted up and
> the second, which remained behind only as an object, was pulled
> up to follow it by the first and by the certainly shaking hand, and
> disappeared. And I saw new feet step onto this spot, which had
> immediately set about addressing this theme again: which, also,
> rightly, was expressed in a careful mincing, whilst also
> immediately ended in a reluctant improvization, until one foot
> suddenly decided to step up. Then the upper bodies appear between
> the cloth-covered seats of the bus; and they formulated the gestures
> appropriate to this space;

> Ich sah die Füße der Verreisenden, unter dem Bus hindurch, vor
> der geöffneten Tür einige Male verschiedenen Abstiegstellen
> wählen, bis sich, in immer neuen Variationen, einer aus dem
> parallelen Fußpaar hinaufhob und der zweite, der nur als Objekt
> zurückgeblieben war, durch den ersten und besonders vor der
> sicher zitternden Hand, nachgezogen wurde und verschwand. Und
> ich sah neue Füße an die Stelle treten, die sich, sofort, zu einer
> neuen Behandlung dieser Thematik entschlossen hatten: das, auch,
> richtig, in einem sorgfältigen Trippeln verwirklicht wurde, aber
> zugleich wegen der vielen eintreffenden Gedanken, in zögernden
> Improvisationen endete, bis sich plötzlich ein Fuß zum
> Hinaufgehen entschloß. Dann erschienen die Oberkörper zwischen
> den leinenüberzogenen Sitzen des Busses; und die formulierten die
> diesem Raum entsprechenden Gebärden; (E 87)

Here individual people are reduced to a series of body parts moving relatively to
each other and to inanimate objects in a particular space. The minute observation
of this movement does not result in it being attributed a specific meaning, but

simply allows it to take place within the text. Throughout the text, the writer experiences a number of similar moments: for example, when he hears a recording of Janis Joplin's version of 'Summertime' as he watches a man park his car (E 258), or when he suddenly sees a fragment of a discarded sandwich lying under a bush (E 273), or when observing a couple from a distance as they move towards each other in a window (E 193-4). Such moments bring a sense of 'the close proximity of poetic structures' ('die nahen Anwesenheiten poetischer Strukturen', E 273), yet there is apparently nothing for the writer to say about them once he has reproduced these meetings and interactions within his text.

Neumann's strategy here is to turn these fragments of reality – a piece of refuse, a limb, a snatch of music – into 'poetic signs' ('poetische Zeichen'), with which to oppose 'the interpretations of events through the sentences of *Realität*' ('die Deutungen des Geschehens durch die Sätze der Realität', E 271), which impose themselves upon human lives. By opening himself to the heterogeneity of these fragments and the strangeness of their meeting he hopes to gain access to an absent *Wirklichkeit* beyond the 'static' language of ideology's *Realität*. In Michel de Certeau's terms, this approach can be read as a 'tactic' that sets itself against the 'strategic' domination of social space by the ruling discourses. The 'tactic' does not overthrow the strategic power of the state, if such a thing can even be expected of a lone individual, but does create a moment in which, from the subjective point of view of the poet, that order power to hold sway.[17] What Neumann describes here in terms of a spatial experience is something akin to that 'getting lost' that Rebecca Solint describes, with reference to Walter Benjamin, and which is not a matter of no longer knowing where one is, but is rather a conscious choice to surrender oneself and to become 'utterly immersed in what is present so that its surroundings fade away'. Such getting lost is 'to be fully present, and to be fully present is to be capable of uncertainty and mystery'.[18] Similarly, through his meditation on fragments of reality and their spatial

---

[17] On the notion of 'tactical' resistance, see Michel de Certeau, *Kunst des Handelns*, trans. Ronald Vouillé (Berlin: Merve, 1988), 23.

[18] Rebecca Solint, *A Field Guide to Getting Lost* (Edinburgh: Canongate, 2006), 6.

interrelation, Neumann succeeds in liberating these fragments from the meaning imposed on them by an ideologically dominated society and allows their interplay to produce a moment of mystery and openness.

Clearly, the experience of being situated bodily in a concrete and localized physical reality is central to this poetic process, as it provides a point of view from which the unpredictable yet productive encounters of fragments of the real world can be experienced. Much the same can be said, for example, of the description of the working relationship between Angel, a Bulgarian, and the autobiographical narrator of Neumann's *The Clandestinity of the Boiler Cleaners*,[19] as they work together as maintenance men in an evangelical hospital in Leipzig. Neumann describes his days with Angel, and the text which results from them, in terms of a 'perception   of   silent   concordances'   ('Wahrnehmung   schweigender Konkordanzen', K 11) that escape the ideological control of the state security apparatus. These 'concordances' are protected by a poetic 'conspiracy' ('Konspiration', K 11) or 'clandestinity' ('Klandestinität'), as the text's title has it, which is exemplified by the relationship between the first-person narrator and his colleague. Whereas state socialist *Realität* neurotically seeks to impose its order upon the material of the world (K 15), the practice of everyday life opens up the possibility of interaction beyond language, which Neumann and Angel experience in their work together in terms of the interrelation of their bodies and the physical objects they handle. As with other aspects of social existence in the GDR, work is described as a process which is ordered and restricted by an hermetic (K 47), ideological text (in this case the discourse of the heroic proletariat), which closes off its true possibilities. In their largely silent toil, hidden away from the rest of GDR society in the bowels of the hospital, Neumann hopes that 'the things and people that meet in work can begin again to experience their possibilities beyond

---

[19] The autobiographical nature of the text is clear from a number of details. For example, in the early part of the text, Neumann describes in detail his son's arrest and imprisonment in 1983. As files of the *Staatssicherheitsdienst* have since shown, this was a deliberate measure aimed at the 'unsettling' ('Verunsicherung') of the author. Joachim Walther, *Sicherungsbereich Literatur: Schriftsteller und Staatssicherheit in der Deutschen Demokratischen Republik* (Berlin: Ullstein, 1999), 403.

the unavoidable yet actually unloved product of that *work*' ('die in der Arbeit sich begegnenden Dinge und Menschen wieder beginnen, ihre Möglichkeiten jenseits des unausweichlichen und eigentlich nie geliebten Ergebnisses der *Arbeit* zu erfahren', K 49 – italics in original). In other words, he aims to overcome the conception of work as a means to an end (the creation of a product or earning a living) in order to explore its potential as poetic process. Although the two workers do talk to each other, their cooperation is also a dialogue of gestures, or 'gesture-words' ('Gebärdenwörter', K 58), material objects such as 'pipelines, supporting beams, stairways, conveyor belts, steam distributors: cleaning vents' ('Rohrleitungen, Verstrebungen, Treppen, Förderbänder, Dampfverteiler: Abschlämmventile', K 65), or even the noises that such objects make (K 64). As in examples cited above from *Eleven O'Clock*, there is no question of attempting to synthesize a new interpretation of the world from the encounter with these linguistic and non-linguistic elements, which might serve as a counter-discourse to the ideology of the regime. Instead, Neumann and Angel seek to experience a 'present tense [...], which lives from the possibilities of encounter' ('Präsensform [...], in der die Möglichkeiten der Begegnungen leben', K 75). To return to the semantic distinction between *Realität* and *Wirklichkeit*, it might therefore be argued that the *Wirklichkeit* valued by Neumann is something having or taking effect in time, but growing out of a concrete experience of situatedness in a particular place.

A key theoretical source for Neumann's interest in such 'meetings', as Grant and Walter Schmitz observe, is the philosophy of Martin Buber.[20] Buber's description of what he terms dialogical life does not focus on the formation or reformation of consensus, in other words of a shared *Realität* in Neumann's terms, but rather on the importance of openness to that which is other than ourselves

---

[20] Walter Schmitz, 'Über Gert Neumann', in Neumann, *Verhaftet*, 97-131 (here 114). Colin B. Grant, *Literary Communication from Consensus to Rupture: Practice and Theory in Honecker's GDR* (Amsterdam: Rodopi, 1995), 144.

('Anderheit'),[21] be it another individual or objects in the world around us.[22] For Buber and for Neumann, this 'turning towards' ('Hinwendung') the other is a means of resisting '[t]he conherent, sterile system, to which everything only has to conform'('[d]as zusammenhängende, sterilisierte System, in das sich all dies nur einzufügen braucht') and which puts language in its service.[23]

Neumann's encounter with and attempt to render the *Wirklichkeit* of the city streets and its challenge to the ideological *Realität* of the state raises, however, the following important question: If such possibilities of encounter in the real world are in and of themselves already a challenge to the 'textual fossil' of the ruling ideology, what specific place does literature itself have, beyond perhaps recording these 'meetings' as they occur? Although Neumann implicitly claims for such encounters a subversive potential, it is clear that it is only in literature as the author conceives it that they attain that potential fully. Paradoxically, Neumann states that the meeting that is crucial to *Wirklichkeit* only truly achieves its full power, despite its foundation in lived experience, when it takes place within a text:[24] these elements that meet to create the effect of *Wirklichkeit*, whether human or non-human, become signs which resonate and enter into a dialogue with each other within literary language. A 'place of language' ('Ort der Sprache') is created out of the elements of geographical place through their transformation into text. Here, 'beyond the erected, static sentences [...] the people [...] mov[e] about in language like punctuation marks and words' ('außerhalb der errichteten, statischen Sätze [...] [gehen] die Menschen in [der Sprache, DC] wie Satzzeichen und Wörter herum[...]', E 205). This process does not lead, as I have already observed, to the synthesis of some new meaning out of

---

[21] On the importance of the notion of 'Anderheit' for Buber's thought, see Hans-Joachim Werner, *Martin Buber* (Frankfurt a.M.: Campus, 1994), 48-52.

[22] See Martin Buber, 'Zwiesprache', in *Das dialogische Prinzip* (Heidelberg: Schneider, 1973), 137-96 (here 133).

[23] Buber, 'Zwiesprache', 154.

[24] 'The dialogue must [...] actually one hundred percent take place in the text' ('Das Gespräch muß [...] eigentlich hundertprozentig im Text stattfinden'). Hesse, 'Gespräch mit Gert Neumann', 20.

the encounter of these 'poetic signs', but rather to an open-ended production of *Wirklichkeit*, which can, however, only truly take place within the work of art.

Literature's role here is perhaps most succinctly exemplified by one of Neumann's Leipzig poems, 'Unexpected Celebration' ('Unverhoffte Feier', 1986), in which a series of discarded objects in the snow is described. The title itself recalls the unexpected emergence of *Wirklichkeit* already described above in the descriptions of everyday scenes in *Eleven O'Clock*, in that a moment of 'celebration' is created through the juxtaposition of heterogeneous elements in the text. The objects in question have been placed in this marginal space by 'work-dark men / who hardly carried the possibility of freedom in their faces' ('arbeitsdunkle Männer, / die im Gesicht kaum Möglichkeit für eine Freiheit trugen').[25] Here Neumann portrays the human ordering of the material world, reaching back into history to the building of the pyramids, in terms of a 'silence of things' ('Schweigen der Dinge'): The imposition of that order closes off the possibility of the emergence of other configurations and, as the description of the workers already cited implies, is equally inimical to true human freedom. The deterioration of the objects discarded by the workers points, however, to the rebirth of freedom: The snow becomes a 'medium white' ('Medium weiß'), a metaphor for the white page on which the poem itself is created,[26] and on which these items are brought together: 'Only / the white claimed a glimmering towards the briefcase / on the edge of the path, which almost touched a paint-covered horsehair brush' ('Allein / das Weiß behauptete ein Glimmern zur offenen Aktentasche / am Randweg, die beinahe ein farbgetränkter Roßhaarbesen berührte'). The objects described enter into a constellation through their contact with the snow, which, like the rotting objects themselves, is a substance without distinct borders and which is 'disappearing' ('schwindend' – it is in the process of melting). The white of the snow is like the white of the page in that on both the

---

[25] Gert Neumann, 'Unverhoffte Feier', in Michael and Wohlfahrt (eds.), *Vogel oder Käfig sein*, 101. Originally in *Schaden*, 12 (1986), 13.
[26] This image is also used in the later text 'Medium Weiß', in Arnold, *Text+Kritik: Sonderband*, 215-20.

snow and the page disparate elements (textual or physical) are brought into relation to each other, but the clear implication is that this medium is the necessary (if fragile) precondition of that interrelation, which produces something new, yet indefinable in its openness: the poem makes the 'celebration' take place, but refuses to offer us any interpretation of its meaning. Unlike in the street scenes of *Eleven O'Clock*, there is no identifiable human perspective here, from which the coming-into-relation of these objects can be made to take place. It is rather the medium of the poem itself which creates, as Gilles Deleuze and Felix Guattari would put it, a 'rhizomatic structure', i.e. 'a figure that connects any point to any other point' in an 'acentred, nonhierachrical, non-signifying system'.[27]

The 'neoromantic'[28] Neumann's conviction that literature can create such moments of openness can be read in terms of a tradition of stretching back beyond German Romanticism, and which finds expression in 'post-modern' versions of the Romantic sublime formulated by the likes of Jean-François Lyotard and Karl-Heinz Bohrer. Figures like Georg Friedrich Hamann and Jakob Böhme, both of whom the narrator reads during the writing of *Eleven O'Clock*, and who were both precursors of early German Romanticism, work with a notion of language and of nature as revealing the divine, yet this revelation can only ever be partial and indeterminate, the 'signature of something not fully present', as John A. McCarthy puts it.[29] Martin Buber is also concerned with revelation, through the process of dialogue, which he opposes to an instrumental attitude to the world, expressed *inter alia* through language. The meaning of things, he explains, is not to be found in them or in the sense we attribute to them, but in the 'between' of a

---

[27] Gilles Deleuze and Félix Guattari, *A Thousand Plateaus: Capitalism and Schizophrenia*, trans. Brian Massumi (London: Athlone, 1988), 21.

[28] Adolf Endler, 'Nachwort', in Hilbig, *Zwischen den Paradiesen*, 322-23 (here 322). The first significant academic analysis of Neumann's work by Günter Saße almost points to certain points of contact between Neumann and Romanticism. Saße, '"Der Kampf gegen die Versteinerung der Materie Wirklichkeit durch die Sprache": Zur Systematik sprachthematisierender Literatur aus Anlaß von Gert Neumanns *Elf Uhr*', in *Jahrbuch zur Literatur in der DDR*, 6 (1987), 196-219

[29] John A. McCarthy, 'Philosophy and Literature in the German Enlightenment', in Nicholas Saul (ed.), *Philosophy and German Literature, 1700-1900* (Cambridge: CUP, 2002), 13-56 (here 15).

meeting with them.[30] This meaning remains indeterminate, however, given that any attempt to define it in instrumentalizing language would spell its destruction. That these are all fundamentally religious thinkers hints at the central issue here: they are concerned with the gap between the real and ideal and, whilst recognizing that the ideal can not be represented in language, seek to show how it makes its absence felt. A similar concern is clearly also central to early Romanticism, and indeed to the work of Symbolists like Mallarmé and Valéry, whom Neumann also refers to in *Eleven O'Clock*: they all seek to use language to point towards the infinite, the ideal, or the totality that cannot be directly represented. For the French postmodernist Lyotard, the Romantic, and not just its specifically German variety, is preoccupied above all with the sublime, following Kant's definition of it as 'the ungraspable and undeniable "presence" of something which is other than the mind'.[31] The work of art, in Lytoard's account creates 'events' or 'encounters',[32] in which something ineffable takes place. Works of art 'allud[e] to an impenetrable' and thereby point beyond established versions of reality to something that escapes representation in them.[33] Bohrer's version of the sublime as a 'suddenness' ('Plötzlichkeit') works with a similar model. In this context, the encounters staged by Neumann in his texts can be read as exemplary of that Romantic tradition that rejects the totalizing discourses of power without seeking to replace them with their own (equally totalizing) version of *Realität*, but seeks rather to create, by bringing together fragments of the world of experience within the text, an intimation of a totality, understood as that of which no perception can exist.[34] In other words, Neumann seeks to make the absence of the absent *Wirklichkeit* felt, without claiming to make that *Wirklichkeit* fully present.

---

[30] Buber, 'Zwiesprache', 192.

[31] Jean-François Lyotard, *The Inhuman: Reflections on Time*, trans. Geoff Bennington and Rachel Bowlby (Standford: Stanford UP, 1991), 75.

[32] Jean-François Lyotard, *The Postmodern Explained*, trans. Don Barry et al. (Minneapolis: University of Minneapolis Press, 1992), 97.

[33] Lyotard, *The Inhuman*, 128.

[34] There are clear parallels here to the notion of Romantic irony. See Kai Hammermeister, *The German Aesthetic Tradition* (Cambridge: CUP, 2002), 83.

Not only does Neumann insist on the function of literature in allowing us
to momentarily glimpse the presence of *Wirklichkeit* in the interrelationship
between things in the world and on the page, his texts can also be said, in their
fracturing of German syntax, to provide a reading experience that is analogous to
the encounter with this *Wirklichkeit*. Neumann stresses this act *qua* act, that is to
say as a 'creative process' ('schöpferisch[er] Prozeß', E 43) over and above any
meaning which the reader may take away from the text, as implied in Neumann's
references to his audience not as 'the reader' ('der Leser'), but as 'the reading'
('das Lesen').[35] The examples already described above, in which Neumann brings
into relation fragments of the reality he finds in the streets of Leipzig as 'poetic
signs' within the literary text, already give some indication of how 'the reading' is
to approach his writing. The author makes a positive virtue of the difficulty of
some of his work on the grounds that 'an understandable way of writing' ('eine
verständliche Schreibmethode') is 'a clear denigration of the reader, [...] since he
is forced to follow one particular interpretative path' ('die klare Entwürdigung des
Lesers [...], da sie ihn ausweglos deuten [muß]', E 252).

The difficulty of Neumann's syntax is more significant, however, than an
avoidance of clear and easily digestible meanings. His textual practice in fact
echoes the strategies already outlined above, in that his sentences often contain
linguistic elements which cannot be easily subordinated to a single coherent
meaning. A number of recurring structural features of Neumann's texts can be
noted in this regard. Firstly, the overuse and sometimes ungrammatical use of
commas creates at certain points a disjointed effect in which the flow of the text is
disturbed, as, for example, in the following descriptive passage from the early
Leipzig story 'The Reports' ('Die Reportagen'):

> But then, after a silence, the familiar, very long, shadows of the
> poplars reached us clearly and sharply; and the sun came, distantly,
> over the horizon and began, slowly, to warm.

---

[35] For example in 'Das nabeloonische Chaos', in Ernst Wichner und Herbert Wiener (eds.),
"Literaturentwicklungsprozesse": Die Zensur in der DDR (Frankfurt a.M.: Suhrkamp, 1993), 144-
71.

> Dann aber, nach einem Schweigen, erreichten uns klar und scharf
> die bekannten, sehr langen, Schatten der Pappeln; und die Sonne
> kam, fern, über den Horizont und begann, langsam, zu wärmen. (S
> 32)

The translation into English, a language which favours a more expressive use of commas, to some extent erases the non-standard features of this style. In the above quotation in German, the parenthetical use of the commas around 'very long' ('sehr langen') is, strictly speaking, correct from a grammatical point of view, yet unusual. The same use of commas around the adverbs 'distantly' ('fern') and 'slowly' ('langsam') is, however, not standard German, and creates not only a rather staccato effect, but also the impression that these elements are to some extent separate from the main statement: they become discrete elements which might easily be excluded, like all parenthetical material, from the statement proper. Elsewhere, even relatively simple expressions are divided into their component parts using commas, for example: 'Will, it, really work?' ('Wird, es, wohl gelingen?', E 329). The four words in this question are, by virtue of the insertion of commas, no longer automatically read as part of one enunciation, although they can still be understood as such. Instead, the impression is created that they are essentially unconnected textual elements placed arbitrarily in this order, even though they happen to make sense. Although such disruptive usage of commas is a recurring strategy, it is not applied systematically according to a particular pattern. Less frequently, a similar effect is created by the separation of a subordinated verb from the sentence with an ungrammatical colon.

More common is the use of ellipses ('...'). On occasion, these seem simply to replace commas at the end of a clause, at other times they precede such a comma and suggest an omission which, although it does not stop the sentence from making sense, is made visible. Frequently, however, these ellipses are used parenthetically, like the commas examined above, in order to introduce further units of sense, as it were, into a sentence. For example:

> the continual agony of building an entire poetic existence on a
> certain, which has no form: apart from, that which in silence ...
> although all around there are forms, which can not however be

understood in the proximity of their necessity, because they are used as rags, with which the shivering souls cover themselves for want of something better ... is dissolved into various victories of poetry, which can, only, be denied.

die fortdauernde Qual, eine ganze poetische Existenz auf einer Gewissheit aufzubauen, die keine Form hat: außer, der im Schweigen ... obwohl rings Formen sind, die aber nicht in die Nähe ihrer Notwendigkeit zu verstehen sind, weil sie gebraucht werden als Lappen, mit denen sich die frierenden Seelen notdürftig zudecken ... ist aufgelöst in verschiedene Siege der Poesie, die, nur noch, zu leugnen sind. (E 148-49)

The ungrammatical use of commas is also again visible here, but the use of ellipses in order to introduce additional material into the sentence clearly also has the function of disrupting the flow of meaning for the reader. German literary language is infamous for its use of the nested sentence, yet the replacement of the commas that might have been inserted before 'although' ('obwohl') and after 'cover' ('zudecken') has the effect of hampering the reader's attempt to establish the connection between the noun 'the continual torture' ('die fortdauernde Qual') and the rest of the passive construction of which it is part ('ist aufgelöst'). It is not merely the distance between these two elements on the page that creates this difficulty, but the ellipses which seem to suspend the grammar of the first part of the sentence without any clear indication as to when the reader will be able to return to it. The material between the two ellipses therefore appears as a foreign body, distinct from the sentence proper. The example cited above is one of the easier-to-follow instances of this use of the ellipsis, but this practice is indicative of Neumann's general approach to German syntax, which he often stretches to the point of incomprehensibility.

A further extended example from the beginning of *Eleven O'clock* illustrates this point. Neumann is on a tram in Leipzig on his way to work, reading Paul Valéry's *Monsieur Teste* (1896) and reflecting on his recent nervous breakdown:

he [Valéry, DC] was today a hope, and a memory of a world of thought, in which the aesthetic, humane, insight into the, only,

living possibilities of saying something to the point of action, in the
sentences and his recognition of language, which realizes itself in a
body, had pushed forward... which I had, through an accident,
which I have to describe as a psychotic accident, and which is that,
inner, event: that clearly leads, led by various inner forces, as an
experience of the poetry of the exterior defended with all,
imaginable, means, suddenly into a psychic chaos, which turns
every inner compulsion to interpret things poetically, into its
opposite, and, destructively, turns it against one's own self, until a
pain and a horror break out, which paralyses the body into
unconsciousness... that I had terribly lost.

er [Valéry, DC] war heute eine Hoffnung, und eine Erinnerung an
eine Gedankenwelt, in der die ästhetische, humane, Einsicht in die,
lediglich, lebendigen Möglichkeiten etwas zu sagen bis zum
Handeln, in den Sätzen und seinem Erkennen als Sprache, die sich
in einem Körper verwirklicht, vorgedrungen war ... die mir aber,
durch einen Unfall, den ich als Psychounfall bezeichnen muß, und
der jenes, innere, Geschehen ist: das deutlich, von verschiedenen
inneren Kräften geführt, als eine mit allen, denkbaren, Mitteln
verteidigte Erfarhrung der Poesie des Außen, plötzlich in ein
psychisches Chaos führt, das allen inneren Antrieb, die Dinge
poetisch zu deuten, zu seinem Gegenteil werden läßt, und,
vernichtend, gegen das eigene Ich lenkt, bis ein Schmerz und ein
Grauen ausbricht, das den Körper zur Ohnmacht lähmt ...
ungeheuer abhanden gekommen ist. (E 17)

The syntax of this sentence (in fact an extract from a much longer sentence)
clearly presents challenges to the reader. The basic statement, one might say, is
'he was today a hope that I had terribly lost' ('er war heute eine Hoffnung, die mir
ungeheuer abhanden gekommen war'). Apart from the long descriptions of the
nature of this hope and the 'world of thought' that Valéry represents, which serve
to separate the subject and verb from the direct object and the relative clause, the
replacement of two commas with ellipses hampers the reader's attempts to
recognize the grammatical structures which are nevertheless still (just about) in
place.

What emerges from a close analysis of Neumann's disruptive approach to
the written language is an attempt on the author's part to break down the flow of
German grammar and to produce sentences which are composed of loosely

connected fragments. The reader sometimes succeeds in making sense of these fragments in relation to each other, but they nevertheless continually threaten to break down into a series of disjunctive linguistic units. On a metaphorical level, these free-floating fragments of language are not unlike the fragments of the real world which Neumann turns into 'poetic signs' in his texts and which, whilst certainly producing meaning in the course of 'the reading', always leave the reader with the impression of something not quite grasped. Their meaning is glimpsed in the interaction of these textual fragments, but can not be pinned down definitively, thereby providing an experience analogous to those momentary experiences of the Romantic sublime that Neumann encounters in his observations of the life of the city.

To what extent, then, can we say that place, specifically the city of Leipzig, matters to Neumann's project? Clearly, Neumann is not interested in defining any kind of local identity, although his continued personal engagement in the lives of ordinary working citizens of Leipzig means that he has, paradoxically, a justified claim to having produced a 'workers' literature' ('Arbeiterliteratur'), although not in the way the SED would have wished. Furthermore, and despite the fact that many of his texts describe moving through recognizable locales which can still be identified by the visitor to the city today, what is important for Neumann's poetics is less the recording of the physical character of the city than the narrator's attempts to transform the urban landscape into a poetic landscape. What is striking about Neumann's approach is above all the extent to which the cityscape comes to mirror the text and the text itself comes to reproduce the cityscape on a formal level. Both are broken down into a flow of more or less loosely connected fragments, whose interconnections and juxtapositions do not create a new meaning to replace that imposed on the cityscape by ideology, but which point to a meaning beyond that ideology that can never be fully grasped. For Neumann, then, it is clearly necessary to turn away from the search for the definition of the meaning of place towards the experience of place as open-ended process, a process that finds its analogy in the act of reading.

CHAPTER 11

'We Have to Limit Ourselves':[1] Negotiating No Man's Land in Helga Schütz' Novel *Border to Yesterday*

Juliane Parthier

The Berlin Wall was one of the most powerful symbols of the Cold War, and its demise after nearly 29 years of existence was met with a mixture of relief and joy. Its remains have been exhibited and sold to tourists, while allotment gardeners, car dealers and holiday makers now populate the former death strip.[2] And yet, not only the material evidence of separation has disappeared. The history and impact of the Wall's existence, too, seem to have largely vanished from public consciousness since unification. In a recent article in the German monthly *Merkur*, Hermann Rudolph bemoaned the insufficient and at times inappropriate commemoration of German division in the media which had reduced the 40-year separation to 'a handful of relevant facts' and dismissed them as an unpleasant episode of the past.[3] Nowadays, he argues, only historical guide books and specialists are able to identify the exact course of the Berlin and inner-German borders, while their impacts on the lives of ordinary people are on the verge of being forgotten, or suppressed, altogether.[4] The mental elimination of Cold War history and its 'icons', which followed their physical disappearance, was not only a consequence of the speed and impact of unification, or of the demise of a politically bipolar world. It also arose, Rudolph suggests, from the uncomfortable thought that Germans on either side of the border somehow accepted the imposition of German division.[5] Over the years, most people had taken to

---

[1] 'Es gilt, sich einzuschränken'. Helga Schütz, *Grenze zum gestrigen Tag* (Berlin: Aufbau, 2000), 72. Referred to in the following as G. All translations are my own.
[2] See Oliver Birger, 'Spurensuche in Berlin: "Was von der Mauer noch steht, ist zuwenig"', *FAZ*, 13 August 2007.
[3] Hermann Rudolph, 'Die verdrängte Teilung', *Merkur* 1 (2007), 1-14 (here 1).
[4] See Maren Ullrich, *Geteilte Ansichten: Erinnerungslandschaft deutsch-deutsche Grenze* (Berlin: Aufbau, 2006).
[5] Rudolph, 'Die verdrängte Teilung', 5.

blanking out the political realities in their daily lives. They thus 'domesticated' Germany's double statehood, not least because they had accepted it as atonement for German war guilt.

Nevertheless, in the German Democratic Republic, the division of Germany also rested on 'a hidden ground of doubt and despair, the conflict of whether to stay or leave, and the ambivalence between disengagement and self-assertion'.[6] These underlying issues were the subject matter of a number of literary texts dealing with German division prior to the fall of the GDR regime.[7] In comparison, the issues of suffering, despair, and stoicism in the face of Wall and division have featured relatively little in literary prose since 1990. While the division of Germany and in particular Berlin has been a farcical or bleak reference point in texts by a number of writers from the former German Democratic Republic,[8] the GDR author Helga Schütz has approached the topic from a different angle. Drawing on personal experience, her novel *Border to Yesterday* (*Grenze zum gestrigen Tag*, 2000) tells the story of a family's life in a provincial GDR location which, due to its close proximity to the Berlin Wall, is a 'taboo' area, a no man's land: invisible on the country's maps and inaccessible to outsiders. Schütz tells of people's ambivalent behaviour within and towards crude manifestations of political power in the GDR; behaviour which has been both defended and discredited during the post-unification debates about the GDR dictatorship. The author describes moments of exasperation and resignation in the face of the impermeable, rising concrete of the Wall in the family garden. Yet she also depicts instances of happy ignorance and covert defiance, indicating the remoteness of politics and ideology from the day-to-day concerns in the family

---

[6] Rudolph, 'Die verdrängte Teilung', 8.

[7] See Birgit Frech, *Die Berliner Mauer in der Literatur: Eine Untersuchung ausgewählter Prosawerke seit 1961* (Pfungstadt: Edition Ergon, 1992).

[8] See, for instance, Thomas Brussig's *Heroes Like Us* (*Helden wie wir*, 1995) and *Sun Alley* (*Am kürzeren Ende der Sonnenallee*, 1999). Older writers like Helga Königsdorf or Brigitte Burmeister refer to the Wall and German division with a view to post-unification changes and continuities in east Germany, while Reinhard Jirgl and Wolfgang Hilbig present us with gloomy, apocalyptic portrayals of East German landscapes.

enclave: a sickly child, dying trees, intrepid animals, love, jealousy, and loss. Schütz 'introduces us to an East German microcosm which now is museum-like but nonetheless rarely depicted'.[9] She belongs to a group of East German writers who have challenged the public and academic discourse about life in the GDR by presenting the personal life-narratives which constituted the day-to-day realities of this life.

In this chapter, I will argue that Helga Schütz's autobiographical novel *Border to Yesterday* explores personal history in relation to places whose history and existence have been 'repressed' in public memory. Her literary return to a provincial, yet politically sensitive location by the Berlin Wall is a highly subjective recollection of the impact of the GDR's 'totalitarian' topography on the daily lives of GDR citizens, offering an alternative and perhaps provocative narrative about how ordinary people dealt with state-imposed limitations in their daily lives. It is a timely intervention because, paradoxically, former 'taboo' places such as the no man's land along the Berlin Wall and inner-German border, but also traces of the Second World War and the post-war military occupation in the provinces of the GDR, seem once more 'invisible'. In the context of more urgent issues of post-unification transformation, they appear to be repressed from public memory.

In this chapter, I will examine how the author acquaints us with her own understanding and experience of borders and other limits on personal freedom in the GDR, where some people negotiated and counteracted state-imposed restrictions in an attempt to lead normal, fulfilled lives. I will argue that, as a result, Schütz's text ascribes greater significance to issues *beyond* the spatial, temporal and political aspects of such limitations.

---

[9] Iris Radisch, 'Morsezeichen aus Altdeutschland: Helga Schütz füttert Enten hinterm Todesstreifen, und die Geschichte der DDR-Literatur beginnt von vorn', *Die Zeit*, 13 (2000).

Helga Schütz has been referred to as one of the more marginal figures on the literary scene of the GDR,[10] although much of her writing enjoyed a considerable readership in both the GDR and the Federal Republic and the author saw herself as a privileged writer, who was allowed a number of trips to the Federal Republic and the USA.[11] In the mid-1960s, she moved with her partner, the filmmaker Egon Günther, and her son to the village of Großglienicke near Potsdam, where, for the next eighteen years, they witnessed the impact of the Cold War at close range. The village and lake of Großglienicke were divided by the Berlin Wall which bordered the family garden. The area was further delimited by the continuing extension of the prohibited zone and the fortification of the border. In retrospect, Schütz ascribes her choice of home close to the death strip to a mix of naivety, ignorance, defiance and compassion – attitudes which she has explored in her post-unification autobiographical fiction about living in the GDR:

> The new machinery of war was ravaging the woods. [...] While around us everything disintegrated and pre-fab apartment blocks appeared, we were living in our beautiful refuge. [...] We failed to realize what was going on because we were so close to the action. [...] Perhaps pity was the prime cause for our love [of the place]. Pity with [...] the land which, bare and bleak, was the border strip, pity with the fact that the trees, animals and we ourselves had had to inhabit a military area for decades.

> Die neue Kriegsmaschinerie wütete in den Wäldern.[...] Während es ringsherum bröckelte und Neubauschachteln entstanden, lebten wir in unserem schönen Refugium.[...] Wir übersahen, was gespielt wurde, weil wir dem Geschehen so nahe waren. [...] Vielleicht war das Mitleid der Urgrund unserer Liebe [zum Ort]. Mitleid mit [...] dem Land, das nackt und kahl Grenzstreifen sein mußte, mit dem

[10] See Radisch, 'Morsezeichen' and Anne Lequy, *'unbehaust'? Die Thematik des Topos in den Werken wenig(er) bekannter DDR-Autorinnen der siebziger und achtziger Jahre. Eine feministische Untersuchung* (Frankfurt a.M.: Lang, 2000), 37 and 148-51. See also Ricarda Schmidt, 'Im Schatten der Titanin: Minor GDR Women Writers – Justly Neglected, Unrecognized or Repressed?', in Axel Goodbody and Dennis Tate (eds.), *Geist und Macht. Writers and the State in the GDR* (Amsterdam: Rodopi, 1992), 155-58.
[11] See Dinah Dodds and Pam Allen-Thompson (eds.), *The Wall in My Backyard: East German Women in Transition* (Massachusetts: U of Massachusetts P, 1994), 103-11 (here 104-7).

Sperrgebietsstatus, den die Bäume, die Tiere und wir in trauriger Solidarität seit Jahrzehnten trugen.[12]

Following the birth of her severely disabled daughter in the late 1960s, Schütz started writing literary prose as a freelance writer. By that time, her former hopes of 'harmony and peace' had given way to growing disillusionment. Subjected to GDR border control and arbitrary government decisions on a daily basis, and concerned about an increasingly fragile-looking peaceful coexistence at the international level, Schütz opted for a 'cautious, hardly detectable rebellion in the niches of everyday life' ('vorsichtige Leuchtwürmerrevolution im Nischenalltag'), and for 'treading lightly, so the missiles wouldn't explode' ('leise treten, damit die Raketen nicht platzten').[13]

According to literary critic Iris Radisch, Schütz was 'neither critical nor loyal' towards the GDR and 'her books did not aim to be among representative, politically ambitious writing'.[14] Schütz did not start out as professional and accredited GDR writer, but came to writing later in life, while holding other jobs and having children. Compared to more established colleagues, she was more sceptical about her role as an intellectual representative of both the GDR state and society. She has been sceptical, too, about the assumed political impact of literature.[15] While claiming she did not aim to be 'critical of our society', Schütz admits to indirect criticism of the GDR regime and to by-passing GDR censorship: 'I wrote within the context of the literature that existed, GDR literature. [...] My writing always had the goal of expanding the limits of what was

---

[12] Helga Schütz, 'Im Grenzgebiet, warum Zuhause', in *Von Abraham bis Zwerenz. Eine Anthologie des Bundesministeriums für Bildung, Wissenschaft, Forschung und Technologie als Beitrag zur geistig-kulturellen Einheit in Deutschland* (Berlin: Cornelsen, 1995), 1933-4 (here 1936-7 and 1940).
[13] Helga Schütz, 'Once I Lived Near the Wall...', in Anna Mudry (ed.), *Gute Nacht, du Schöne: Autorinnen blicken zurück* (Frankfurt a.M.: Luchterhand, 1991), 15-29 (here 29).
[14] Radisch, 'Morsezeichen'.
[15] 'I don't know if literature can actually change anything. Its task is more to create a sense of solidarity among people'. Dodds and Allen-Thompson (eds.), *The Wall in My Backyard*, 108.

possible'.[16] However, her reputation as a critical, or 'truthful', writer presented the author with a dilemma:

> I had to write about the many things that didn't appear in our media, and so I had to work more like a journalist. The subject matter ended up being very provincial. I could never concentrate simply on form; I was constantly interrupted by daily matters.[17]

The depiction of everyday life was to become a hallmark of Schütz's writing and largely contributed to the success of her novels in East and West before and after 1989. Insisting on the validity of personal experience and on forgoing ideology, Schütz provides her readers with narratives they can relate to. Feeding on the history of her own life, she tells stories of lives worth living in the face of adverse circumstances, such as the Second World War and its repercussions, or the restrictions of GDR society during the time of the Cold War. Like other texts about everyday matters ('Alltagsprosa'), Schütz's novels of the 1980s, such as *Julia or Training to Sing in Harmony* (*Julia oder die Erziehung zum Chorgesang*, 1980) and *In Anna's Name* (*In Annas Namen*, 1986), reveal the fragile state of affairs, the lacking quality of life and the effects of leading 'double lives' in the GDR,[18] as well as reflecting the stagnation of everyday life and the acquiescence and philistinism prevalent in GDR society during its concluding decade.[19]

Compared to the political engagement of her more prominent contemporaries such as Wolf or Stefan Heym around the time of the fall of the GDR regime, Schütz kept a relatively low profile. She did not share their concerns regarding the continuation of the GDR to the same extent, nor was her reputation discredited during the literary debates of the early 1990s. 'My world was still

---

[16] Dodds and Allen-Thompson (eds.), *The Wall in My Backyard*, 107-8.

[17] Dodds and Allen-Thompson (eds.), *The Wall in My Backyard*, 107.

[18] Eva Kaufmann, 'Adieu Kassandra? Schriftstellerinnen aus der DDR vor, in und nach der Wende: Brigitte Burmeister, Helga Königsdorf, Helga Schütz, Brigitte Struzyk, Rosemarie Zeplin', in Elizabeth Boa and Janet Wharton (eds.), *Women and the Wende: Social Effects and Cultural Reflections of the German Unification Process* (Amsterdam: Rodopi, 1994), 216-25, (here 217-18).

[19] Schütz, 'Once I Lived Near the Wall...', 22-23.

intact' ('Meine Welt war noch immer in den Fugen'), she said shortly after unification.[20] While she approved of the fall of the Wall and welcomed measures to tackle environmental damage in the (former) GDR, she was nevertheless disappointed with missed chances and reforms concerning other, broader issues such as demilitarization and European unity.

Meanwhile, she returned to the mundane practicalities of everyday life after unification and referred to apparently more important tasks, such as inspecting her Stasi file, in the subjunctive: 'I should grapple with that whole dirty network. [...] I should accuse and apologize. But I was concerned with [rotting] tomatoes in the Havelland region' ('Ich müßte das ganze dreckige Netz anpacken.[...] Ich müßte Anklagen und Abbitten leisten. Doch mir ging's um die [vergammelnden] Havelland-Tomaten'). Daily matters continued to interfere with her writing, too. Hopes to now return to imaginative storytelling, away from everyday life and provincial subject matter, were dashed because 'life hadn't become easier and more transparent; on the contrary, most things were more obscure and ambiguous now' ('Das Leben war nicht leichter, nicht klarer, im Gegenteil, das meiste war undurchsichtiger, verschwommener geworden').[21]

Schütz's former reservations about politics and ideology, her preoccupation with daily matters, family issues and personal history have thus been characteristic also of her literary returns to the GDR. The author's autobiographical writing since unification depicts specific places that may not be named but, since 1990, can be easily identified on a map: Steinstücken for instance, in her novel *The Shining Elbe* (*Vom Glanz der Elbe*, 1995), or Großglienicke in *Border to Yesterday*. Both places share a close proximity to the Berlin Wall, albeit on opposite sides of it: Steinstücken is a former West Berlin enclave and Großglienicke a village divided between the Russian and British zones of occupation.

---

[20] Schütz, 'Once I Lived Near the Wall...', 19.
[21] Holly Liu, '"In einem gewissen Sinne hat der Osten uns lebenstüchtiger gemacht..." Im Gespräch mit Helga Schütz', *Berliner LeseZeichen*, 4 (2000) <http://www.luise-berlin.de/Lesezei/Blz00_04/text02.htm>.

Much of Schütz's writing deals with the appropriation, violation and repression of places. Her prose tells of politically motivated acts of demarcation and partitioning of space and addresses the concealment of unpleasant or unfavourable traces of history.[22] She writes about the marginalizing effect of such acts on the lives of ordinary people, families who made their homes in the immediate vicinity of the border. Paul A. Chilton has pointed out that the German term 'Grenze' has a narrower semantic range compared to the English 'border' which can also mean 'margin'. The latter denotes a (peripheral) area rather than a two-dimensional line between opposed places or systems.[23] Life 'on the margins' thus means life in a curiously undefined, ambiguous, 'in-between' space, resembling a no man's land invisible on a map.

Ten years after unification, Helga Schütz revisits this periphery by the Berlin border in *Border to Yesterday*. Drawing on personal memories, her portrayal of a family's life next to the death strip is a depiction of hope, perseverance and despair in the face of crude demonstrations of power by a rigid political system. There are two reasons for the apparent time-lag of Schütz's return to the subject of the GDR: firstly, the distance required to understand and re-evaluate one's own life after incisive events; secondly, the ongoing need for personal but unsentimental commemoration of the GDR and German division amid politicized debate on the one hand and forgetfulness on the other: 'The general ideas had been communicated, but not the subtleties. They needed time, distance' ('Im Groben war alles gesagt, im Feinen nicht. Fürs Feine brauchte es Zeit, Distanz').[24]

Like Großglienicke in the Cold War, the (unnamed) focal point of Schütz's novel is an invisible place, 'a blank spot on the maps' ('[a]uf den

---

[22] See, for instance, Schütz, 'Im Grenzgebiet'. The topic of German division and the Berlin Wall also features in some of her pre-unification texts, for instance in *Julia* and *In Anna's Name*.

[23] Paul A. Chilton, 'Grenzsemantik', in Rüdiger Görner and Suzanne Kirkbright (eds.), *Nachdenken über Grenzen* (Munich: iudicium, 1999), 19-32 (here 27-28).

[24] Schütz, 'Once I Lived Near the Wall...', 19. See also Friedrich Schorlemmer, 'Erinnern und Vergessen. Der lange Schatten der DDR und die Vergangenheitspolitik', *Freitag* 41 (2007).

Landkarten ein weißer Fleck', G 11). From about 1964 to the fateful year of 1976, the female narrator, her partner Hugo, their children Niklas and Betty, and a number of adopted animals live in an awkwardly situated, heavily guarded paradise: an old house with a garden, enclosed by the Berlin Wall and a mined lake. Faced with the daily presence and increasing fortification of this border, the family are involuntary witnesses of their growing geographical isolation:

> [The border] cuts us off from the world. [...] Early in the morning we often briefly think the word death. Especially in winter, when the bare trees allow us to look in the distance.

> [Die Grenze] schneidet uns ab von der Welt. [...] Meist denken wir kurz in der Frühe das Wort Tod. Besonders im Winter, wenn die kahlen Bäume uns weit blicken lassen. (G 6-7)

Ironically, they are also cut off from some of the normalities of GDR life. Border area restrictions mean that friends, family, and even the postman and the emergency services need official permission to visit. Taking photos, picking mushrooms and playing games are illegal pastimes this close to the border and may or may not be penalized. 'Nothing was certain' ('Nichts war gewiß', G 177), the narrator sums up one such experience of arbitrariness after the family have been charged with 'bawling drinking songs' ('Brüllen von Kneipenliedern') on a walk in the border area. With a mixture of sarcasm and resignation, she comments on the seemingly absurd political logic behind their arrest: 'Presumably Moscow was being pressured by the Far East, hence strict orders of the day for the Berlin border. Perhaps we were meant to be an example.' ('Wahrscheinlich schlug Fernost auf Moskau, und es gab strenge Tagesbefehle für die Berliner Grenze. Vielleicht sollten wir ein Exempel sein', G 177).[25] Once the last remaining window to the (Western) world, the lakeside by the family garden, is properly closed off, their enclosure is complete:

> Now the ring is closed. [...] Instead of barbed wire there is concrete now. Neat, opaque, sturdy. [...] Any climbing expert will tell you:

---

[25] There is, however, the odd experience of humanity, too. When the family risk their lives while freeing a dog from the barbed wire, a border guard cautiously joins in the operation (G 10).

you won't manage that. Once up there, you'll slip back to where you belong.

Nun ist der Ring geschlossen. [...] Statt Stacheldraht nun Beton. Sauber, undurchsichtig, stabil. [...] Jeder Kletterexperte sieht sofort: Das packst du nicht. Von dort oben rutschst du wieder dahin, wo du hingehörst. (G 17)

'Ring' and 'circle' are recurrent metaphors in Schütz's novel. The hopelessness which the ring image evokes is enhanced by the perpetual movement of the border patrol dogs 'round and round the Wall. [...] Until the end of time' ('Immer um den Mauerring herum. [...] Bis ans Ende der Zeit', G 23). Curiously, the family's complete walling-off leads to a reversal of directions and their ideological appropriation, thus rehabilitating 'the difference between politics and geography' ('Unterschied zwischen Politik und Geographie', G 21). Where the family live, the sun rises in the West and 'one learns to turn a blind eye' ('Man übt das Augenverschließen', G 7) to the border and its implications, to get on with the challenges of everyday life. Mastering this technique to perfection, the female narrator is eager to compensate on the domestic front for state-imposed restrictions. In an attempt to create a sense of normality in their enclave next to the death strip, she tirelessly applies herself to the routines of daily domesticity. She heats the house, feeds the family and animals, and waters her plants and trees in the garden. She cares for the needs of her daughter Betty, who cannot walk and suffers from absence seizures and a lack of oxygen: 'I am always there, always vigilant' ('Ich bin immer da und immer wachsam', 77), she insists. Betty's fragile health seismographically reflects the state of things in the family's microcosm. It is reason for perseverance and optimism in the 'age of resignation' ('Zeitalter der Resignation', G 193) that is the GDR after 1961:

Worries about Betty are part of our life just like the concrete [wall], this declaration of power in our enclosure. So far and no further, it seems to say. There are terrestrial limits to our hopes, but none overhead. Betty's rosy mouth is reason enough for us to become jubilant.

> Die Sorgen um Betty gehören [zu unserem Leben] dazu wie der
> Beton, der Machtbeweis, im Gehege. Bis hierhin und nicht weiter.
> Unsere Hoffnungen haben im Irdischen Grenzen, aber nicht in der
> Luft. Bettys rosiger Mund läßt uns jubeln. (G 174)

However, Betty's lifeline – oxygen – is increasingly cut off by the government's continuous and clandestine efforts to fortify the Wall at nature's expense: 'The lakefront where pines, birches and willows used to grow lies flat in the midday sun. There is a dead silence' ('Das Ufer, wo früher die Kiefern, Birken und Weiden standen, liegt glattgewalzt in der Mittagssonne. Totenstille', G 85).[26] Yet although the family's home ground is delimited and corrupted by political and military power, the issues at stake are private concerns, irrespective of politics and its appropriation of space. The Wall's reinforcement is first and foremost a threat to Betty's health and a sign of disrespect for nature. Hence to the family, 'the Wall itself is more acceptable than the fact that trees fell victim to it' ('Die Mauer würde die Familie noch eher akzeptieren als die [dafür] umgeschlagenen Bäume').[27] While the existence and potential danger of the border are acknowledged, this is, Schütz insists, 'a story where people's happiness is to do with the girl's recovery, not politics' ('[sind] Menschen plötzlich glücklich [...] aus Gründen, die mit der Gesundung des Mädchens zu tun haben und nicht mit der Politik').[28]

A gardener by training, the narrator's outlook on life is shaped by her understanding of nature, a perpetual process of growth and decay which human life is only part of. Nature's resistance towards the troubles of history has been a source of hope, surprise and optimism in the narrator's life: amid the Dresden firestorm of February 1945, a camellia miraculously started blossoming in the gardens of Pillnitz Castle. From her garden, flowers and trees are spilling over the Wall into the death strip in the 1970s, and anyway,

---

[26] Schütz refers to the addition of a second wall to set up the death strip – a mined corridor for border patrol vehicles, dogs and other deterrents.
[27] Liu, '"In einem gewissen Sinne"'
[28] Liu, '"In einem gewissen Sinne"'

[t]he eels and zanders live like they always have done. The birds
are oblivious to laws in any event. No trouble with gravity, no
despair over borders.

Die Aale und Havelzander leben wie in alten Zeiten. Die Vögel
haben sowieso wenig Gesetz im Leibe. Keine Not mit der
Schwerkraft, keinen Kummer vor Grenzen. (G 7)

Seemingly insurmountable by humans, the border proves to be a corridor
rather than a barrier for such casual border-crossers. The wind, too, 'carries many
a thing to us' ('trägt uns manches zu', G 7) across the lake. Yet the frontier can
deceive those who ignore it: a dog nearly dies while trying to squeeze through the
barbed wire, and the family's adopted cat falls into a death trap by the Wall.
Unlike their daring visitors, the area's inhabitants seem less tempted to transgress
the line. Perhaps this is because, although borders are intrinsically vulnerable, the
inhabitants themselves are equally vulnerable to the consequences of
transgression and so only in moments of desperation will they challenge them.
Like other occupants of precarious 'in-between' places, the narrator and her
family may find themselves 'incessantly prepared to jump the border, but [...] do
not actually intend to take the plunge' ('beständig auf dem Sprung entlang ihrer
Grenze, aber [...] sie wollen [den Absprung] gar nicht finden').[29] In fact, the
increasing physical limits imposed on their living space in the name of supposed
peace-keeping seem to enhance the value of the (family) garden which, in social
and cultural history, has been

[...] the only place where one could live in peace with the
world.[...] It is the primeval place, *hortus conclusus*, the enclosed
and peaceful place, paradise. The garden's quietude presupposes
that the garden is also a prison.[30]

Especially in dictatorships, the intrinsic closedness of the garden has provided the
individual with a place for inner emigration, a niche (from) where they could

---

[29] Rüdiger Görner, *Grenzen, Schwellen, Übergänge: Zur Poetik des Transitorischen* (Göttingen:
Vandenhoeck & Ruprecht, 2001), 58.
[30] Georg Seeßlen, 'Rückzug ins Paradies: Der Garten als Ort der geschlossenen Welt', *Freitag*, 27-
28 (2007).

escape or defy authority. Although the garden of Schütz's narrator is such a place, it is continuously exposed to silent intruders: the searchlights of watchtowers and pricked-up ears of border guards. Hence a visitor's comment that her garden is 'the most genuine place in the world' ('der ehrlichste Platz der Welt') leaves the narrator perplexed (G 89).

Where political circumstances are secondary and daily matters rule, the responsibility to keep up optimism lie with her, she believes. Referring to early experiences of guilt and indispensability ('Unabkömmlichkeit, die mir in den Knochen steckte', G 195) during and after the Second World War (see also G 236), she aims to create a sphere that is immune to state intervention by drawing an invisible 'chalk circle' around her family:

> An archetypal mother and centre of a small community, she is able
> to put everything in order and radiate happiness. She only has to fit
> their small universe into the next larger one and it will be immune
> to the world.[31]

Compared to the state-imposed restrictions of territory in the name of dubious peace-keeping, the narrator imposes limitations on herself and her family to appease at the human and humane level. Her balancing of powers is a demanding task. It requires a strong sense of responsibility, the ability to dissimulate, and the odd white lie. It also depends on her successful suppression of reality, as in the case of Betty's health: 'Betty is a good, a happy child. If the doctor knows anything different, I will have to avoid her' ('Betty ist ein gutes, frohes Kind. Wenn die Stationsärztin etwas anderes weiß, muß ich ihr aus dem Wege gehen', G 80), she says when confronted with alarming test results. Furthermore, the narrator's endeavour to maintain optimism and peace on the small scale ('Frieden im Kleinen') requires imagination and defiance: 'You could sow beans and cultivate hops in the shadow of the concrete' ('Du könntest im Betonschatten Kletterbohnen stecken oder Hopfen aufziehen'), she ponders as the

---

[31] Regina General, 'Wunder haben keine feste Haut. In Helga Schütz' Buch "Grenze zum gestrigen Tag" geht es um Behinderungen vielfältigster Art', *Freitag*, 9 (2002).

Wall 'grows' higher (G 85). And after the lake has been lost to the fortified border, she stubbornly builds a pond in the garden and settles plants and mandarin ducks in it.

It is evident from the above that 'limitation' exceeds its topographical denotation in Schütz's novel. The fact that private issues seem to override political ones cannot conceal that the daily presence of the Wall puts the family's stamina and patience to the test. In the words of the author, 'a novel about the Berlin Wall is possibly concerned with limitations of an altogether different kind' ('Ein Roman, der von der Mauer handelt, meint möglicherweise ganz andere Grenzen').[32] Rare outbursts of frustration reveal the complexity and burden of the narrator's role(s):

> My anger comes straight from my harried heart. Everything is crowding together. Betty's cough. The imperishable concrete. The ashes in the cellar every morning. Hugo's ignorance over the past few weeks. He has only been interested in his opera and the Vietnam War. He didn't even have time to photograph the ducks.

> Mein Zorn steigt direkt aus meinem gepreßten Herzen. Es drängt sich so vieles zusammen. Bettys Husten. Der ewige Beton. Die Asche jeden Morgen im Keller. Hugos Ignoranz in den vergangenen Wochen. Er kümmert sich nur noch um die Oper und den Krieg in Vietnam. Er hatte nicht einmal Zeit zum Entenfotografieren. (G 101)

The passage above leads one to suspect, too, that 'borders' have come in the way of the relationship between the narrator and Hugo. The latter is a maverick composer who meddles in politics and, perhaps, has long stopped loving only one woman. His professional and political intrepidness contrasts with her sedentary existence, her dedication to what might be called traditionally 'female' areas of life. The dwindling intimacy of her relationship intensifies the narrator's sense of physical and social isolation in her enclave by the Wall: 'Nobody is allowed near me and I cannot flee' ('Niemand darf zu mir kommen und ich kann nicht fliehen', G 202). Thus she seeks out a smallholding nearby which is

---

[32] Liu, "'In einem gewissen Sinne'".

supposed to be her secret, alternative retreat. Yet her self-imposed exile fails to convince anybody, including herself, and she soon flees the unfamiliar 'territory without a visible border' ('Territorium, wo man die Grenze nicht sieht', G 180).

Yet next to the Wall and other constants, life continues and the narrator is confronted with further experiences of detachment and loss. Her son Niklas flies the nest, and days after the GDR singer ßß's infamous Cologne concert of 1976, after which he was refused re-entry into the GDR, her partner Hugo leaves for a work trip to Switzerland. The transit area at East Berlin's Schönefeld Airport 'is a room which you enter and never return from. Unless a miracle happens' ('ein Raum, da geht man hinein und kommt nicht wieder. Es müßte schon ein Wunder geschehen', G 270). The narrator's apprehension proves well-founded: Hugo is denied re-entry into the GDR, for no explicit reason but amid rumours that he signed a politically sensitive petition (G 280-82). His involuntary absence coincides with the sudden death of their daughter Betty in hospital. Even this final act of parting is subjected to the GDR's rigid ideology and clumsy bureaucracy which, under the circumstances, equals mockery: 'I hope you appreciate your relatives' permission to enter the border area [to attend the funeral]' ('Hoffentlich wissen Sie die Berechtigungsscheine für Ihre Angehörigen zum Betreten des Grenzgebietes [für die Beerdingung] zu schätzen', G 279), an official asserts.[33] And after a subsequent drunken attempt to demolish the Wall with a boulder, the narrator is met with incomprehension by the local registrar:

> It is inconceivable to him how I, a worker, could become delinquent so rapidly. Unmarried, without income, and on the side of elements hampering progress and peace.

> Er will nicht begreifen, wie ich, eine Arbeiterin, so rapide auf die schiefe Bahn geraten konnte. Unverheiratet, ohne Einkommen und dann noch auf Sciten von Elementen, die den Fortschritt und Frieden stören. (G 291)

---

[33] Betty's father Hugo is not allowed to attend her funeral. To make things worse, the narrator's other accomplices – her cat and horses – also die.

The loss and isolation she suffers intensify the narrator's need to retrace
and remember her own history in relation to places which she and her family have
inhabited or fled. She provides us with glimpses of a family history marked by
fragmentation and displacement in and after the War. For instance, there is the
family's expulsion from Silesia, another no man's land bitterly missed by her
older relatives (G 211). There is the temporary flight from Dresden to a Harz
village via the zonal border at Ellrich in 1947.

On the interrelation of memory and place in Schütz's work, N. Ann Rider
has noted that 'landscapes are the tactile link to German history':[34]

> For Schütz, obtaining access to moments absent in memory
> requires recognition of the physical nature of historical experience.
> Typically in Schütz' work physical geography – notably,
> architecture and landscape – becomes the medium through which
> the physical body engages in history. Place stimulates the sense
> perception which, in a Proustian manner, activates involuntary
> memory.[35]

As her narrator cleans out the oven in the morning, landscape-like
markings on cinder pieces trigger contrasting memories of her adolescence in
wintry post-war Dresden: 'Debris-lined streets. A cleared square with little stalls
and decorated [...]. An oasis: the Dresden Christmas market' ('Trümmergesäumte
Straßen. Ein freigeräumter Platz mit kleinen Buden und geputzten
Fichtenbäumchen [...]. Wie eine Oase der Striezelmarkt', G 184). Trees, a wooden
pillar, an old boat and building stones are used to witness and date episodes of
happiness in the midst of the ruined city:

> Through a window in the cellar we are able to enter [the soot-
> blackened city-hall tower]. Little Paul has taken my hand. [...] [The
> wind] blows the scarf off my head. [...] The weather and the times
> were unimportant now. A heart and the date, 13 February 1952,
> engraved in a stone at the top.

---

[34] N. Ann Rider, 'The Journey Eastward: Helga Schütz' *Vom Glanz der Elbe* and the Mnemonic
Politics of German Unification', in Carol Anne Costabile-Heming et al. (eds.), *Textual Responses
to German Unification* (Berlin: de Gruyter, 2001), 17-34 (here 30).
[35] Rider, 'The Journey Eastward', 29.

> Wir haben durch ein Kellerfenster [im rußgeschwärzten Rathausturm] einen Einstieg gefunden. Paulchen hat mich an die Hand genommen. [...] [Wind] reißt mir das Tuch vom Kopf [...]. Das Wetter und die Zeit spielten keine Rolle mehr. Ein Herz und das Datum 13.2.52 ganz oben in einem Stein. (G 185)

The narrator's recollection of such moments clashes with official depictions and interpretations of post-war realities. The metaphor of the unruly scarf is used to counter linguistic clichés used to label history and its images:

> Mountaineers had taken photos from the city-hall tower. 'The view from the heavily damaged city-hall tower' [or] 'The whole extent of the destruction', as the captions in magazines and books would read from now on. Ghost-like, my scarf keeps wafting through those images.

> Bergsteiger hatten vom Rathausturm herab eine Serie Fotos aufgenommen. Blick vom schwer beschädigten Rathausturm. Das ganze Ausmaß der Zerstörung. So lauteten fortan in Illustrierten und Büchern die Bildunterschriften. In diesen Fotos geistert mein Tuch. (G 185)

Like the narrator's adult life next to the Berlin Wall, her Dresden youth is depicted as being entangled in, yet also unbroken by, history on a larger scale ('Großgeschichte'). Amid depictions of post-war confusion and Cold War 'icons', Schütz presents us with a somewhat innocent account of life in places which have been damaged as a result of political and military showdowns.

In *Border to Yesterday*, place offers a vital link between the present and the past, even though the traces of that past are often deliberately obscured by the GDR authorities. On and underneath the alleged no man's land around her, Schütz's narrator uncovers numerous (hi)stories. Apart from buried military boots and uniforms, for instance, her garden holds another surprise: the family home sits on a line where glaciers from eastern and western directions once met: 'We are living on the edge of an ice layer' ('Wir leben auf einer Eisrandlage', G 92). A prehistoric mirror-image of Cold-War lines of confrontation, a premonition of displacement and isolation as furthered by the GDR authorities. In the name of peace and progress, the narrator learns, old homesteads have been demolished and paddocks flattened overnight: 'Too close to the border. Modern lights and two watchtowers will replace them' ('Zu nahe an der Grenze. Moderne Leuchten und zwei Wachtürme sollen hingesetzt werden', G 243).

Schütz' concern with politically induced marginalization and displacement is closely linked to her criticism of militarism in the past and present. On her explorations of the surrounding prohibited zone, her narrator discovers traces of military destruction everywhere: ruins in the park, anti-tank trenches and the remains of an ordnance factory in the woods, and the skidmarks of Russian tanks across the heath. A scarred landscape, inhuman and deserted, where children nevertheless loved to play, where rare plants grow and birds and deer have settled. An area bearing witness to Nazi corruption and guilt:

> In the woods we found a cross made from birch [and helmets]. Soldiers' graves. I learn that seven deserters were shot here at Carolinenhöhe, eighteen-year-old boys who had been drafted for the *Volkssturm* in 1945. They had refused to fight in the war at that stage.

> Wir haben im Wald ein Kreuz aus Birkenstämmen [und Helme] gefunden. Soldatengräber. Meine Nachfrage [...] bringt zutage, daß hier bei Carolinenhöhe sieben Deserteure erschossen wurden, achtzehnjährige Jungen, die man 1945 zum Volkssturm eingezogen hatte. Sie hatten sich geweigert, den Krieg noch mitzumachen. (G 71)

An area, too, which tells of the hypocritical way in which the GDR dealt with such remnants of the Nazi past: the narrator's attempts to find out the exact circumstances of her discovery are met with reluctance and anxiousness at the local municipal office, where the secretary advises her to let bygones be bygones:

> The cross [...] has repeatedly been removed by the officials. They don't dare touch the helmets though, hoping instead that their steel plate will merge into the ground one day, sink into the sand, overgrown by heath land [...]. Hoping for the metal to rust and be forgotten. [...] The officials know who the [soldiers'] unresting relatives are, but the matter shall not be publicized. [...] The secretary only hints at certain things. She'd rather not be quoted. I advise you to let the matter rest [she says].

> Das Kreuz ist [...] von offizieller Seite immer wieder beseitigt
> worden. An die Helme traut sich keiner ran. Man hofft, daß das
> Blech eines Tages im Waldboden verschwindet, im Sand versinkt,
> mit Heide überwuchert [...]. Hofft auf Rost und Vergessen. [...] Der
> Name der rührigen Verwandten [der Soldaten] ist den zuständigen
> Leuten bekannt, man will jedoch den Vorgang nicht öffentlich
> machen. [...] Die Gemeindesekretärin läßt manches nur
> durchblicken. Sie möchte nichts gesagt haben. Ich rate Ihnen, die
> Sache im Dunkeln des Waldes ruhen zu lassen [sagt sie]. (G 71-72)

The secretary's behaviour both reveals and reflects the GDR's duplicity towards places which represented 'tricky' ('verzwickte') episodes of the past. While those young deserters were potential anti-fascists and Red Army allies, they refused to obey military orders, she insists. She thus calls for discretion in the politically sensitive area around the Berlin Wall: 'Not yet another thing in the deep woods and so close to the border' ('Nur nicht noch was mitten im Wald und so dicht an der Grenze', G 72). After all, GDR border guards may be tempted to follow the historical example and desert, or refuse to shoot at defectors, she implies.

In Schütz' text, the repressive way in which the GDR dealt with disagreeable episodes and settings of history also refers to the country's relationship with the Russian occupational forces. For one, the coexistence of the Russians' military presence and a flourishing barter economy in her novel reflects the ambivalent treatment which the occupational forces received both at state and private levels in the GDR (G 28 and 38-39). Yet light is also shed on the more secretive and repressed aspects of Russian-GDR relations since the Second World War. For instance, the brutal punishment of deviant young Russian soldiers meets with silent approval in the German Democratic Republic. Officials successfully prevent a grass-roots initiative to uncover and restore the ruin of a temple near Sanssouci. The excavations might disclose a secret KGB compound from where defectors are sent to Siberian imprisonment (G 271 and 281).

In her novel *Border to Yesterday*, Helga Schütz reverts to the time and place of the GDR for a retrospective of personal and family history. Her choice of a momentous setting for her novel is counteracted, though not trivialized, by her non-ideological depiction of (attempted) normality in the shadow of the Berlin Wall. Her recollection of history on a small scale does without the allegories of brutality of the GDR regime which dominated the 'totalitarian' discourse about the GDR in the 1990s. Hers is a non-judgemental depiction of the diversity of human behaviour and strategies to deal with the ideological and spatial constraints of the GDR. Her narrator's strategy is what I have termed 'negotiating no man's land', both in the narrower and wider sense. The family home by the Wall displays 'the particular vitality of a border area whose inhabitants actually profit from the border's impulses'.[36] The void of the adjoining death strip is invaded by overflowing plant and animal life from her garden, suggesting permeability. The narrator trespasses and explores the surrounding 'prohibited zone', unearthing relics of suppressed episodes of history. However, she does not only wrest territory and truth from the hostile landscape around her. In a metaphorical sense, the narrator and her family eke out a degree of normality, serenity and happiness from an otherwise bleak political and geographical situation and outlook. 'Each line [of the novel] tells of the dictatorship without having been damaged by it',[37] one critic remarked.

Schütz's novel is a personal account of the fragmenting and displacing effects which GDR politics, militarism and environmental ignorance have had on the lives and living spaces of ordinary people. The author believes, however, that she has 'not written a historical novel' ('keinen historischen Roman geschrieben'). Rather, she maintains, 'it is also a story of today, only perhaps about timeless issues' ('Es ist doch auch ein Buch von heute, nur geht es vielleicht um zeitlose Angelegenheiten').[38] Schütz's novel is therefore an alternative, highly subjective account of lives whose histories do not correspond to official chronologies. Similar to other women's writing after unification, her subjective

---

[36] Wilfried von Bredow, 'Beiderseitigkeit – Vom Verschwinden und Wiederauftauchen politischer Grenzen', in Görner and Kirkbright (eds.), *Nachdenken*, 57-71 (here 69-70).
[37] Radisch, 'Morsezeichen'.
[38] Liu, '"In einem gewissen Sinne"'

take on history serves to question presumed historical certainties and to challenge the authority of abstract discourse about the past.

> The dominant gesture [...] is one of questioning: closed chapters of the past are opened up to enquiry, and certainties about history are replaced by a recognition of complexities and ambiguities which make final judgements problematic.[39]

Perhaps like no other medium, literature can achieve both, 'Remembering *and* leaving-alone, forgetting *and* reminding [of the past]' ('Erinnern *und* In-Ruhe-lassen, Vergessen *und* Wach-halten').[40] Schütz's narratives of autonomous, self-determined lives in adverse circumstances can be understood as an ongoing, if subtle, demand for a non-ideological approach to discourse about the GDR. As the GDR's political geography has been increasingly disappearing under forgiving grass and modern infrastructure, her novel can be read as a plea against forgetting and suppressing that past.

---

[39] Helen Bridge, *Women's Writing and Historiography in the GDR* (Oxford: OUP, 2002), 227.
[40] Schorlemmer, 'Erinnern und Vergessen'.

CHAPTER 12

From a Topography of Hope to a Nightmarish 'Non-Place': Chronotopes in Christa Wolf's 'June Afternoon', 'Unter den Linden' and *What Remains*

Renate Rechtien

Christa Wolf is without doubt one of the leading contemporary writers to have emerged from the former German Democratic Republic. As a member of a generation whose personal biographies have closely mirrored the history of twentieth century Germany, she was raised under National Socialism, forced to flee her childhood home in the former eastern territories of the Reich at the age of sixteen, and ended up more or less by chance in the socialist part of divided Germany. Even though initially forged under the impact of the guilt she had incurred as a child of the Third Reich, her commitment to socialist ideas and her attachment to GDR society have been defining characteristics of her work. Wolf has mainly written prose narratives, and her battle for the development of realist forms that would pose a credible alternative to Socialist Realist dogma played a major role in producing a shift towards modernism in GDR literature as a whole. Her insistence on the principle of 'subjective authenticity', her contention that the author should always be present in the text to give it a 'fourth dimension' of moral integrity and her extensive explorations of issues of memory, history, and identity from the perspective of psychological and emotional experience, are amongst her most significant contributions in this regard. Wolf's growing and eventually irretrievable disillusionment with GDR socialism repeatedly precipitated deep personal crises which coincided with points of caesura in the history of GDR socialism and its eventual demise. Confronted with the growing isolation and alienation of committed writers in her country, but increasingly aware of her own entanglement as a writer and public persona in the very processes she set out to criticize, she has been prompted to explore with ever greater intensity the interplay between 'rift[s] in the fabric of time' ('Ri[sse] im Gewebe der Zeit') and rifts in the self by writing autobiographically.[1]

Wolf's quest for the self has involved spatial as well as temporal considerations, and she has viewed both dimensions as markers of identity that shape subjectivity and selfhood. Time, she asserted in her seminal essay of 1972, 'The Reader and the Writer' ('Lesen und Schreiben'), is a subjective experience, 'tied to us, subjects who live in objective circumstances' ('an uns gebunden, Subjekte, die in objektiven Verhältnissen leben').[2] Place plays a similar role, as the narrator of her first major prose work, *The Quest for Christa T.* (*Nachdenken über Christa T.*, 1968) observes:

> But they're not so unimportant, the places we live in. They aren't only the framework for our actions, they involve themselves in the actions, they change the scenery; and not infrequently, when we say 'circumstances', what we really mean is a particular place which paid no attention to us.

> Aber so unwichtig sind die Orte nicht, an denen wir leben. Sie bleiben ja nicht Rahmen für unsere Auftritte, sie mischen sich ein, sie verändern die Szene, und nicht selten ist, wenn wir ‚Verhältnisse' sagen, einfach irgendein bestimmter Ort gemeint, der sich nichts aus uns macht. (WA II, 153)[3]

Given, moreover, that socialist space, as David Crowley and Susan Reid have noted, was always a political space 'claimed by the State on behalf of the

---

[1] Wolf's entire oeuvre is pervaded with reflections on this theme, a most recent example of which is 'Donnerstag, 27. September 2001', in Christa Wolf, *Mit anderem Blick* (Frankfurt a.M.: Suhrkamp, 2005), 171-90 (here 171). See also Cheryl Dueck's extensive study of this theme in *Rifts in Time and in the Self: The Female Subject in Two Generations of East German Women Writers* (Amsterdam and New York: Rodopi, 2004). For an extensive examination of the development of the autobiographical dimension in Wolf's writing, see Dennis Tate, *Shifting Perspectives. East German Autobiographical Narratives before and after the End of the GDR*, (New York: Camden House, 2007), 194-235.

[2] Christa Wolf, 'Lesen und Schreiben', in Christa Wolf, *Werkausgabe*, ed. by Sonja Hilzinger, 12 vols. (Munich: Luchterhand, 1999-2001), IV, 238-82 (here 242). Unless otherwise stated, translations from Wolf's texts are my own. Further references to this edition of Wolf's collected works are given as WA.

[3] Christa Wolf, *The Quest for Christa T.*, trans. Christopher Middleton (London: Virago, 1982), 136-37 (adapted).

working people', but controlled by national regimes (such as the Socialist Unity Party in the GDR) through 'pervasive efforts to permeate not only places of work and public ceremony but also the most intimate spaces of the everyday with ideological meaning',[4] spatialization in Wolf's writing has inevitably been highly charged with political meaning. In this regard it is worth remembering that Wolf's battle for subjective authenticity in the 1960s and beyond involved the rejection of notions of space and time along conventional socialist realist lines. Influenced by what Einstein's Theory of Relativity had done for physics, namely to break with established concepts of time and space, she conceived of writing as a process which springs from what she called 'depth', to be understood as the composite of an author's experiences, including 'memory, fantasy and social or moral consciousness'.[5] Blurring the boundaries between past, present, and future, the realism she had in mind has the potential of involving both the writer and the reader in a creative process of change, resisting the ossification of art and literature into a finished 'product' and conceiving of writing as a dynamic and open process akin to life itself.

This chapter will examine the significance of place in two of Wolf's early texts which illustrate particularly pertinently the radical shift in her approach and style. It argues that her rejection of the theories of Georg Lukács and her experimentation with a prose writing that is subject-centred, process-oriented, and non-normative as well as increasingly aware of the polysemantic nature of language, echoes Mikhail Bakhtin's radical rethinking of the novel in his four seminal essays published in *The Dialogic Imagination*.[6] It examines in particular Wolf's exploration of the chronotope as a spatio-temporal constellation that

---

[4] David Crowley and Susan E. Reid (eds.), *Socialist Spaces: Sites of Everyday Life in the Eastern Bloc* (Oxford and New York: Berg, 2000), 3. Full title and page references for this introduction?
[5] See Karen McPherson, 'Introduction', in Christa Wolf, *The Fourth Dimension: Interviews with Christa Wolf,* trans. Hilary Pilkington (London and New York: Verso, 1988), vii-xxvii (here xi).
[6] Mikhail Bakhtin, *The Dialogic Imagination*, ed. by Michael Holquist, trans. Caryl Emerson and Michael Holquist (Austin: U of Texas P, 1981). For an excellent introduction to the significance of Bakhtin's rethinking of the novel in Russian culture, see Caryl Emerson, *The First Hundred Years of Mikhail Bakhtin*, (Princeton: Princeton UP\, 1997).

affords the modern prose work precisely the 'depth' Wolf was aiming for, without forcing it into normative generic straightjackets. The short stories 'June Afternoon' ('Juninachmittag', 1965) and 'Unter den Linden' (published in 1974, but written during the late 1960s) both view GDR socialism through the prism of alternative 'visions' which, ambiguous and multifaceted in nature, transform the stultifying and stifling conditions of really existing socialist spaces into an imaginative realm of new potentialities. Both claim for the writer and for literature a place at the heart of socialist society, but one liberated from Party dogma and ideology. This is symbolically expressed not least by the fact that both narratives are set in or near East Berlin, the capital of the socialist state and the place which Wolf has most emphatically associated with a sense of home and belonging.[7] By way of conclusion, the chapter will contrast the topography of hope which is ultimately re-established in these earlier texts with the dashed hopes and growing despair of Wolf's text *What Remains* (*Was bleibt*, 1990), published after the fall of the East German regime. Anticipation of the demise of the GDR during a period of existential crisis in the late 1970s has turned the city as the place around which all the author's utopian longing had gravitated over time into a hellish 'non-place'.

Critics have generally associated Christa Wolf's break with socialist realism and her adoption of modernist techniques and forms with *The Quest for Christa T.,* the prose work which marked the beginning of her international success.[8] However, it is actually with 'June Afternoon', an experimental short prose text written three years earlier, that this transition was made.[9] As the author stressed in a recent interview, it was this narrative which led to the discovery of

---

[7] In a recent interview, Wolf stated in this regard: 'I lost my Heimat a long time ago, it was on the other side of the river Oder. My home is Berlin, and I would not wish to live anywhere else, not even always in the country. [...] I have lived in Berlin since the 1950s; my life, my whole development has taken place in this city, and I have gone through good as well as difficult times here.' Interview with Hanns-Bruno Kammertöns and Stephan Lebert, 'Bei mir dauert alles sehr lange', *Die Zeit*, 29 September 2005, 17-20 (here 18).

[8] A recent example is Cheryl Dueck's *Rifts in Time and in the Self.*

[9] 'June Afternoon' was written between June and August of 1965 (WA III, 560)

'my kind of realism' ('meine Art von Realismus').[10] From the outset, this carefully crafted piece of prose writing goes firmly against the grain of Socialist Realist norms. An assertive, confident narrative voice establishes immediately, for instance, that readers expecting a conventional story, '[something firm, tangible, like a pot with two handles, to be held and drunk from [...]' ('[et]was Festes, Greifbares, wie ein Topf mit zwei Henkeln, zum Anfassen und zum Daraus-Trinken [...]'), will not be satisfied (WA III, 87).[11] Nor does the spatial setting conform to the Socialist Unity Party's cultural policies which demanded that works of art and literature must focus on the world of socialist production and highlight the achievements of workers and peasants in their daily struggle of furthering socialism's progress. Almost like a painter, the author sketches instead an intimate, dreamy garden scene in which a family relaxes in the beauty and quiet of their opulent and lovingly tended garden. Apart from brief interactions and verbal exchanges amongst the members of the family and a few conversations with their neighbours, there is neither a plot nor action. The diary-like concentration on a single afternoon is, in fact, an early example of Wolf's lasting fascination with the narrative potential of everyday experience, which she has only recently again made fruitful with the publication of a substantial volume of diary-like texts entitled *One Day in the Year* (*Ein Tag im Jahr*)[12]. As I have argued elsewhere, the temporal framework of the everyday, which emphasizes the cyclical nature of human action and experience and evokes repetition, sameness and stasis, provides a fruitful alternative to linear notions of time which have underpinned both the Socialist Realist and the Bourgeois Realist tradition,

---

[10] 'Bei mir dauert alles sehr lange', 19.
[11] Christa Wolf, 'June Afternoon', in Wolf, *What Remains and Other Stories*, trans. Heike Schwarzbauer and Rick Takvorian (Chicago: U of Chicago P, 1993), (adapted), 43-65 (here 43). All further references to this edition are given as WR.
[12] Christa Wolf, *Ein Tag im Jahr. 1960-2000* (Munich: Luchterhand, 2003).

suggesting that human action should be geared towards the achievement of an ultimate goal.[13]

Made up largely of interior monologue and revolving with its stream of consciousness style around the reflections and self-reflections of the narrator, Wolf's text resists clear-cut generic boundaries and frees the subject from the grip of authorial omniscience or plot-line, permitting the subjectivity of the writing self to determine the story's shape and meaning. The central figure is clearly based on the author herself, since she is a writer and an avid reader who is looking for fresh inspiration.[14] In fact, the story's concentration on literature – which is underlined by the fact that the central figure refuses to leave her garden chair all afternoon, barely able to conceal her irritation whenever she is forced to combine her desire for self-abandonment in literature with her mothering role or her responsibilities as a good neighbour – is itself an indication that the subject of writing and the issue of the role of the writer and her place in socialist society are principal concerns of the text. By addressing the reader directly, with phrases such as 'if you understand what I mean' ('falls Sie verstehen, was ich meine', WR 43; WA III, 87), 'believe me' ('Sie können mir glauben', WR 45; WA III, 89), or [e]xcuse me' ('[v]erzeihen Sie', WR 54; WA III, 99), moreover, the story invites the reader to respond to and take part in the creative process. In clear defiance of Socialist Realist doctrine, the creation of meaning is conceived of as an open process between writer and reader. This is immediately underscored also by Wolf's polysemantic use of language. When she offers her reader a 'vision, perhaps, if you understand what I mean' ('[e]ine Vision vielleicht, falls Sie verstehen, was

---

[13] For an extensive discussion of Wolf's fascination with everyday experience, see Renate Rechtien, ' "[...] eine Autobiographie nach anderen Gesichtspunkten als denen der äußeren Historie und Chronologie." Christa Wolfs Alltagsprosa als autobiographisches Projekt', in Peter Barker, Marc-Dietrich Ohse, and Dennis Tate (eds.), *Views from Abroad: Die DDR aus britischer Perspektive* (Bertelsmann: Bielefeld, 2007), 223-34.

[14] Helen Fehervary has identified the book the narrator is absorbed in as Marie-Louise Kaschnitz's *Long Shadows* (*Lange Schatten*, 1960). In fact, Fehervary has argued that Kaschnitz assumes the role of a 'third person' in the text, extending the relationship between narrator and reader by that of another female authorial presence. See Fehervary, 'Christa Wolf's Prose: A Landscape of Masks', in Marilyn Sibley Fries (ed.), *Responses to Christa Wolf: Critical Essays* (Detroit: Wayne State UP, 1989) 162-85 (here 185).

ich meine', WR 43; WA III, 87), she leaves it to the reader's imagination and to an engagement with her text to decide what kind of vision might be invoked here. Subjective, fragmentary, open-ended, non-normative, non-generic, reader-response oriented, and ambiguous in its use of language, the realism Wolf was developing in the mid-1960s, could well have been inspired by Mikhail Bakhtin's radical rethinking of the novel in the early part of the twentieth century. If it was – although Wolf never refers to Bakhtin as an influence - the fact that Bakhtin reinterpreted nineteenth-century German aesthetics in the light of Einstein's Theory of Relativity and aimed, in particular, at dethroning the authority of Georg Lukács, will clearly have been of some attraction to her.[15]

Wolf's use in 'June Afternoon' of an idyllic chronotope as a strategy of emphasizing place is especially interesting. A term coined by Bakhtin to express his belief in the fundamental inseparability of time and space, the chronotope intrinsically connects all temporal and spatial relationships expressed in literature, constructing a particular time-space constellation that links a narrative to other literary works over time and across traditions.[16] The chronotope's significance is that it is 'the organizing center' and 'the place where the knots of narrative are tied and untied' and where 'the meaning that shapes narrative' lies. Its function, according to Bakhtin, is that it

> materiali[zes] time in space, emerges as a center for concretizing representation, [...] a force giving body to the entire novel. All the novel's abstract elements – philosophical and social generalizations, ideas, analyses of cause and effect – gravitate toward the chronotope and through it take on flesh and blood, permitting the imaging power of art to do its work. Such is the representational significance of the chronotope.[17]

---

[15] See Emerson, *The First Hundred Years of Mikhail Bakhtin*, especially 110-53.
[16] M.M. Bakhtin, 'Forms of Time and of the Chronotope in the Novel', in *The Dialogic Imagination. Four Essays*, ed. by Michael Holquist, trans. Caryl Emerson and Michael Holquist (Austin: U of Texas P, 1981), 84-258 (here 84).
[17] Bakhtin, 'Forms of Time and of the Chronotope', 250.

In the idyllic chronotope, emphasis is given to unity of place, slowing down the passage of time and highlighting stability, rootedness and belonging. The idyll illuminates the fundamental aspects of everyday life, foregrounding family relationships over the generations, parent's loving care and protection of their children, and life in harmony with the rhythms of nature.[18] The idyllic garden scene Wolf constructs in 'June Afternoon' appears, at first glance, to subscribe to literary traditions which employed the idyll to full effect.[19] The central image of a perfect garden complete with clichéd detail such as a deck chair and a snail (WR 45; WA III, 89), a nuclear family consisting of father, mother, and two children, the playful and loving engagement of family members in the pursuit of leisure, the care and attention bestowed on the garden, and human beings living in perfect peace and harmony with nature, all these elements at the very least appear to flirt with the bourgeois *Bildungsroman*, the provincial novel or the folkloristic *Heimat* novel. Given that the place is expressly described as '[t]he archetype of a garden' and '[g]arden incarnate' ('Das Urbild eines Gartens. Der Garten überhaupt', WR 43; WA III, 87), a link can even be made to the oldest story in Western culture and civilization, to the biblical story of creation and the Garden of Eden.

It is soon apparent, however, that something rather more complex is at play in 'June Afternoon'. As Georg Seeßlen has recently stressed, the garden as sign and topos is particularly rich in metaphoric potential and interpretative possibilities, and it has occupied a prominent position in European literary traditions from the bible to postmodernism.[20] Whilst Wolf may well have aimed at

---

[18] Bakhtin, 'Forms of Time and of the Chronotope', 225-26.

[19] According to Bakhtin, 'the influence of the idyll on the development of the novel of modern times has proceeded in five basic directions: (1) the influence of the idyll, idyllic time and idyllic matrices on the provincial novel; (2) the destruction of the idyll, as in the *Bildungsroman* of Goethe and in novels of the Sternean type (Hippel, Jean Paul); (3) its influence on the Sentimental novel of the Rousseauan type; (4) its influence on the family novel and the novel of generations; and, finally, its influence on novels belonging to certain other categories [...].' Bakhtin, 'Forms of Time and of the Chronotope', 228-29.

[20] Georg Seeßlen, 'Rückzug ins Paradies: Der Garten als Ort der geschlossenen Welt', *Freitag*, 27-28 (2007).

embedding her story in Western culture in this widest sense, the garden she constructs appears to be located somewhere in between the worlds of dream, fantasy, or fiction and sober reality. Described as 'the dream of being a green, rampant, wild, lush garden' ('der Traum [...] ein grüner, wuchernder wilder, üppiger Garten zu sein'), and as 'never more real than this year' ('nie wirklicher [...] als dieses Jahr', WR 43; WA III, 87), it invokes memories of Romantic literature alongside comparisons with realist forms, alluding to a literary vision beyond the constraints of genre and tradition.

Topographically, the garden is easily identified in the real world as the Wolfs own in Kleinmachnow, a Berlin suburb where the family moved in 1962. The narrator's observation early on in the text, for instance, that the vine the family is growing needs an unusual amount of thinning out in this particular summer, 'since it was acting as if it grew on a Mosel hillside and not on a skimpy trellis under a Brandenburg pine' ('weil er sich gebärdete, als stünde er an einem Moselhang und nicht an einem dürftigen Staketengitter unter einer märkischen Kiefer', WR 44; WA III, 44), locates the scene geographically in East Germany. Further topographical clues increasingly distance the story from the idyllic chronotope, introducing dramatic tension and drawing into the scene the political realities of divided Germany. The narrator's irritation with the fighter planes overhead, which constantly frustrate her longing for peace and quiet, for example, place the garden underneath the busy air corridor that connected West Germany to West Berlin during the country's division, whilst the helicopters that circle over the German-German border draw further attention to deeper uncertainties about the future of the small socialist half of Germany in the context of the Cold War (WR 46, 47, 48; WA III, 90, 91, 93). Clearly, the political realities created by the postwar world order are still sufficiently unfamiliar to the narrator in her new environment to be thoroughly disorientating, since she deliberates for some time on the confusions created by the fact that the commercial airlines, subjectively speaking, appear to be flying from 'west to west' ('von Westen nach Westen', WR 46; WA III, 90), whereas the coordinates of the compass irrefutably establish that their path leads 'clearly visible to everybody, [...] from east to west' ('für jedermann sichtbar von Osten nach Westen', WR 46, WA III, 90).[21] The jumbo jet planes, finally, appear to be signalling that the forces of modernity in league with Western capitalism threaten to destroy the very quality of life the narrator of 'June Afternoon' is set to defend (WR 47, WA III, 91).

Throughout the afternoon, the perspective in fact veers between the idyllic family chronotope and its counterpoint in literary history and tradition, the theme of the destruction of the idyll. The fact that the family has not lived in this place for long, undoes the idea of rootedness and belonging to a particular place: 'In all the time we have known it [the garden, RR] – of course it has only been three years –' ('Seit wir ihn [den Garten, RR] kennen, das sind allerdings erst drei Jahre', WR 43; WA III, 87). The central figure's irritation with her neighbours betrays her deeper apprehensions about the gulf that has continued to separate the concerns of intellectuals and writers from those of the working population (WR 63; WA III, 108) as well as the socialist visions of Party technocrats (WR 48; WA III, 96). Her annoyance with her husband, her frustrations about the demands made on her by her younger daughter, and her anxious concerns about whether she has set an adequate role model as a mother for her older daughter, are just some of the elements which overwrite the idea of happy family life in harmony with nature. The garden as the chronotopic place 'where the knots of narrative are tied and untied' and where 'the meaning that shapes narrative' lies, in effect, increasingly turns into a place filled with repressed anxiety, fear and foreboding. As a bounded site that is encircled by a border, it offers an inside and an outside perspective, is surrounded by a threatening world, is potentially paradise, but also a prison, and it ultimately points beyond itself to another border which also at once protects its people and imprisons them, namely that of the nation state GDR. For the narrator as a writer, the all-pervasive presence of the garden fence also contrasts

---

[21] There are clear similarities here in terms of both narrative technique and subject matter to Virginia Woolf's *Between the Acts* (1941). In this narrative, the central figure also looks fearfully up into the sky, where aeroplanes flying over an idyllic garden scene fill her with a sense of foreboding in anticipation of the outbreak of the First World War.

disconcertingly with the personal and intellectual freedoms she desires. Rather than providing seclusion and privacy, the fence appears to imprison her, her static position in the garden chair pointing to stasis and a sense of paralysis. Memories of the horrors of the Second World War triggered by the aeroplanes, anxieties about the future of divided Germany in the context of the Cold War, alarm about the seemingly unstoppable advance of Western capitalism, a profound sense of un-ease about growing social rifts and unresolved issues in GDR socialism, as well as personal concerns about her family, eventually culminate in a profound sense of fear:

> Yet one begins to be afraid if one still sees no ground; one jettisons superfluous ballast, this and that, only in order to get up again. After all, who is to say that the hand which will pull one away from everything is already set to pounce? Who is to say that, this time, it is our turn? That the game will go on without us?

> Aber man kriegt Angst, wenn immer noch kein Boden kommt, man wirft Ballast ab, dieses und jenes, um nur wieder aufzusteigen. Wer sagt denn, daß diesmal wir gemeint sind? Daß das Spiel ohne uns weiterginge? (WR 65; WA III, 111)

On one level of the text, therefore, historical contingencies in conjunction with the forces of modernity and the political realities of divided Germany create a profoundly heightened awareness of the fragility of the self in the face of death. But the story also hints at the author's concerns about her role as a writer and the future of literature in the GDR. The significance of the fact that the writer here speaks not from the centre of society, but from its margins, is open to interpretation. It could suggest that the writer has merely withdrawn from public life out of her own volition in order to find fresh inspiration and much needed respite. But it is at least as likely that she is paralysed by a fearful sense of foreboding and is no longer able to write. 'June Afternoon' was written between June and August 1965, and thus in the atmosphere of growing tension preceding the infamous Eleventh Plenum of the Central Committee of the Socialist Unity Party in December 1965, which abruptly terminated the tentative reforms of the previous years and reinstated the Party's strict adherence to bureaucratic centralism. At the Plenum, Wolf was practically the only intellectual who openly stood up to the Party's defamatory statements and punitive actions against its committed writers and artists. Speaking on behalf of GDR writers and film-makers, she found an inner strength which, in retrospect, she has attributed to the shock of realizing that the Party would stop at nothing in order to subject artists and writers in the GDR fully to its control, even if this amounted to an attack on their personal integrity and the destruction of their ability to work. She summarized her sentiments on leaving the Plenum as follows:

> But it was necessary for me to understand from within how this mechanism worked. [...] When I came out of there – I still remember exactly what I thought, when I came down the stairs: having my hands slapped away.

> Aber es mußte passieren, daß ich von innen her sehen konnte, wie der Mechanismus funktioniert. [...] Als ich dort rauskam – ich weiß noch ganz genau, was ich dachte, als ich die Treppe runterging: die Hände weggeschlagen.[22]

The narrator's association in 'June Afternoon' of a woman's suicide with this same image, I would argue, powerfully conveys the author's sense of foreboding of the repression that was to occur at the Plenum: 'No matter which game she had had her hand in, it had been slapped away, and the game had gone on without her. The entire feather-light afternoon hung on the weight of this minute' ('In welchem Spiel sie ihre Hände auch gehabt hatte, man hatte sie ihr weggeschlagen, und das Spiel ging ohne sie weiter. Der ganze federleichte Nachmittag hing an dem Gewicht dieser Minute' (WR 65; WA III, 110).

Ultimately, however, the story ends optimistically, since the narrator resolves at the end of the day to shed her fear and psychological ballast and concentrate on what is important to her in the here and now. But the claim that the

---

[22] 'Auf mir bestehen. Christa Wolf im Gespräch mit Günter Gaus', in Hermann Vinke (ed.), *Akteneinsicht Christa Wolf. Zerrspiegel und Dialog. Eine Dokumentation* (Hamburg: Luchterhand, 1993), 242-63 (here 249).

writer's place is at the heart of society and the writer's protest about the lack of freedom from Party control and its hegemonic ideological claims has been inscribed into her text. Place, by way of the chronotope, plays a defining role in the narrative. Not only does it lend cultural depth to Wolf's story, it also reveals other, hidden stories and overwrites, as on a palimpsest, her previous longing for a future in a socialist paradise with far more realistic and disconcerting possibilities.

With 'Unter den Linden', an aesthetically and thematically highly sophisticated and multifaceted story, Wolf embarked during the late 1960s on the project of putting into practice her resolution to examine how what she calls 'the mechanism' works. First published in 1974 as part of a trilogy of stories which, as the title of one of the others in the collection suggests, she conceived of as 'self-experiment[s]' ('Selbstversuch[e]'), it constitutes part of the author's ongoing search for the self and examines in particular the intricate interplay between hegemonic power structures and socio-political mechanisms of control on the one hand and the individual susceptibility to authoritarian patterns of behaviour and thought on the other. Highly intertextual and drawing on a range of literary influences such as German Romanticism, love poetry, the fairytale, Ingeborg Bachmann, as well as Freudian psychoanalysis, 'Unter den Linden' blurs genre boundaries and mixes reality, fantasy and dream-world to a point where the transitions between these different realms have become unrecognizable. As in 'Juninachmittag', the reader is addressed as an intimate 'you' ('du'), but the text's subject-matter here is clearly of a more sensitive nature, since the reader who is invoked is a loved one, addressed as 'dear' ('Lieber') (WR 78; WA III, 392). The dialogic relationship constructed between writer and reader is thus an intimate, even conspiratorial one, suggesting that the text's only reader might be a close friend or even the author herself. The text's purpose, this suggests, is ultimately a process of self-examination. In contrast to the earlier story, the narrator here has just emerged from a period of deep crisis, with the text's motto[23] and her assertions that she can now 'freely tell the truth' ('Ich kann frei die Wahrheit sagen', WA 69; WA III, 383), after she has recently been readmitted into 'the fellowship of the fortunate' ('den Bund der Glücklichen', WR 69; WA III383), indicating that she has shed fear and self-doubt and has found new inner freedom. This is underscored by the confident beginning of the story and the almost defiant tone in which the narrator, a figure resembling a female *flaneur*, stakes a personal claim on one of East Berlin's historically, politically, and architecturally most prestigious public places: 'I have always liked walking along Unter den Linden. And most of all, as you well know, alone' ('Unter den Linden bin ich immer gerne gegangen. Am liebsten, du weißt es, allein', WR 69; WA III, 383).

This setting is of course highly evocative, triggering associations that go to the very core of issues of German national history and identity:

> Emerging as a focal point for the residential expansion of Berlin in the seventeenth century, transformed into a via triumphalis in the early nineteenth century, serving as regal, imperial thoroughfare for the Kaisers before the First World War, and co-opted by the Nazis for grand ceremonies in the 1930s, Unter den Linden lay in ruins at the end of the Second World War. From then until the end of the century, Unter den Linden became a different sort of battleground, one involving competing ideologies and visions of the socialist and capitalist city.[24]

Since Unter den Linden has also always held a particular attraction for German writers and artists, its topographical significance is further enhanced by the associations it invokes from German literature and culture: these reach back from Heinrich Heine's *Letters from Berlin* (*Briefe aus Berlin*, 1822), to the

---

[23] This is a citation from the Romantic poet Rahel Varnhagen: ‚I am convinced that it is part of life on earth that everyone be hurt where he is most sensitive, by that which is unbearable: Essential is the way in which he overcomes this.' ('Ich bin überzeugt, daß es mit zum Erdenleben gehört, daß jeder in dem gekränkt werde, was ihm das Empfindlichste, das Unleidlichste ist: Wie er da herauskommt, ist das Wesentliche', WR 69; WA III, 383).
[24] Paul Stangl, 'Restoring Berlin's Unter den Linden: Ideology, World View, Place and Space', *Journal of Historical Geography*, 32 (2006), 352-76 (here 353).

Romantic writers Rahel Varnhagen and Bettina von Arnim,[25] to the oldest love poem in Germany's cultural history, Walther von der Vogelweide's 'Unter den Linden'. Thus, the writer here no longer speaks from a private place off the beaten track, but from the very core of her country's political, social and cultural history. Symbolically, I would argue, she seeks to reclaim this place from socialist space, embedding it and her story in the deeper socio-political and cultural history of Germany and resisting the pressures that would limit GDR culture to schematic provincialism.

She lays claim to the road as 'my street' ('meine Straße', WR 70; WA III, 384):

> It has never bothered me that the street is famous [...]. I am aware that it has suffered this misfortune on account of its location: East-West axis. This street and the one appearing in my dreams have nothing in common.

> Daß die Straße berühmt ist, hat mich nie gestört [...]. Ich begreife, daß sie dieses Mißgeschick ihrer Lage verdankt: Ost-West-Achse. Sie und die Straße, die mir im Traum erscheint, haben nichts miteinander zu tun (WR 69; WA III, 383)

What is at stake is clearly a journey of self-discovery and self-revelation: 'For we esteem nothing more highly than the pleasure of being known' ('Denn höher als alles schätzen wir die Lust, gekannt zu sein', WR 69; WA III, 383).

In a complex process involving the interplay of memory, association, dream and fantasy, the narrator travels, with clear allusion to Freudian dreamwork, along a road that 'leads into unknown depths' ('diese Straße [führt] in die Tiefe', WR 77; WA III, 391), into the heart of her emotional experience and the realm of her dreams and memories, and it is from this perspective of 'depth' that she reflects on the realities around her. The narrative weaves together the strands of several parallel stories which connect the lives of a number of people whose paths crossed at a particular point in time, amongst them the narrator's

---

[25] Both writers lived on Unter den Linden during periods when they resided in Berlin. Wolf has felt a particularly deep affinity to these women writers.

own. The linchpin of all three stories is the 'fate' of a young woman whose character is based on someone the author once knew: a student has an affair with her lecturer, a married man, and justifies a brief period of absence from her studies, which she spent with this man, with a forged sick note; she is penalized with suspension from her studies and sent to work in a lightbulb factory.

Therese Hörnigk has rightly noted that it is the dream-like atmosphere of 'Unter den Linden', with its suspension of real time (WR 76; WA III, 390), which furnishes the aesthetic means that permit the author to weave the stories together.[26] However, she leaves unconsidered the role of place in unlocking the deeper issues the narrative explores. In this regard, Mikhail Bakhtin's observations on the chronotope of encounter provide a fruitful additional dimension, which draws attention to the particularly rich interpretative possibilities of the road as metaphor and symbol in literary history:

> The road is a particularly good place for random encounters. On the road [...] the spatial and temporal paths of the most varied people [...] intersect at one spatial and temporal point. People who are normally kept separate by social and spatial distance can accidentally meet; any contrast may crop up, the most various fates may collide and interweave with one another. [...]. Time [...] fuses together with space and flows in it (forming the road); this is the source of the rich metaphorical expansion on the image of the road as a course: 'the course of a life', 'to set out on a new course', 'the course of history' and so on; varied and multi-levelled are the ways in which road is turned into metaphor, but its fundamental pivot is the flow of time.[27]

In 'Unter den Linden', these potentialities clearly play a role and Wolf builds in particular on the Romantic tradition in order to explore issues of chance and fate that have been associated with travel along a road in real as well as in metaphorical terms.

On a superficial level, random encounters on the narrator's walk along Unter den Linden produce a spectrum of mixed feelings about life in the socialist

---

[26] Therese Hörnigk, *Christa Wolf* (Göttingen: Steidl, 1989), 152-53.
[27] Bakhtin, 'Forms of Time and of the Chronotope', 243-44.

GDR in the late 1960s: she humorously appreciates the absurdities of the 'Great Changing of the Guards' ('Groß[e] Wachablösung', WR 71; WA III, 385) and its indebtedness to the traditions of Prussian militarism, she marvels with a mixture of pride and estrangement at the cultural and social diversity of the people who have come to visit the GDR's capital city, 'strange characters […], [n]ot all of [whom] had been baptized with Spree water and grown up under pine trees' ('Merkwürdige Gestalten […], [n]icht alle waren sie mit Spreewasser getauft und unter Kiefern aufgewachsen', WR 72; WA III, 386), and notes with strained bemusement that the young generation of socialist citizens bears little resemblance to her own:

> Strange birds with brightly colored plumage: the same jeans, the same light-blue sweaters tied around their waists, the same flowered shirts – viewed from behind distinguishable neither by their narrow hips nor by their unkempt hair of equal length.

> Seltsame Vögel mit grellbuntem Gefieder: die gleichen blue Jeans, die gleichen hellblauen Pullover um die Taille geknotet, die gleichen großgeblümten Hemden – von hinten weder an ihren schmalen Hüften noch am gleich langen, zottligen Haar zu unterscheiden. WR 72; WA III, 386)

On the deeper level of the narrative, however, the narrator re-encounters in the course of her journey people from a past she has been at pains to forget, but failed to repress: 'I must have kept it a secret, but the story is still on my mind. It follows me around like a tune that is played in my head again and again' ('Ich werde es wohl verheimlicht haben, aber die Geschichte geht mir nach, wie ein Thema, das wieder und wieder in mir angeschlagen wird', WR 73; WA III, 387). This brings to light truths about herself and her personal role in the wider scheme of events which are decidedly less comfortable. In clear allusion to Kafka's *Trial* (*Der Prozeß*, 1925), she realizes that she has come to this road at this particular juncture in her life in order to put herself on trial. Couched in the language of self-incrimination and self-indictment, she must unravel the past in order to find orientation for the future:

> I [...] suspected that I had come here on her account in order to visit certain localities which served as the scenery in her [the young woman's, RR] drama. That which, legally speaking, is called a return to the scene of the crime.

> '[ich] hatte [...] den Verdacht, ich sei ihretwegen hierhergekommen [...] gewisse Örtlichkeiten zu besichtigen, die in ihrem [dem des Mädchens, RR] Drama als Kulissen mitspielten: Was man bei Gericht Lokaltermin nennt. (WR 74; WA III, 388)

When the first-person narrator finally 'gets to the bottom of it' ('endlich auf den Grund gekommen [ist]', WR 78; WA III, 392), she makes some unwelcome discoveries. She remembers that she played a passive role in the fate of the young woman. She herself had had an affair with a married man at the time, a surgeon and high-ranking Party official, who was directly involved in passing judgement on the young woman's case. For reasons she retrospectively considers to have been misplaced romantic love and personal cowardice, she neither protested nor took a deeper interest in the 'drama' which unfolded in the other woman's life. With hindsight, her behaviour strikes her as something between that of a bystander ('Mitläufer') and a self-interested conformist.

The two parallel stories in 'Unter den Linden' represent subject positions which are deemed morally equally questionable: Peter, the young woman's lover, is exposed as a 'typical' apathetic opportunist, and Max, as 'Mr Everyman [...] Colleague Everyman [...] Comrade Everyman' ('Herr Jedermann [...] Kollege Jedermann [...] Genosse Jedermann', WR 101; WA III, 416) exemplifies the uncritical and conformist Party functionary who has shed all moral principles in order to rise up the Party hierarchy. As parallel figures, these characters in effect represent facets of the narrator's identity, reflecting and re-fracting unacknowledged or repressed parts of her 'self'. As she approaches the most intense moments of her self-imposed trial in the hall of mirrors of her projections and self-projections, she begins to understand that one of her more noble character traits, namely her deeply felt longing for self-determination and her insistence on the supreme authority of the subject, has in practice resulted in a rather less laudable tendency to turn a blind eye: 'The beautiful freedom of not having to know what I know – I chose it a long time ago.' ('Die schöne Freiheit, nicht wissen zu müssen, was ich weiß – ich habe sie mir seit langem genommen', WR 97; WA III, 412). As she walks through East Germany's capital city or, as it were, backwards along 'the course of her life', in Bakhtin's terms, she begins to break imposed and self-imposed 'taboos' and starts to understand how 'the mechanism' works: the scene in the state library, for instance, exposes the multiplicity of ways in which individuals, in their everyday lives, unquestioningly obey obscure instructions issued by fanciful authorities who appear to make up the rules as they please:

> Don't turn around [...]. Sometimes the laws dictating your behaviour in certain places change overnight and that's the way it is. [...] There's no end of things that can happen to you.

> Dreh dich nicht um [...] Manchmal wechseln die Gesetze über Nacht, nach denen man sich an bestimmten Orten zu verhalten hat, und es hat nichts weiter zu bedeuten. Was einem nicht alles passieren kann. (WR 79; WA III, 393)

Allusions to her 'dream censor' and her 'censor' ('Mein Traumzensor', 'mein Zensor', WR 96-97; WA III, 411) clearly point to the issue of censorship and self-censorship,[28] whilst her exploration of the psychological pressures exerted on individuals in authoritarian systems trigger a range of associations suggestive of the machinations of the GDR state, not least those of its secret police, the *Stasi*: 'One only knows one has been summoned and must obey. The time, place, and purpose of the meeting are not disclosed' ('man ist bestellt und hat Folge zu leisten. Stunde, Ort und Zweck der Verabredung werden einem nicht mitgeteilt', WR 70; WA III, 384). The observation that 'coincidences today are not what they used to be' ('Zufälle sind heute auch nicht mehr, was sie mal waren'), since

---

[28] In her interview with Hans Kaufmann, Wolf openly spoke out against censorship in the GDR, explaining at length how their more perfidious psychological mechanisms impinge on the writer's ability to work. WA IV, 401-37 (here 433). See also David Bathrick, *The Powers of Speech: The Politics of Culture in the GDR*, (Lincoln and London: U of Nebraska P, 1995), 40.

> [a]t any intersection […] a certain blue Wartburg can coincidentally have a small accident, and one is coincidentally nearby, becomes a possible witness of the innocence of the driver … something like that

> [a]n jeder Straßenkreuzung zum Beispiel kann ein bestimmter blauer Wartburg zufällig einen kleinen Unfall haben, zufällig steht man in der Nähe, kommt als Zeuge für die Unschuld des Fahrers in Betracht … In dieser Art (WR 98; WA III, 413)

appears to point in a similar direction. Since 'Unter den Linden' was written at a time when Wolf was embarking on her extensive exploration of the lasting impact of fascism on the behaviour and psychological patterns of members of her generation in *A Model Childhood* (*Kindheitsmuster*, 1976), the self-investigations and self-revelations of 'Unter den Linden' were clearly intended to inform and inspire her inquiry into these issues on the much larger canvas. But, as 'little experiments with new tools' ('Kleine Proben auf anderen Instrumenten', WA IV, 433)[29] as she called them, they certainly furnish some interesting insights into socio-political and cultural realities in the GDR and invite above all members of her generation to begin breaking the silence. The young woman, whom the narrator has expressly chosen as a confidante and companion on her journey, of course plays a crucial role in this regard. Described as one of the few who are 'in the know' ('die 'Bescheid [wissen]', WR 79; WA III, 393), she is a pivotal figure who provides not only an alternative and probably more honest moral vision, but also embodies hope for the possibility of change over the generations and, in Bakhtin's terms, in 'the course of history'. The chronotope of encounter and of the road, as Bakhtin has explained, has often appeared in the history of the novel in juxtaposition with that of the threshold, suggesting hope in the potential of new beginnings.[30] In this respect, Wolf was evidently able to draw strength and optimism from literary history, since her self-exploration in 'Unter den Linden',

---

[29] Wolf, *The Fourth Dimension*, 36.
[30] Bakhtin, 'Forms of Time and of the Chronotope', 243-44.

as was indeed the case with 'June Afternoon', ends hopefully. In the end, her narrator experiences a kind of epiphany and finds herself:

> Now everything was cleared in a flash. I had been meant to find myself – that was the point of the summons. Cell by cell this new joy filled my body.

> Nun klärte sich mit einem Schlage alles auf. Ich sollte mich wiederfinden – das war der Sinn der Bestellung. Zelle für Zelle füllte sich mein Körper mit der neuen Freude. (WR 118; WA III, 434)

With *What Remains*, Wolf returned to her search for the self from the perspective of renewed and now existential crisis. Written originally during the summer of 1979 in the wake of the Biermann affair, which resulted in fresh reprisals against Wolf and other writers and intensified efforts on the part of the regime to keep them in check, the text was revised for publication a decade later in the immediate aftermath of the GDR's demise. The narrative consequently extends over the last decade of the existence of the state of which Wolf had regarded herself an integral part. Placed under surveillance by the secret police who watch her every move, bug her phone, open her mail and break into her flat when she goes out, the writer here has, in contrast to the first-person narrator of 'June Afternoon', been robbed of the one place where she was hitherto able to recover or even hide from a threatening world, which is also the place most closely associated with identity, selfhood and belonging, namely home. Indeed, it is evident from the outset that the narrator of *What Remains* no longer believes in her country's future: 'One day I would be old. And how would I remember these days then?' ('Einmal würde ich alt sein. Und wie würde ich mich dieser Tage dann erinnern?', WR 232; WA X 223). The testing out of boundaries which in the earlier texts had determined how much of the truth could be divulged and what literary guises or narrative personae had to be devised in order to combine self-revelation with self-concealment, has now given way to the 'pure fear, real panic' ('hell[e] Angst [...] panisch[e] Angst', WR 232; WA X 224) of having missed the boat and of not having done enough whilst there was still time.

The fact that the narrator's most intimate private sphere, her home, has been violated by the state symbolizes poignantly the fact that all former hopes that the writer would have a distinctive place in socialist society have now been dashed. And yet, the text's very existence constitutes an act of defiance, since the writer continues to write against all possible odds. In contrast to the earlier stories, however, the place from which she now speaks is beyond the metaphoric or semantic ambiguities associated with the chronotope. It is a 'non-place' or a nightmarish place that conjures up visions of hell:

> Only then did I realize that a secret fire had glowed in the interior of this city before, I didn't know its name yet, but ever since the day when it was to be extinguished, when all its accompanying fires were to be suffocated and each of its hidden sparks stamped out, I had been hopelessly under its spell. As of yet I had to live with all the others in a lost city, in a merciless city which had not been saved, sunk to the bottom of insignificance. At night I heard the stomp stomp of the robot who laid his iron hand on my breast. The city had turned from a place into a non-place, without history, without vision, without magic, spoiled by greed, power, and violence. It divided its time between nightmares and senseless activities – like those kids in the cars who were more and more coming to symbolize my city.

> Da erst wurde ich gewahr, daß vorher ein geheimes Feuer im Innern dieser Stadt geglüht hatte, noch kannte ich seinen Namen nicht, aber seit dem Tag, an dem es ausgelöscht, als alle seine Nebenfeuer erstickt, jedes seiner verborgenen Fünkchen ausgetreten werden sollten, war ich rettungslos seiner Magie verfallen. Noch mußte ich mit allen anderen in einer verlorenen Stadt leben, einer unerlösten, erbarmungslosen Stadt, versenkt auf den Grund von Nichtswürdigkeit. Nachts hörte ich das Stampfen des Roboters, der mir seine eiserne Hand auf die Brust legte. Aus einem Ort war die Stadt zu einem Nicht-Ort geworden, ohne Geschichte, ohne Vision, ohne Zauber, verdorben durch Gier, Macht und Gewalt. Zwischen Alpträumen und sinnlosen Tätigkeiten verbrachte sie ihre Zeit – wie jene Jungs in den Autos, die mehr und mehr meiner Stadt Sinnbild wurden. (WR 248; WA x 241)

However, even though the place which had shaped the writer's history and her multiple identities for more than four decades was clearly lost to Wolf by the late 1970s, her perspective on the significance of the writer's voice and her role, has not been abandoned altogether. It is true that the confident and optimistic gestures of the earlier texts have given way to the subjunctive mood of a tentative future: 'would I know when the time was right? Would I ever find my language?' ('würde ich spüren, wenn es an der Zeit ist? Würde ich meine Sprache je finden?' WR 231; WA x 223). Plagued by serious doubts about her survival as a writer, writing itself appears to be hanging in the balance; it has become a matter of life and death. But this very existential crisis ultimately leads to the discovery of one possibility that remains. Although written in the form of an interior monologue, the text dialogically invokes a future reader who, as Stephen Brockmann has noted, will in effect 'be engaging in a dialogue with the dead'.[31] But it is a relationship that can, at the end of the day, rescue at least a degree of meaning: from the perspective of ongoing self-reflection and self-indictment, the writer can bear witness and thus take on her staunchest enemy, 'the remorseless stream of time and forgetting':[32]

> With pure fear, real panic, I now tried to cling to one of these doomed days and not let go, no matter what I ended up holding in my hands, be it banal or weighty, whether it surrendered at once or struggled to the last.

> In heller Angst, in panischer Angst wollte ich mich jetzt an einen dieser dem Untergang geweihten Tage klammern und ihn festhalten, egal, was ich zu fassen kriegen würde, ob er banal sein würde oder schwerwiegend, und ob er sich schnell ergab oder sich sträuben würde bis zuletzt. (WR 232; WA x 224-25)

What remains, then, is the hope that the reader of the future will keep alive the memory of the past, including the history of the culture whose socio-political conditions have disappeared. This clearly confronts the narrator of *What Remains* with a new responsibility. Amongst the most significant insights she makes at the end of the day is her understanding that the symbiosis she had envisaged between

---

[31] Stephen Brockmann, 'Preservation and Change in Christa Wolf's *Was bleibt*', *The German Quarterly*, 67.1 (Winter 1994), 73-85 (here 73).
[32] Brockmann, 'Preservation and Change', 73.

the generations in 'Unter den Linden', which was represented there by the fictional merging of the identity of the young woman with her own, was based on self-deception and wishful thinking. The dialogue with a young female colleague in *What Remains*, by contrast, confronts her with the understanding that the younger generation of writers has long since constructed its independent identity, and that it is now up to each of them to manage the process of remembering the past in their own distinctive way.

SELECT BIBLIOGRAPHY

This select bibliography lists publications cited in this volume that are of particular interest for the study of place in literature generally and in German-language literature specifically.

Ahmed, Sara, *Strange Encounters: Embodied Others in Post-Coloniality* (London: Routledge, 2000)

Ahmed, Sara et al. (eds.), *Uprootings/Regroundings: Questions of Home and Migration* (Oxford: Berg, 2003)

Anderson, Benedict, *Imagined Communities Reflections on the Origin and Spread of Nationalism*, revised edn (London: Verso, 1991)

Applegate, Celia, *A Nation of Provincials: The German Idea of Heimat* (Berkeley and Los Angeles: U of California P, 1990)

Augé, Marc, *Non-Places: Introduction to an Anthropology of Supermodernity*, trans. John Howe (London: Verso, 1995)

Bachelard, Gaston, *The Poetics of Space*, trans. Maria Jolas (Boston: Beacon, 1994)

Bakhtin, Mikhail, *The Dialogic Imagination*, ed. by Michael Holquist, trans. Caryl Emerson and Michael Holquist (Austin: U of Texas P, 1981)

Barnes, Trevor, and James S. Duncan (eds.), *Writing Worlds: Discourse, Text and Metaphor in the Representation of Landscape* (London and New York: Routledge, 1992)

Bender, Barbara (ed.), *Landscape and Politics* (Oxford: Berg 1993)

Blanchot, Maurice, *The Space of Literature*, trans. Ann Smock (Lincoln: U of Nebraska P, 1990)

Boa, Elizabeth, and Rachel Palfreyman, *Heimat: A German dream: Regional Loyalties and National Identity in German Culture, 1890-1990* (Oxford: OUP, 2000)

Böhme, Hartmut (ed.), *Topographien der Literatur: deutsche Literatur im transnationalen Kontext* (Stuttgart and Weimar: Metzler, 2005)

Bollnow, Friedrich, *Mensch und Raum*, 2nd edn (Stuttgart: Kohlhammer, 1971)

Braidotti, Rosi, *Nomadic Subjects: Embodiment and Sexual Difference in Contemporary Feminist Theory* (New York: Columbia UP, 1994)

Brown, Peter, and Michael Irwin (eds.), *Literature and Place 1800-2000* (Bern: Lang, 2006)

Carter, Erica, James Donald, and Judith Squires (eds.), *Space and Place: Theories of Identity and Location* (London: Lawrence & Wishart, 1993)

Casey, Edward W., *The Fate of Place: A Philosophical History* (Berkeley: U of California P, 1997)

Cassirer, Ernst, 'Mythischer, ästhetischer und theoretischer Raum', in Alexander Ritter (ed.), *Landschaft und Raum in der Literatur* (Darmstadt: Wissenschaftliche Buchgesellschaft, 1975), 17-35

Cosgrove, Dennis, 'Landscape and Landschaft', in *GHI Bulletin*, 35 (2004), 57-71

Crowley, David and Susan E. Reid (eds.), *Socialist Spaces: Sites of Everyday Life in the Eastern Bloc* (Oxford and New York: Berg, 2000)

Daniels, Stephen, and Denis Cosgrove (eds.), *The Iconography of Landscape* (Cambridge: CUP, 1988)

de Certeau, Michel, *The Practice of Everyday Life*, trans. Steven F. Rendall (Berkeley, California and London: U of California P, 1984)

Deleuze, Gilles and Félix Guattari, *A Thousand Plateaus: Capitalism and Schizophrenia*, trans. Brian Massumi (London: Athlone, 1988)

Ferguson, Marjorie, 'The Mythology about Globalization', *European Journal of Communication*, 7 (1992), 69-93

Foucault, Michel, 'Of Other Spaces', trans. Jay Miskowiec, *Diacritics*, 16.1 (1986), 22-27

Frech, Birgit, *Die Berliner Mauer in der Literatur: Eine Untersuchung ausgewählter Prosawerke seit 1961* (Pfungstadt: Edition Ergon, 1992)

Görner, Rüdiger, and Suzanne Kirkbright (eds.), *Nachdenken über Grenzen* (Munich: iudicium, 1999)

Görner, Rüdiger, *Grenzen, Schwellen, Übergänge: Zur Poetik des Transitorischen* (Göttingen: Vandenhoeck & Ruprecht, 2001)

Harvey, David, *The Condition of Postmodernity: An Enquiry into the Origins of Cultural Change* (Oxford: Blackwell, 1989)

Hillebrand, Bruno, *Mensch und Raum im Roman: Studien zu Keller, Stifter, Fontane mit einem einführenden Essay zur europäischen Literatur* (Munich: Winkler, 1971)

Hubbard, Phil, Rob Kitchin and Gill Valentine (eds.), *Key Thinkers on Space and Place* (London: Sage, 2004)

Huyssen, Andreas, *Present Pasts: Urban Palimpsests and the Politics of Memory* (Stanford: Stanford UP, 2003)

Jameson, Fredric, *The Postmodern Condition or The Cultural Logic of Late Capitalism* (London: Verso, 1991)

Jarvis, Brian, *Postmodern Cartography: The Geographical Imagination in Contemporary American Culture* (London: Pluto, 1998)

Kern, Hermann, *Labyrinthe. Erscheinungsformen und Deutungen. 5000 Jahre Gegenwart eines Urbilds* (Munich: Prestel, 1999)

Ladd, Brian, *The Ghosts of Berlin: Confronting German History in the Urban Landscape* (Chicago and London: U of Chicago P, 1997)

Lefebvre, Henri, *The Production of Space*, trans. Donald Nicholson Smith (Oxford: Blackwell, 1991)

Lequy, Anne, *'unbehaust'? Die Thematik des Topos in den Werken wenig(er) bekannter DDR-Autorinnen der siebziger und achtziger Jahre. Eine feministische Untersuchung* (Frankfurt a.M.: Lang, 2000)

Lobsien, Eckhard, *Landschaft in Texten. Zur Geschichte und Phänomenologie der literarischen Beschreibung*, (Stuttgart: Metzler, 1981)

Lutwack, Leonard, *The Role of Place in Literature* (Syracuse: Syrcause UP, 1984)

Massey, Doreen, *Space, Place and Gender* (Cambridge: Polity, 1994)

———, *for space* (London: Sage, 2005)

Mecklenburg, Norbert, *Erzählte Provinz: Regionalismus und Moderne im Roman* (Königstein: Athenäum, 1982)

Meyer, Hermann, 'Raumgestaltung und Raumsymbolik in der Erzählkunst', in Meyer, *Zarte Empirie: Studien zur Literaturgeschichte* (Stuttgart: Metzler, 1963)

Mitchell, W. J. T., 'Spatial Form: Toward a General Theory', *Critical Enquiry*, 6.3 (1980), 539-67 (551-53)

———, (ed.), *Landscapes and Power* (Chicago: U of Chicago P, 1994)

Moretti, Franco, *Atlas of the European Novel 1800-1900* (London: Verso, 1999)

Nelson, Cary, *The Incarnate Word: Literature as Verbal Space* (Urbana: U of Illinois P, 1973)

Norquay, Glenda, and Gerry Smyth (eds.), *Space and Place: The Geographies of Literature* (Liverpool: Liverpool John Moores UP, 1999)

Page, Norman and Peter Preston (eds.), *The Literature of Place* (Houndmills: MacMillan, 1993)

Reichel, Norbert, *Der erzählte Raum: Zur Verflechtung von sozialem und und poetischem Raum in erzählender Literatur* (Darmstadt: Wissenschaftliche Buchgesellschaft, 1987)

Ritter, Joachim, *Landschaft. Zur Funktion des Ästhetischen in der modernen Gesellschaft* (Münster: Aschendorff, 1963)

Robertson, Robert, 'Glokalisierung: Homogenität und Heterogenität in Raum und Zeit', in Ulrich Beck (ed.), *Perspektiven der Weltgesellschaft* (Frankfurt a.M.: Suhrkamp, 1988), 192-220

Röttgers, Kurt and Monika Schmitz-Emans (eds.) *Labyrinthe. Philosophische und literarische Modelle* (Essen: Die blaue Eule, 2000)

Said, Edward W., *Orientalism: Western Conceptions of the Orient* (Harmondsworth: Penguin, 1995)

Scherpe, Klaus R. (ed.), *Die Unwirklichkeit der Städte* (Reinbek bei Hamburg: Rowohlt, 1988)

Schwartz, Joan, and James Ryan (eds.), *Picturing Place: Photography and the Geographical Imagination* (London: I.B. Tauris, 2003)

Soja, Edward W., *Postmodern Geographies: The Reassertion of Space in Critical Social Theory* (London: Verso, 1989)

———, *Thirdspace: Journeys to Los Angeles and Other Real-and-Imaged Places* (Cambridge: Blackwells, 1996)

Solint, Rebecca, *A Field Guide to Getting Lost* (Edinburgh: Canongate, 2006)

Taberner, Stuart, (ed.), *German Literature in the Age of Globalisation* (Edgbaston: Birmingham UP, 2004)

Till, Karen, *New Berlin: Memory, Politics, Place* (Minneapolis: U of Minnesota P, 2005)

Tuan, Yi-Fun, *Space and Place: The Perspective of Experience* (London: Arnold, 1977)

Ullrich, Maren, *Geteilte Ansichten: Erinnerungslandschaft deutsch-deutsche Grenze* (Berlin: Aufbau, 2006)

Von Oppen, Karoline, and Renate Rechtien (eds.), *Local/Global Narratives* (Amsterdam: Rodopi, 2007)

Von Schirnding, Albert, *Literarische Landschaften* (Frankfurt a.M.: Insel, 1998)

Von Ungern-Sternberg, Armin, *"Erzählregionen": Überlegungen zu literarischen Räumen mit Blick auf die deutsche Literatur des Baltikums, das Baltikum und die deutsche Literatur* (Bielefeld: Aisthesis, 2003)

Webber, Andrew, *Berlin in the Twentieth Century: A Cultural Topography* (Cambridge: CUP, 2008)

Wegner, Phillip E., 'Spatial Criticism: Critical Geography, Space, Place and Textuality', in Julian Wolfreys (ed.), *Introducing Criticism in the 21st Century* (Edinburgh: Edinburgh UP, 2002), 179-203

Wilson, Rob, and Wimal Dissanayake (eds.), *Global/Local: Cultural Production and the Transnational Imaginary* (Durham, NC: Duke UP)

Wolff, Larry, *Inventing Eastern Europe: The Map of Civilization on the Mind of the Enlightenment* (Stanford: Stanford UP, 1994)

INDEX

David John Clarke

Dr. David Clarke is Lecturer in German at the University of Bath, England. Dr. Clarke holds a Ph.D. from Swansea University (formerly the University of Wales, Swansea).

Renate Rechtien

Dr. Renate Rechtien is Lecturer in European Studies and German at the University of Bath, England. Dr. Rechtien holds a Ph.D. from the University of London, Goldsmiths College, England.